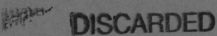

The
Changing
Brahmans

The Changing Brahmans

Associations and Elites among the Kanya-Kubjas of North India

R. S. Khare

Foreword by
Milton B. Singer

The University of Chicago Press
Chicago and London

To Bābā Rāmā Dāss of Kón, who showed how to handle old as well as new, noble as well as mean, ". . . from whom the world does not shrink and who does not shrink from the world and who is free from joy and anger, fear and agitation . . ." (Bhagavad Gita XII:15).

International Standard Book Number: 0-226-43433-8
Library of Congress Catalog Card Number: 72-128711

The University of Chicago Press, Chicago 60637
The University of Chicago Press, Ltd., London
© 1970 by The University of Chicago
Printed in the United States of America

Contents

FOREWORD   *ix*

PREFACE   *xv*

INTRODUCTION

1 The Problem and Its Formulation   *3*

I THE KANYA-KUBJA ASSOCIATIONS

2 History and Distribution   *31*
3 Sabhas and Educational Bodies   *47*
4 The Caste Journal   *72*

II TRADITION AND MODERNITY: STATUS STRATIFICATION
AND THE KANYA-KUBJA ACHIEVER

5 Traditional Hierarchy   *95*
6 Modern Occupational Prestige   *115*
7 Modern Class Standards and Styles   *129*

III TRADITION AND MODERNITY OF THE MODERN
KANYA-KUBJA ORGANIZATION

8 The Sabha as an Interjacent Organization   *161*

CONCLUSION

9 Review and Reformulation   *195*

APPENDIXES

A Minutes of a Typical
Sabha Executive Committee Meeting   *223*

B Distribution and Main Languages
   of the Major Caste Journals   *224*
C Frequency Distribution of Agnatic Ancestral Groups   *225*
D Summaries of Class Indicators of Some Modern Elites   *228*
GLOSSARY   *231*
REFERENCES   *237*
INDEX   *247*

viii

Foreword

BRAHMANS BY traditional reputation are supposed to be priests and pundits, meticulous observers of ritual prescriptions and custodians of Vedic learning. Of the four major orders, or *varnas*, of Hindu society, the Brahman order has been assigned by Manu and other scriptures the role of cultivating and transmitting the great tradition of Sanskritic Hinduism. In view of this reputation, the "changing" Brahmans described in this study may come as a surprise. There are some priests and pundits among them, but many more are lawyers and physicians, judges and government servants, and politicians, engineers, business executives and university teachers. Are they then "fallen" Brahmans who have abandoned their scriptural traditions for secular modern occupations and ideologies? This is a possible interpretation of the changes, one which appeals to those influenced by the theories of Marx, Maine, and Weber on the incompatibility of "traditional" and "modern" societies. These theories, incidentally, were based largely on nineteenth-century reports on the "traditional" character of Indian soicety.

Dr. Khare chooses not to follow these theories or the interpretations based on them. And he has many good facts and reasons at his command for not doing so. In spite of having gone into modern and secular occupations, the Kanya-Kubja Brahmans his study describes continue to follow "exacting tradition in social ceremonies" and generally continue to regard themselves and to be regarded by others as good, even devout, Brahmans. Their secular activities and success, moreover, bring them increased prestige and status among their caste and kin members. How is this possible? On the classical theory of contradictions between traditional and modern societies, these facts would appear para-

doxical and anomalous. At most they would indicate a temporary, transitional phase in an incomplete process of modernization. Khare's study suggests an alternative interpretation. The
Kanya-Kubja Brahmans, he says, are "pragmatists" as well as
"traditionalists" in responding to the opportunities and constraints of modernization. They have the capacity to manipulate
both modern and traditional values and resources according to
the situation. They can perform efficiently and honestly in the impersonal roles of "officers" in modern "organizations" and yet
find time and ways to help caste and kin and to maintain their
religious traditions.

One of Khare's major contributions is to demonstrate how the
norms of "bureaucratic" impersonality get translated into a code
of morality and virtue within traditional Indian culture. He shows
that while caste and kinship affiliation are two axes of the moral
code, they are not necessarily a "free passport" to jobs and other
favors but are limited and even cancelled out by considerations
of economic status, residence, esprit de corps, and other factors.
His detailed analysis of this thesis and the system of social stratification it entails is an original and important contribution. In
the course of the analysis he provides much revealing information that is rarely found in such studies. I refer specifically to his
data on prestige indicators for elite status, his analysis of the
formal and informal arenas in an elite residence, the candid direct quotations from bureaucrats on why ambiguity and indeci-
sion are virtues, the statistical data on the percentage of fathers'
observances still followed by their sons in different occupations,
the cultural rules of behavior governing relations between superiors and inferiors in a modern office, and the very complete
account of how kin networks were found and used by one father
to help his son get a job.

Dr. Khare offers a second and subsidiary explanation of the
apparently paradoxical behavior of these changing Brahmans in
his description and analysis of their caste associations, or *sabhas*.
His account of the "interjacent" character of these associations
shows how they help solve problems for their members, problems
that come with modernization—providing employment agencies,
marriage brokers, educational institutions, caste historians and
custodians of the faith. This modernizing role of caste associations
among non-Brahmans as well as Brahmans has been stressed by

M. N. Srinivas and S. and L. Rudolph, among others, but seldom with such rich ethnographic detail and supporting documentary data as Dr. Khare's account contains.

The mixtures of modern and traditional features, of secular and sacred, impersonal and personal in the operation of these associations is reminiscent of fraternal organizations in the United States. Perhaps these American organizations also play an analogous interjacent role, mediating between the religious and cultural traditions of the fraternal groups, on the one hand, and the impersonal bureaucracies of government, business, and the professions, on the other.

Dr. Khare calls his approach "social anthropological." Certainly an intensive field study of eighty-two families supplemented by mail information about the "networks" of another 100, systematically employing many concepts and methods of social anthropology, is entitled to this designation. Yet his study has certain features which need to be noted since they are not commonly to be found in social anthropological studies and may account for the distinctiveness of this study. When Khare came to the University of Chicago in 1963–64 as a research associate, he already possessed some unusual qualifications to undertake a social anthropological study of the Kanya-Kubja Brahmans. These qualifications included a doctorate in anthropology from the University of Lucknow; an extended five-year period of intimate association with them when he taught anthropology in one of their colleges in Lucknow, a period during which he also did a village field study and collected some information; a fluent knowledge of the language, which happens to be his mother tongue; and a wide-ranging curiosity, anthropological insight and detachment. These qualifications more than offset the usual disadvantages of studying one's own society. Accordingly, when he proposed to return to do an intensive study of how some of these Brahman families relate their traditions to modern changes, my colleagues and I encouraged him.

Another respect in which this study is distinctive is the way in which it combines description and analysis of institutionalized behavior and role as observed in daily life with the sociologists' theory of modern formal organizations. Using the Weberian ideal-typical criteria for a rational-bureaucratic organization, Khare traces in considerable detail the extent to which the Kanya-

Kubja Brahmans conform and fail to conform to these criteria, especially in the context of their caste associations. The conclusion Dr. Khare draws from this part of the study is not the usual one that these Brahmans are bureaucrats *manqués* because they have allowed the "ascriptive" considerations of kinship, caste, and religion to influence their behavior. The caste associations, after all, are not formal organizations of the same kind and degree as the "offices" of modern government, business, and the professions. As one sabha officer quoted in the study so lucidly points out, officers of a caste association are "unpaid, honorary and voluntary workers" who are motivated by a mission to promote the common welfare of their caste and kin and not by an official set of rights and duties. The author agrees with this opinion and also underlines the "sacral" and ascriptive features of the caste associations. But he also points out their modern secular features and functions. And it is this coexistence and interplay of the traditional and modern in the context of the caste associations, as well as in other contexts, that supports his more general conclusion that at the level of daily living the Kanya-Kubja Brahmans deal with these mixtures and interactions "without the fierce conceptual conflicts that a social anthropologist thinks exist between the idealized a priori categories like ascription and achievement, caste and class, tradition and modernity, and kinship and bureaucracy. It is not that such conflicts are not noted by the modern caste members, but they almost always have several ways of dealing with them within a scheme of cultural priorities."

This conclusion may not quite settle the debate among students of Indian society about whether the competition between caste associations of different castes represents a disintegration of the caste system (Leach), its "democratic reincarnation" (S. and L. Rudolph), or its adaptiveness to changing conditions (M. N. Srinivas). At least the conclusion does show, as Khare points out, that the ethnographic reality is not simple and that castes "can be deparochialized but not completely universalized."

Dr. Khare also seems to me essentially right when he notes that the manner in which the changing Brahmans of his study combine tradition and innovation represents an all-Indian tendency in which "the modern Indian achiever, whether a politician or an administrator or a professional, is not a new man (and he does not want to be); he is a link of cultural continuity between his ascendants and descendants. . . . [He] neither makes a tabula rasa of the old, nor does [he] commit himself unreservedly to the modern and Western." An increasing number of recent studies are pointing to this same conclusion. We can only be grateful to the author for giving us, among other worthy gifts, in this and in his other studies of the Kanya-Kubja Brahmans a richly documented case study to help lay the ghost of the overworked dichotomy between traditional and modern societies.

MILTON SINGER

Preface

THIS BOOK has two interrelated purposes. Based on available documentary and field data, it seeks to present a microsociological account of Kanya-Kubja Brahman caste associations. The second purpose is wider; for it relates to the problem of studying social change in a complex and diversified society, especially where tradition and modernity confront and compete in social reality. I have attempted to answer these questions: What is the relationship between the modern organizational and the traditional sociocultural bases of Kanya-Kubja behavior? And, how do the processes of social change operate on the supposed dichotomy of tradition and modernity under the Indian situation?

My approach is social-anthropological, seeking to see how far its concepts and techniques can be used in the analysis of social change in caste associations. Whenever necessary, I have turned to the other social sciences—especially sociology—for useful conceptual differentiations; but, as should be clear from textual discussions, I have avoided their "wholesale transportation." Thus, I have tried to be cautious about the wide—rather sweeping—ambience accorded to "caste and kinship" under social anthropological emphasis, and about the relative polarities and rigidities in the use of such sociological concepts as "ascription," "voluntary organization," and "achievement." Yet the analytical implications of such concepts, as I note in the Introduction, are found to be helpful for explaining the organization of Kanya-Kubja caste associations (the *sabha*s)[1]—a dynamic meet-

---

1. Hindi (or Sanskritized Hindi) terms and phrases are italicized and translated at their initial appearance in the text; and in addition a glossary of these terms is also provided.

Often I have transliterated words by retaining their local renderings

ing ground of institutionalized and "organizational" (bureaucratic) behavior. The study also tries to indicate the usefulness of
such "adapted" conceptual tools beyond the sabha contexts.

My contact with the Kanya-Kubja Brahmans started in 1957,
when I was an anthropology teacher at Kanya-Kubja College.
My interest in their social organization was aroused in 1958 by
the behavioral patterns of Kanya-Kubja colleagues and students.
With candor the latter introduced me to their own caste group.
My teaching assignments at the college lasted until the fall of
1963; and during this period I continued, off and on, the data collection on the caste group through the help of my Kanya-Kubja
friends. The topics of my inquiry varied from hierarchy and hypergamy to family rituals. Between January 1965 and June 1966
I approached Kanya-Kubja Brahmans with a systematic and
more intensive field program, including the problem of their
caste associations.

The substantive field material upon which this study is based
was collected during this period in Lucknow and Kanpur. Living
in Lucknow, I made frequent trips to Kanpur and several to the
Fatehgarh-Farrukhabad (Kannauj) and Hardoi areas. About
eighty-two prestigious Kanya-Kubja families were intensively
studied through prolonged and repeated observations and interviews. Often a single interview lasted for several hours. I now observed Kanya-Kubja Brahmans beyond the confines of the college, which became so familiar during the 1957–63 period. As
Brahmans and as officers, businessmen, contractors, priests, and
clerks, and such, Kanya-Kubjas were found to confront and resolve dilemmas of sociocultural change. Incentives and constraints
of their adaptive relationships appeared in varied empirical situations. In matters ranging from a daughter's marriage to a son's
employment, they exhibited capacities to manipulate value param-
eters and caste and kin resources on the one hand, and economic
and organizational influences, on the other. As pragmatists as
well as traditionalists, they handled the effects of modernization
in various ways.

(e.g., Kachchā, rather than Kaccā); and the diacriticals have been dropped
in the case of the frequently used sabha and Kanya-Kubja (rather than
sabhā and Kānya-Kubja). The plurals of all of these foreign words have
been formed according to common English usage.

This is the background that aroused my interest in studying their modern caste organization, an organization that was at once found to be a *part* of the wider spectrum, constrained and channelized by their dominant *social* concerns. I looked for politization and its concomitants in the sabhas, but was unsuccessful. This book starts with an examination of caste associations but expands to include the wider sociocultural context, for this alone provides the appropriate background for evaluating their significance. Since Kanya-Kubja Brahman associations were found to be different from the reported patterns of politization from other parts of India (cf. Rudolph and Rudolph 1967), I was prompted to reconstruct their past as best I could to understand the trends of their organization over time. I started doing this by mail in 1967.

My field informants (up to 1966), as usual, were always helpful. I had no direct refusal, only two polite evasions, and one postponement. Except in the beginning in 1958, when I started interviewing some old and orthodox Kanya-Kubjas (who thought that it was "undesirable" that a man of another caste should study them), I was well understood in terms of the aims of my investigations. Many keen Kanya-Kubjas went out of their way to provide information and to suggest alternative lines of inquiry. A drought-stricken Kanya-Kubja from rural Bihar, an old and bedridden Kanya-Kubja *vaidya* (indigenous physician) from Hyderabad, a retired sociology teacher from Madhya Pradesh, an old lady from Rajasthan, and an affluent family of Lucknow, were, among scores of others, my ready helpers. After becoming better acquainted with me (with the help of a mutually known person as a reference point), my informants did not hesitate to discuss their intracaste social problems, ranging from marriages to caste sabhas, and to their offices. They displayed a striking capacity to observe their own society in a detached manner. Personalities and families were brought in with directness, as I became "one of them" after a long exposure. Men with a grudge often discussed anomalous situations, but always with a useful perspective.

I have tried my best to reciprocate this confidence of my informants. Studying a modern, educated caste group imposes onerous limitations; and if I have failed somehow somewhere, it is inadvertent, and I extend my apologies. However, it was the field work phase of my inquiry that allowed me to reconstruct sabha details and the related empirical situations of tradition and modernity. Written words, printed materials, and interview notes were also compared for authenticity—always with the help of the Kanya-Kubjas. Those who represented the caste and those who constituted it cooperated readily in the endeavor. They welcomed me openly for the purpose of studying anything from marital to familial situations, to caste sabha affairs. Language was no barrier, and contacts could be as frequent as desired. I constantly tried to maintain the role of an "inquisitive learner," keeping opinionated debates to a minimum; however, discussions and self-praise among my informants were cautiously handled—the first was encouraged to a degree, and the latter was only used as a "catalyst" for further discussion. Reflective thinking and explanations were always encouraged.

My informants as well as my correspondents were heterogeneous, including the rural and the urban, the educated and the illiterate, the prestigious and the "commoner," the rich and the poor. This was a cumulative effect of the time span (1958–63 and 1965–66) involved and the diversified topics pursued. Geographic distance was limited during the intensive field work, mainly in the central and western districts of Uttar Pradesh. Thus, unable to find time and money for an extended trip to outlying concentrations of the Kanya-Kubjas, I first worked on the local bases of heterogeneity. It stood me well when in 1967 I put together my all-Indian mail-communication network. With the acquisition and study of *Kanya-Kubja* (the caste journal) files (1957–67), the distributional patterns easily became evident; the information about who could be contacted where, and through whom, was easily organized. The journal editor Pt. Rama Shankar Misra, "Sripati Ji," became an enthusiastic contributor and coordinator. The response of the first "mail out" to some fifty persons outside of Uttar Pradesh was extremely gratifying. The first contacts led to several newer ones, reaching a high of 150. From Delhi to Bangalore, and from Ajmer and Ahmedabad to Calcutta, my correspondents tried to inform me of their local cultural patterns. In an overview now, because of their strong forces for keeping cultural continuities, these outlying concentrations seem to be the interconnected parts of an "expanded locality"—a "paralocality"—of the Uttar Pradesh Kanya-Kubja Brahmans.

Still, as is evident at some places in the book, information received has remained either incomplete or vague or doubtful. About ten mail contacts trailed off with incomplete information; my efforts to relocate or revive them remained unsuccessful. Hence, I lacked precise numerical information on some outlying caste sabhas. Readiest response did not always mean durability of contact and/or reliability of information. Limitations of written messages were sometimes acutely evident, although I tried to remedy these with more intensive and/or alternative mail contacts.

Thus, as a combination of intensive field studies and extensive mail contacts, this book is based on eighty-two intensive family studies and 100 prolonged mail contacts (of several months' duration). The former are from the Lucknow-Kanpur region; the latter cover the rest of the important Kanya-Kubja concentrations. However, no sample representation is claimed, except that the material does allow a wider degree of spatial comparison. Apart from the techniques listed above, I have noted several procedural points in the text at appropriate places.

The most important single source of published information on Kanya-Kubja Brahmans was the caste journal *Kanya-Kubja* and the related literature published by Akhil Bhartiya Sri Kanya-Kubja Pratinidhi Sabha, Lucknow, over the last thirty-five years. What were ephemeral items for the common caste reader were invaluable leads for this study. The various volumes of the journal noted in the References were kindly sent to me by the editor. In 1965 he allowed me to use special publications of the society for a detailed study of the Kanya-Kubja elites. My several conversations with him educated me more in specific caste problems than a stack of old files could have. I availed myself of several chances, however, to study records at his office to reconstruct Kanya-Kubja social history. The biographic volumes (*Chāruch-aritāvali*) are now out of print and are available only at the editor's office in Lucknow.

In contrast, only limited material was available to me on the Kanara Saraswat Brahmans. Miss Maureen L. P. Patterson of the South Asia Library of the University of Chicago provided me with their journal, *The Kanara Saraswat;* and I am thankful to her for this and for the comparative data on caste journals in India (see appendix B).

Classification and systematization of the field and documentary data took almost one year (July 1967 to May 1968). Subject cards of different colors were used to discover areas of incomplete or lacking information. Once these were known, appropriate correspondents were contacted for elaboration, verification, and completion of available leads. (However, since the same network was used for supplementing data on areas outside the scope of this book, correspondents had a wide variety of subjects to engage in—according to their knowledge and inclination.) Subject cards on caste association matters were sorted against those on caste, kinship, and modernity, allowing a check between *possible* and *meaningful*—empirically verifiable and culturally significant—alternatives of behavior under the forces of social change. Such a scheme allowed me to emphasize interjacent dynamics of social change as explained later in the text.

My work on this book was greatly facilitated by two year-long grants (1967–69) made by the Faculty Research Committee of the University of Wisconsin, Madison. These made possible the necessary arrangements for collection of data through the mail and the processing of data and writing of reports by specialist and secretarial help. M. Kamal, as part-time project help, collected and classified *Kanya-Kubja* data, including the retrieval of extensive kinship-network material given in chapter 8. The committee offered further facilities during the summer of 1968, enabling me to do the writing in conducive surroundings. I am thankful to the committee for its helpful and understanding attitude.

However, the gainful use of the above facilities was made possible only through the most cooperative responses of my scores of Kanya-Kubja Brahman friends in various cities and villages of India. Naturally, this study would have been impossible if these people had not continually contributed—both directly in my field work and indirectly through the mail. They helped me to establish rewarding contacts from a distance and freely gave me information on the points that I raised repeatedly in my letters. All was with a considerateness that befits, as they would say, "educated Brahmans." I take this opportunity to express my profound thanks to all of them. However, I shall be failing in my duty, unless I record my special gratitude to Pt. Rama Shankar Misra, "Sripati Ji" of Lucknow; Professor S. D. Dube of Indore; Pt. Bhuvaneshwar Prasad Pandey of Ichchatu; Pt. T. R. Shashtri of Lucknow; Mrs. U. Tiwari of Jaipur; and fifteen modern caste elites who must remain anonymous for understandable reasons. All of these people have told me so much over the years about their "life ways" that only an aspect can be covered in this attempt.

On the completion of my first draft I took the opportunity of informally discussing the planning and the content of the book with my colleagues in Madison, particularly Professor Joseph Elder, whose comments were helpful and reactions encouraging. Despite his own work, Professor Elder closely read the entire manuscript, discussed its contents from the sociological perspective, and made several suggestions for its improvement. He helped me to keep from straying into unnecessary generalities, and emphasized the value of intensifying the inquiry. Professors Miller, Hitchcock, and Hart of Madison, and Professor Nicholas of Michigan State University were also consulted at one stage or another.

When it came to preparing the final draft, Professors Milton Singer and Bernard Cohn of the University of Chicago were most helpful. While presenting an aspect of this study during the annual meeting of the American Anthropological Association (Seattle, 1968), I received encouragement from Professor Cohn. Despite his heavy engagements, Professor Milton Singer graciously invested time and energy to comment extensively on its content and style. He repeatedly helped me to improve the effort in his inimitable gentle style. He gave me confidence when I needed it and provided analytical clarity whenever necessary. Moreover, I have received intellectual stimulation from his writings— particularly those on cultural transmission and structural change in India. I am most grateful to him for all such stimulus, without which this study would have missed so much, and especially so for his writing of the Foreword.

However, the presentation is entirely mine and I alone am responsible for whatever shortcomings exist in the effort.

Mr. Calhoun and Mr. Goodrich of Manitowoc County Campus have helped me to improve the readibility of the manuscript in several ways, particularly for a Western audience. The book underwent several revisions and for their patience and skill in typing the different drafts, I also thank Miss M. Rosemary and Mrs. Evelyn Martin of Manitowoc, and Miss Mary Kay Peters of Green Bay. The figures were ably drawn by Paul Bouschard.

Following the traditional Hindu manner, I shall only implicitly thank my family which has, as always, helped me most, directly as well as indirectly, during the course of writing.

R.S.K.

Introduction

1 The Problem
and Its Formulation

THIS is a study of some caste associations (*sabhas*)[1] of the Kanya-Kubja Brahmans that betray, more than anything else, a continuous process of adjustment between traditional and modern behavioral patterns. In accounting for such a wide process, this description of sabha organization will provide the basis for investigating both "modern organizational" behavior of the Kanya-Kubja group and traditional structure and its effect on this behavior. The emphasis will be on showing how such interrelations are established in social reality by the Kanya-Kubjas and how they can be systematized within social anthropology.

Here I am primarily concerned with the educated, urban, and orthodox sections of this north Indian caste group. They belong to the Panch Gauda Brahmans, "which are found north of the Vindhya ranges," according to a traditional genealogy (Misra 1959, p. 9). The same source describes Kānya-Kubja Province (*désh* or *pradésh*) as "lying between Kannauj, Ayodhya and Avadh, and Delhi and Agra" (for descriptions of other castes of the same geographic designation see Crooke 1896; and Fox 1967, for a Kanya-Kubja Bania trader caste). Unless specified otherwise, "Kanya-Kubja" in this study refers to the Brahman group.

1. The popular Hindi term "sabha" may refer to any kind of assembly of men (or, by implication, things). Here, it will be used as a technical term to describe voluntary groupings of a caste and is to be preferred over "association" or "organization," to avoid the transplanting of certain unnecessary complexities, especially at the expense of some more important, but implicit, native connotations of cultural *emics* and *ethos*. Moreover, in the stage in which such sabhas are found to be now, they probably are most aptly designated by the native term. In the following discussion such meanings are mostly obtained by the contexts in which the term "sabha" appears; but "association," however, does appear in the text when appropriate.

3

They are considered here as a caste rather than a sub-caste, primarily because they present complexes of status-rank organization, occupational patterns, marriage requirements, and prescribed rites and rules of orthodoxy and orthopraxy (i.e., an emphasis on ritualized religion) which they hold as peculiar to themselves (see Khare 1960). Therefore, the main criteria, cultural and social ones (rather than those of size and distribution), are regarded as sufficient grounds for treating the Kanya-Kubja Brahmans as a caste group.

Counted among the socioeconomically progressive groups of Uttar Pradesh they have been exposed to Western education since the 1850s and to diverse occupations in far off places since the late eighteenth century.[2] Although a detailed social history of the group is largely absent,[3] it is repeatedly recorded in traditional genealogies that a significant section of these Brahmans has for long lived in cities such as Lucknow, Kanpur, Unnao, Sitapur, Hardoi, Fatehgarh-Farrukhabad, and Agra, and that these urbanites have increasingly helped in attracting their rural counterparts into the towns or cities.[4] Their diversity of and excellence in modern occupations have placed them under various forces of modernization, including Anglicization and Westernization, urbanization, bureaucratization, and politization. The members take pride in the fact that their caste has produced such diverse "achievers" as chief ministers, state governors, members for the Indian mission at the United Nations, and secretaries

2. A personal communication and a genealogy of 1790 of a Kanya-Kubja elite from Hyderabad, among others, provide the basis for such an observation.

Court service, the military (Khare 1966), and trade are constantly mentioned as prestigious jobs by genealogists as well as by my old informants.

3. However, there are several good biographic and genealogical accounts in Sanskrit and Hindi that give, at least, a rough idea of their history. Information is much more definite after the 1860s, the period being covered by several writers of *gotra-vamshāvalis* ("clan" genealogies) as well as by some sabha workers (*Kanya-Kubja* 1910–20).

4. This effect was most dramatically evident to me when I took field trips (May-June 1965) to such places of original concentration (*susthān*) as Kannauj and its neighboring villages. The exodus, over a period of time, has been in some places as much as 76 per cent of the total Kanya-Kubja Brahman population. However, those who remain in the village are primarily there because of their significant land holdings or some other sizeable economic resource.

4

and under-secretaries to the central and state governments—and as many before as after the Independence. In addition, there have been numerous judges, lawyers, engineers, physicians, university professors, writers, journalists, businessmen, and philanthropists.[5] The awareness of such a "heritage" is repeatedly mentioned by those parents who are involved in educating their children "with the aim that they reach as exalted social positions as their forefathers."[6]

On the other hand, these modern Kanya-Kubjas display a particularly strong tendency to follow all the traditionally important rules and rituals of marriage, including an extensive emphasis on kinship gift presentations, an emphasis on higher dowry transactions, and the continuing close observance of the multiple caste hierarchy. Orthodoxy in commensalism goes to the extreme, although it may be comparatively lax with the younger generation now, especially when the youths do not live with their parents or some older relative. The latter still recall with pride how those who travelled abroad for further studies in the 1900s were "excommunicated" on ritual bases. As I shall de-

5. Although it is tempting to give names of the numerous outstanding "achievers" of this caste, I shall refrain from it in deference to my informants. However, one can conveniently name such persons as the late Pt. Ravi Shankar Shukla (Chief Minister, Madhya Pradesh), the late Sir Girija Shankar Bajpai (Governor, Bombay), Sri Shyama Behari Misra, and D. P. Misra.

A detailed account of almost one thousand eminent persons from all parts of India is found in the *Chārucharitāvalis* (biographic accounts) compiled and published by the present editor of *Kanya-Kubja*, the caste journal, during the 1930s. Several of them were again updated in a golden jubilee number of the journal (1957). These accounts are based on extensive travel and person-to-person inquiry by the editor.

6. Throughout this book, statements, such as this, appearing within quotes are (unless otherwise specified) pieces of information directly from my interview notes. Whenever possible the informant has been identified by a pseudonym and some other actual additional characteristic. For understandable reasons, those who preferred to remain anonymous have so remained in the discussion.

Despite this extreme caution, if some inference can be drawn by any person of this caste group, I can only offer again (as I did in 1960) my apology with the plea that my aim has consistently been to record and analyze their own social group as objectively as possible. Although my own caste identification is different, I have almost always enjoyed the Kanya-Kubja Brahman's sagacity and open-mindedness, even when investigating such currently unpopular topics as casteism and individual favoritism.

5

scribe later, the variety and pervasiveness of this traditionalistic element in an elite's behavior, whether at home or in work, can not be overemphasized.

These two broad tendencies provide the backdrop for our inquiry on organizational behavior among these Brahmans. Whereas the presence of these tendencies in any Indian social group is a sociological commonplace, their relative emphasis may be specific to every group. Their caste sabhas, though originally approached as representatives of modern organizations, were later discovered to be an excellent entrée into the dynamics between the traditional and modern behavior of the caste group. There were much more intricate and substantive organizational relations found at the individual, informal, noncollective, and unorganized level. Thus, this study for the above reason and for several others detailed later finds it useful to focus on intracaste kin and nonkin groups (for a definition, see below) with an emphasis on individually achieved positional ranks and behavioral patterns. The reference levels, however, may be both groups and/or individuals found within or outside the traditional caste system.

THE NEED FOR THIS TYPE OF STUDY

During the process of developing this inquiry, I became aware of the limitations of existing published resources. The need for detailed accounts has been felt by social anthropologists working on social change in India (e.g., Bailey 1963a and b). Although recent social anthropological studies provide hypothetical-ideal schemes for explaining the meaning and function of modern caste organizations in India, the lack of sufficient empirical studies has consistently been felt during the last decade. Naturally, this study tries in its own modest way to reduce such a gap.

Even with the growing interest in such organizations, as far as I know, there are few full-length intensive studies from the social anthropological viewpoint planned or under progress. One detailed study has been completed, however, by a political scientist interested in the south-Indian Nadars.

The published data relating to Indian caste associations has appeared mainly in successive decennial Census of India *Reports* from 1872 onwards. Its emphasis was mainly that of recording "organized" efforts for claiming and disputing rank precedence (for a series of historical facts, see Ghurye 1961, pp. 186–87, 205–11, 313–25, and historical sources mentioned therein). Thus, census reports and the daily newspapers formed the primary basis for making observations on caste associations, even up to the late 1940s. Since it is not the aim of this work to trace the varied historical trends in the study of caste and its modern adaptations (for a recent and useful overview of trends in caste studies, see Cohn 1968), and especially since numerous caste associations making higher caste-rank claims are not of direct relevance to this case study, let us go on to the more relevant sources of the last two decades.

The 1950s saw the vigorous pursuit of the empirical approach for crystallizing some powerful methods and concepts, and not merely for collecting information on varied "customs and practices." Such a beginning is very well represented in the now famous studies by Marriott (1955) and Srinivas (1955). As Singer (1968, p. viii) recently observed about this period, the basic social units of Indian society (joint family, caste, and village community) were no longer looked on as structural or cultural isolates but as being "intimately interconnected with one another and with other units, through social networks of various kinds." This "non-isolationist point of view" became the point of departure for many succeeding studies, the notable being Singer (1959), Leach (1960), Srinivas (1962), Mason (1967), Crane (1967), and Silverberg (1968), even if each collection has its specific orientation and discusses disparate topics. The same approach is further extended in Singer and Cohn (1968), where attention "is directed to the specific patterns of interconnection which can be traced through empirical studies of particular groups in particular localities, and to the changes in such patterns" (Singer 1968, p. viii). Cohn (1968, p. 25) aptly sees the same collection as "one of many indications of the variety of directions we are going in. Politics, study of entrepreneurs, systematic study of cultural rules, sociolinguistics, and law, are all underlaid by new and more rigorous methods of quantification and model construction and are all tempered by wider comparative knowledge." The present study may basically fall in this line, although with appropriate particularizations.

However, discussions of caste associations have taken place mostly in the context of "social mobility" (as a means to this end) and/or political modernization (e.g., for general observations, see Srinivas 1962, 1966, 1968). They have been discussed as a consequence of wider sociocultural processes of change as operating on the traditional caste institution. Macrosociological observations and approaches have been employed to examine the sabhas for their general functions and interrelations (see Rudolph and Rudolph 1967). However, this study intends to approach the subject in a specific microsociological perspective, although such an empirical approach may not deter us (as we shall see later) from discussing the findings in more general terms.

More directly relevant, and more specific, references for our discussion are mostly contained in disparate articles appearing since 1960, and most of them will be mentioned at appropriate places. However, Leach (1960), Srinivas (1961, 1966, 1968), Nandi (1965), Kothari and Maru (1965), Rudolph and Rudolph (1960, 1967), Rudolph (1965), Bailey (1963a, 1963b), Fox (1967), Hardgrave (1966, 1967), among others, represent, even if in a fragmentary way, a train of current specialized thinking on the caste organizational problem. More general interdisciplinary suggestions come from, for example, Weiner (1962), Dalton (1967), Almond et al. (1960), Smith (1963), Apter (1965), and Shils (1961).

Finally, an examination of the bibliographies (1965, 1966, 1967) published by *The Journal of Asian Studies* further indicates that even now the studies of Indian caste associations have not received their due attention. The topic is covered in about a dozen studies, mostly in articles and a few unpublished dissertations. No published book was reported that dealt exclusively with sabha organization.

AIMS OF THE STUDY

We are concerned with two apparently basic questions in this study: first, what are the factual details of sabha organization among these modern Brahmans and, second, why are these sabhas as they are? In answer to the first question I shall present a full-length case-study of the all-Indian Kanya-Kubja caste association (along with its various local sabhas and sabha-sponsored bodies) and its organizational characteristics. A complete answer to the second question is not easy, but is more significant, for it allows us to understand the meaning of and the reasons for the presence or absence of organizational complexity in such sabhas. Moreover, it also brings into focus the diversity of the organizational behavior of this group. We shall answer it by an extended discussion of status stratification and modern sabha organization under ideal and actual conditions. This, thus, offers the two-fold aim for this study.

The characteristic that intrigued me very early in this inquiry was the absence of organizational elaboration and complexity in the Kanya-Kubja sabhas, especially because, if their modern achievements are any indicator, they are expected to be more concerted in organizing their caste for increasingly instrumental and prestigious political ends under the post-Independence democracy.[7] The significance of this study, therefore, rests, at least in part, in finding out the reasons for such an organizational state of the Kanya-Kubja sabhas, and in determining the way their traditional and modern elements produce interjacence and interpenetration in a functionally useful way.

This study deals with the above problems and, while so doing, it employs, transvalues, and adapts certain sociological and social-anthropological concepts; it does not import them wholesale.[8] Besides, it also presupposes discussion of some social institutions of the Kanya-Kubjas, including signs of change and

7. See Rudolph and the Rudolphs (1965, pp. 975 ff.; 1967) who made a logical and forceful case for "the democratic incarnation of caste in India," by spelling out a series of presence-absence factors and by encouraging one to look forward to a new "decompressed and deparochialized" way of group assertion for catalyzing democratic policy in India. However, the details as provided by the case of the Kanya-Kubjas help illuminate this proposition in a negative way; that is they do *not* necessarily use their modern conditions for their political or organizational ends, yet they do maintain their network of kinship cohesion by using the same modern conditions. Further discussion will be undertaken on this in the concluding chapter.

8. With modern theoretical and conceptual developments in both sociological and social anthropological fields, with freer borrowings from either side, and especially with the topic with which I am concerned in this study, the use of the terms "sociological," "social anthropological," and "anthropological" is interchangeable with manifestly specific overtones or undertones concerning certain research techniques, concepts, and theoretical theses. For example, as I shall use the terms "achieved" and "ascriptive," "formal" and "informal," "bureaucracy" and "formalization," I shall avoid a priori sociological rigidities or polarities and shall use them flexibly.

9

nonchange in this century. As both of these aspects need appropriate prefatory treatment, I shall proceed as follows: First, I shall introduce the general frame of reference that I wish to use in my description and exposition. This I shall do here without entering into an extended discussion of conceptual problems, for in the final chapter of this book I shall return to consider those upon which this study crucially bears. This discussion will be followed by a consideration of certain aspects of directly involved institutions and organizational activities of the modern Kanya-Kubja.

INSTITUTIONAL AND ORGANIZATIONAL BEHAVIOR

This book is concerned, first of all, with certain aspects of the organizational behavior of a caste group; this, then, makes it essential that we define and differentiate between institutional and organizational behavior.[9] Since this differentiation has been conceptually refined for over a century, it appears as the most fundamental element of modern sociological thinking (see, for example, the chapter sequence in Parsons et al. [1961] on the theories of modern sociology). Social anthropology has recognized the same basic differentiation, although it has almost exclusively emphasized institutionalized relationships, because it has been concerned chiefly with the study of relatively small-scale primitive and peasant communities. However, as it is becoming evident that social anthropology can also contribute modestly but significantly to understanding more complex cultures and mod-

9. This dichotomy is clearly established by Durkheim in terms of the mechanical and organic (1933, first English edition), although its presence is evident in the writings of the historical jurists ever since the beginning of the last century. This thought, actively pursued by Toennies in his *Gemeinschaft und Gesellschaft*—a work reviewed by Durkheim—basically persisted in Lewis Morgan's "gentile" and "political," and Sir Henry Maine's "status" and "contract." Max Weber takes up the same two poles of social order and provides a huge panoply of distinctions for differentiating between social stability and change, "with a focus on the rationalization of the world" (see Naegele 1961, pp. 189–90). Linton differentiated, as we know, between ascription and achievement, between what Weber also called "closed" and "open" systems, and what has become so fundamental for modern role analysis.

Recently Marriott (1968) recognized the necessity of "closed" and "open" systems of stratification in Indian villages and cities, respectively. He uses it for understanding the trends in modern caste mobility. Especially important is his idea of realizing the existence of the multiplicity of referent groups and their ethos in the modern Indian stratificatory system.

ern communities, its major concepts may have to be appropriately refocussed in the context of the specific demands of the inquiry, as in this study in regard to the concepts of "institution" and "organization."

Social anthropologists are in wont of using the term "institution" to refer to social relationships which are well-established, relatively enduring, and guided by cultural directive. Institutions involve social usages which are characteristic of the society which possesses them. Whereas some social usages may be more institutionalized than certain others, the social anthropologist is supposed to be dealing with *some* degree of institutionalized relationships (see Beattie 1964, p. 35), even in the context of change where erosion or defensive strengthening of institutions may be going on. In this basic sense, the present inquiry adheres to the accepted social-anthropological usage of the term "institution," especially in dealing with the study of tradition, caste, and kinship under changing circumstances.

However, since this study is concerned mainly with modernity and "modern organizations" and since it is through a study of the latter that change and nonchange in tradition, caste, and kinship are approached, the concept of "organization," as used here, requires some clarification, especially as it accents those aspects that may be considered "sociological." First it may be noted that social anthropology recognizes the basic dichotomy of social relationships as conceived by Toennies, Durkheim, Weber, and others, and that it stresses differences and dynamics between primary and secondary, and kinship and contractual groups. However, social anthropology does not use the term "organization" with exactly the same emphases and meanings as sociology does. The former may use it to emphasize empirical, dynamic, adaptive (or· variant), and comparatively "flexible" social relationships as against those of "structure" which may signify relative stability, constancy, continuity, and persistence (usually at an abstracted level). Social anthropology may also use the term "organization" for planned action for an institutional aim which is shared by a set of persons. Within institutions organized actions may be contracted for desirable common goals. (Traditional caste *panchāyats* [councils] may illustrate such an organization.) The dynamics between institutional and contractual relationships may be widely and variously recognized within social anthropology (see Bohannan 1963, pp. 146–49).

But in this study, sociological emphases are accentuated in the concept of "organization." This is done *not* to dissociate or to push the social anthropological usage into the background, but to reformulate it according to the requirements of the subject of our study.

Modern caste associations (sabhas) are not to be confused with traditional caste councils (panchāyats: these bodies never existed among the Kanya-Kubjas; and, in general, they have been found to be absent among the Brahmans [see Ghurye 1961]). Most of all, they are organizationally different, involving different criteria of formal rank, roles, and relationships. The latter characteristically involve "bureaucratic" or "modern organizational" rationality (as against only institutional) as commonly recognized by sociologists. Modern complex societies, according to sociologists (e.g., see Horowitz 1965), are increasingly marked by social groups which are called "modern organizations" (Etzioni 1962, 1965). The latter are, according to Etzioni (1965, p. 3), "social units (or human groupings) deliberately constructed and reconstructed to seek specific goals," and have: "(1) divisions of labor, power, and communication responsibilities, divisions which are not random or traditionally patterned, but deliberately planned to enhance the realization of specific goals; (2) the presence of one or more power centers which control the concerted efforts of the organization and direct them towards its goals . . . (3) substitution of personnel, i.e. unsatisfactory persons can be removed and others assigned their tasks." Sociologists like social anthropologists recognize that even institutions require some degree of planned, purposive action, have a network of power relations, and may deliberately structure and restructure social units with replaceable membership; however, they also emphasize that a modern organization has these characteristics in much greater measure and uses them much more frequently, and as rationally and effectively as possible.

The term "organization" will be often used in this specialized sense to differentiate analytically (but is not so tightly compartmentalized in reality) the institutional and organizational behavior of modern Kanya-Kubja Brahmans in their homes, offices, and sabhas. This will be done first to extricate sabhas from being viewed merely as extensions of caste and kinship, and second to view them as modern organizations of a *special* kind. Under

the latter emphasis, *empirical dynamics, rather than the ideal gap,* of institutional and organizational relationships will be under consideration—a matter of crucial social-anthropological concern. I shall return repeatedly to discuss organizational behavior of the modern Kanya-Kubjas but mostly in relation to what is institutional; this is both indicative of the social reality and suggestive of the overall accent on the social anthropological approach. While I shall examine in greater detail the ideal and actual criteria of modern organization in chapters 3 and 8, here it is necessary for the sake of clarity that I suitably introduce the concepts of caste and kinship.

Kinship exemplifies the ascriptive solidarity group based on the involuntary single event of birth. It is the most fundamental, basic, common, and automatic system of social relationship. It probably displays the highest degree of institutionalization—a process under which, as noted above, some social usages are more institutionalized than certain others (cf. Beattie 1964). Kinship displays inherited as well as involuntary aspects of social relationships. It, therefore, characterizes a "closed" segment of social relations, differentiating work, or occupation, or office from home; primary groups from the secondary; and the sociological notion of "complex" from the "simple."

Caste in India basically employs a kinship criterion and is viewed as a closed system because the incorporation of new members is entirely by birth (Bailey 1963a). A particular caste is therefore considered as an ascriptive group. This view is taken for granted, as it has been found consistently applicable to the majority of social groupings in India. This view of caste is particularly advantageous for studying intercaste or caste-noncaste group relations. However, when only one caste is being studied intensively, as in this book, there can be another way of looking at a caste group. It can be viewed from within, rather than from outside, or from above, or below. In this view, any caste member, much like an ego in kinship genealogy, provides the starting point (cf. Mayer 1966) for moving from kin to nonkin, from subcaste to caste, and from caste to wider relations. The first striking feature that thus appears is that a caste group has at least—and necessarily—two types of social groupings inside it: one which forms an incestuous, nonmarriageable kinship group of relatives of both the sides (agnatic and uterine) of one's parents (evidently the

13

size or range differs in various parts of India); and the other which is composed of individuals with whom one can marry. The latter group, however, shares one very striking and important character with the former: all those nonkin members belong to a caste group by sharing the same event (of birth) by which one's kin-group members are included.[10] But beyond this sharing, the right-obligation distinctions are exclusive between the kin and the non-kin, especially in northern India, the region from which the Kanya-Kubjas come.

A caste group is thus internally differentiated into the two kin and nonkin groups, between which new boundaries are created (and old and distant ones are blurred) with every birth, marriage, and death in every generation. Again from the contemporary ego's point of view such boundaries are relatively stable, although they change first at birth, again at marriage, once again at the marriage of a son, and finally at death. Such a view becomes complicated if the egos are many, because the nonkin to some are also the kin to some others. But this network, with multiple points—some nearer and direct and others distant—is the common kinship arrangement. (For example, in most cases one approaches a nonkin caste member for a marital connection through this network of kinship.)

Despite such a complex kinship network, a caste group's non-kin zone is so large that it is impossible for a person to know all his nonkin at the same time. Institutionalized kinship is as efficient in continuous inclusion as it is in continuous exclusion. Most remarkably, the birth-ascriptive membership (which actually is a principle of kinship anomalously extended and applied to the entire caste) provides the common link to all members of one caste; but the increasing size, occupational diversity, spatial dispersion, and hierarchical differentiation[11] severely curtail the actual knowledge about nonkin caste members.

10. Anomalously, it is a "kinship" character, because the fact of birth, rather than any other, ordains once and for all one's caste calling; it is in exactly the same way as irreversible as the father-mother relationship for a newborn. This application of a universally recognized kinship rule (e.g., see Bohannan 1963, pp. 54 ff., 124 ff.) is anomalous because, logically extending, all the members of the same caste should be some type of kin-brothers and kin-sisters, and hence all should form a common nonmarriageable group. Yet the culture does not extend the kin roles and relationships to all those within a caste group. This contradiction has been described variously (see DeVos 1966, pp. 325–84; Leach 1960).

11. Hierarchical principles have been studied variously to indicate b

ELEMENTS OF SABHA ORGANIZATION

The dynamics between tradition and modernity are a fundamental characteristic of the Kanya-Kubja caste sabhas. They reflect it in their aims as well as in their organizational elements. Accordingly, their sabhas aim to promote modern occupational excellence at the individual level, on the one hand, and kinship cohesiveness for marriage, kinship, and traditional hierarchy, on the other. Organizationally, their sabhas simultaneously employ status stratification (see chapters 5, 6, and 7) and formal bureaucracy as the most important "means" of collective action. As interacting elements, they produce a range of behavioral complexity owing mainly to: first, the simultaneous employment of intercaste ascriptive hierarchical principles with those of diverse achievements; second, the presence and the simultaneous reckoning of multiple references to group levels, values, and relationships; and third, the situational dynamics of all of these dimensions, accommodating "societal guidance" presented by the modern Kanya-Kubja elites. The first dimension exhibits situations of both conflict and complementarity, depending upon the context, and it shows the relative emphasis laid on modern achievements, including those in the traditional sector. One's positional rank is, therefore, a complex of the two; and it is this positional "complex" that appears under the sabha organization. This positional complex is all together a processual, situational, and a consciously guided consequence.

In this study, a caste sabha, a "modern organization"[12] professing varied all-caste aims[13] for competing with other castes and modern organizations (cf. Bailey 1963a), is viewed in both ascriptive and achievement contexts. A sabha is conceived as an

---

they create simultaneous fission and fusion, exclusion and inclusion, and cultural integration and variation within a caste group (e.g., Hsu 1963, Pocock 1957, Marriott 1955).

12. My general preference for using the term "modern organization" or "organization" over "formal organization" or "bureaucracy" basically stems from its comparatively neutral value and simplified polarity against kinship groups (Etzioni 1965, pp. 3–4).

13. Since a following chapter will inquire into some relevant historical circumstances generally held responsible for such a need among different caste groups, here we will only indicate that the alternative means as well as aims that were brought in by the British rule and its educational system after the 1850s provided the sufficiently diverse raw material for the caste sabhas that we find today.

interjacent organization, where institutional and organizational activities interface or *interjacére* without having to move towards eventual replacement of one type by the other, mostly by striking some kind of "functional balance," and by refraining from making a sabha a truly "commitment organization."[14] However, some degree of conflict is inevitable in the two types of social action,[15] and we have to ascertain it in the context of the Kanya-Kubja sabhas, by considering "caste" as a category that is open and responsive to the constant flux of social change, whether implicit or unintended, explicit or intended (Merton 1949, pp.

14. As Gusfield (1967) has recently indicated, our notions about such social-change polarities as tradition and modernity are largely misplaced. Moreover, the assumptions concerning the "natural" dominance of the latter usually emerge from our continuing predispositions to establish Western–non-Western, modern-traditional, industrial-nonindustrial, complex-simple, and finally, and most ubiquitously, "progressive-backward" dichotomies, and from indiscriminate equivalence and superimposition of one dichotomy over another for assessing social change. Even such a simple idea as, that non-Western can also be modernistic, and modernizing —if only under a different frame of reference—is thus far hard to find in the studies of social change. The idea of interjacence tries to emphasize the organizational and functional properties of the traditional vis-à-vis the modern without acquiring a necessary predisposition one way or the other.

Functional balance refers basically to such constant evaluations by the individuals as: "what will this new action do for me and my group, if it is undertaken?" A Kanya-Kubja youth, for example, makes such decisions continuously in his domestic life and in his career. As a modern "elite" (achiever) he decides, for example, to break certain commensal and ritual rules of behavior (for it is helpful to diversify social contacts and be considered a "liberal" in his career), but the same person decides not to disobey his norms of kinship and affinity (for the repercussions of his decision would be much wider and more disruptive, hurting his near and dear ones). However, when such decisions are multiplied daily by the thousands, the group, as a whole, displays parallel tendencies. Thus it is interesting to observe that kinship, as an institution, now not only has the social function of ordering relationships between certain people, but also has the purpose of retaining the order by responding to the changed social circumstances.

Commitment organizations—an idea developed by Ralph C. Beals— are of various types, the total commitment organizations being exemplified by certain "pure" communist orders. Here it chiefly refers to the strength of one's involvement with organizational aims and activities (for a recent discussion of how "profession" and "organization" relate, see Hall 1968).

15. It might be, as Parsons (1951, pp. 44–45) indicates, due to the partial independence of "personalities" and "societies" as systems. Further, it may be due to the discrepancy between the normative and the actual, the construct, and the idea.

6 ff.). For such a purpose, caste as a social category will have to be considered at the level of actualizations (for an ideal model, see Leach 1960, pp. 1–10).

Thus, I shall try to examine the Kanya-Kubja data in terms of the interjacency between the ascriptive and the achieved, and between the institutional and the organizational aims, activities, and achievements, especially as the sabhas provide a very fertile ground for such exchanges. Since the nature of this condition will most probably depend on the contextual characteristics of the caste group, I shall narrow the actual scope of such terms as the "institutional" and the "organizational," by emphasizing the caste-specific rather than the comparative view of the modern Kanya-Kubja group. The paucity of suitable material for a systematic comparison makes the above stipulation a matter of necessity rather than of choice.

There remains one final problem limiting the scope of this inquiry, which arises primarily out of the above references to the Kanya-Kubja Brahmans. I have spoken of them as constituting a homogeneous social group whose boundaries are quite defined. However, this is only a simplification, for even in the last century these Brahmans were well-known for their migrations, occupational diversities, ritual orthodoxy, and urbanization. They had an early introduction to Westernization (see Crooke 1896; District Gazetteers 1903–27; *Kanya-Kubja* 1905–57).

Their total number of 1,303,348 according to the census of 1891 was distributed as follows: Kanpur (168,360), Unnao (120,301), Hardoi (110,358), Sitapur (98,766), Ballia (86,382), Rae Bareilly (82,284), Farrukhabad (67,025), Kheri (64,237), Barabanki (57,083), Etawah (51,910), Shahjahanpur (43,545), and Lucknow (39,428). What major increments and movements have occurred among them since then is largely a matter of guesswork, as the later census reports do not give any specific data on the Kanya-Kubja Brahmans. The modern Kanya-Kubjas produce, however, a mythical figure of two million. There is no systematic attempt by the sabhas to know what is the present population of their group. However, we shall get glimpses of their actual diversity in the following discussion, especially of the urban and the educated.

Although the Kanya-Kubja Brahmans are traditionally designated as being of western Uttar Pradesh in various genealogies

17

(*vamshāvali*), the data bear out that they settled in different and far off places, especially since the last century. Their families frequently moved in and out of Uttar Pradesh, and thousands lived permanently outside the province, although most of these continued to maintain their kinship connections with the "people back home." The social autonomy of such emigrated groups increased as their size enlarged, resulting in an extension of spatial boundaries of the caste group. Caste sabhas also appeared at such places mostly as independent welfare bodies. Several such distant organizations will be accounted for, although their coverage is not uniform for the obvious reasons of limitations of time and expense. With the availability of some reliable sources of data collection, however, I decided to cover some of the better-known organizations as best as I could; and these sabhas, far and near, only together present, as I discovered later, more comprehensive dynamics of institutional and organizational behavior. At this point it should also be clear that my coverage of "the caste group" is limited mostly to those who are actual participants in the sabha activities. This is most true of the sabhas studied from a distance, while those bodies in Lucknow and Kanpur are obviously covered in situ, i.e., in association with the local Kanya-Kubja population. However, all this has resulted in a major preoccupation with the urban Kanya-Kubjas, especially since I could not find even a single instance of sabhas organized and manned exclusively by their rural counterpart.[16] In turn, my preoccupation with such sabhas has led to an emphasis on the roles of urban Kanya-Kubja elites in such organizations.

I shall now, before plunging into the description of the caste sabhas, briefly outline some of the major institutional aspects of Kanya-Kubja caste and kinship, and their interrelatedness with modern social achievement. Both aspects are of contemporary distribution and significance, and both have had by now a century of interjacency with these Brahmans. I shall briefly focus on traditional caste hierarchy, marriage, and kinship to describe the traditional complex, and on occupations, positional ranks, and style of elite behavior to describe the modern one.

16. Obviously I do not claim either that the rural sabhas could not exist at all, or that they are actually nonexistent today. From the informants' versions, the Kanya-Kubja sabha phenomenon has almost invariably been an urban affair. However, this "dichotomy" of rural-urban is less effective today, as there are increasing two-way contacts between these sectors.

THE TRADITIONAL COMPLEX: HIERARCHY, MARRIAGE, AND KINSHIP

Since some aspects of the internal Kanya-Kubja ranking schemes will be discussed later, here we will only outline the most significant elements of hierarchization, primarily as they are found to influence, positively or negatively, the organizational behavior of these Brahmans. The purpose of the following description is therefore intended to serve mainly as an introductory statement rather than as a discussion of the interrelationships and contributions of these elements towards the sabha organization.

A part of the internal caste-ascriptive elements of hierarchy is an *ideal* three-tier hierarchy of *gotra*[17] clusters (the *Uttama* or *Khatkul* [six houses]; the *Madhyama*, *Dhākara*, or *Dash-gotra Wālé* [half-house]; and the 56 "unknown" gotras—see chapter 5). These gotra clusters (actually only the first two) provide sixteen exogamous gotras for the contemporary Kanya-Kubja Brahman. The members of every gotra have varied titles (*āspads* or *alla*) like Shukla, Misra, Bajpai, and Awasthi—all originally linked with specific ritual sacrifices prescribed for the Brahmans in the sacred texts. Originally considered as achievable by performing these sacrifices, these titles are today ascribed by birth. Such a change is important for our study. Thus today a child born in a Misra family will have Misra as his surname, irrevocably, while, as I noted elsewhere (1960, pp. 357–58), earlier ". . . *āspads* changed as soon as any ancestor in the lineage got name and fame by performing a particular type of sacrifice or obtaining special adeptness in Sanskritic texts." Genealogies (e.g., Bajpai 1946) show that the present Bajpais' ancestors had such surnames as Pāthak, Awasthi, Dixit, and Bajpai successively. One āspad may be found predominantly in only one or two gotras, but it may also be found in several more, making it complex to relate gotras with āspads. Conversely, one gotra is also found to have several āspads. The persons of the same gotra are strictly prohibited from marrying each other, while

17. Gotra as a kinship category can roughly be regarded as an exogamous "clan"; however, when examined closely certain problems are evident (Madan 1962). For the Kanya-Kubja Brahmans, their exogamous character is uniformly emphasized, much more so than Madan alludes. Moreover, certain gotras cluster together and hierarchize against certain others (Khare 1960, pp. 353 ff.).

persons of the same āspad, but of different gotras, can do so. The gotra groups are further subdivided into hundreds of *ānk* or *purushā* ancestral groups which are reckoned in terms of *susthān* (places of original concentration). (All of these are enumerated in a published or unpublished vamshāvali [genealogy] usually written by a traditionally learned caste pundit in Sanskrit and/or Hindi.) The ānks include, at most, one or two names of "actual" human ancestors "which are of the recent past," although it is not possible to tell exactly how many generations ago such an ancestor actually lived. In some cases the ancestral link may be further reckoned under the category termed purushā (i.e. an ancestor still more recent). The Kanya-Kubjas emphasize that only those who were renowned and/or who migrated from some "original" (i.e. older) place of concentration could be named as the founders of new ānks. However, it is not possible to ascertain from a genealogy whether the oldest and the most recent names are included, or only those who are in some way the most eminent, or both. Nevertheless, the important fact is that they are uniformly present in plural numbers (ranging from twelve to 264) in each gotra (see appendix C). Once again achieved positional rank was "originally" responsible for the inclusion or exclusion of a certain ancestor as ānk or purushā, although distant migration was also considered as a contributory factor (see also Khare 1960, p. 360).

Extensive migration and Muhammadan rule are the popular reasons for the social necessity of having numerous ānks and purushā in terms of one or several places of original concentration. This element complicates the internal ranking further. My effort to geographically locate the vamshāvali-mentioned susthāns has not been very successful because most of these places are those, according to informants, "which have either changed their names or are now nonexistent"; thus only rough locations are possible in some cases in the districts of Hardoi, Rae Bareilly, Kanpur, Lucknow, Shahjehanpur, Unnao, and Farrukhabad (which includes Kannauj). The susthāns, like the gotras and ānks, have thus become "mythical" categories, recorded most elaborately in the Kanya-Kubja genealogies, but not always confirmable now.

However, the importance of susthāns and of those relatives who lived in or near them became the most crucial "verifiers" of the internal caste ranks of the emigrants.

Although it is not known exactly what different reasons were responsible for their spatial mobility, according to the accounts available through genealogies (Narain P. Misra 1959; Bajpai 1946) these Brahmans did not *collectively* move either in the medieval period or, as indicated by the published biographies (R. S. Misra 1940), in this century. Their movements have almost always occurred through individual families. In this regard this study corroborates the contentions of both Stein as well as Srinivas (1966, pp. 43–45). And, as Srinivas noted, these emigrated families did have to face the question: where will the mobile family find brides for sons and grooms for daughters? The initial response of the isolated, emigrated Kanya-Kubjas was, "back home." But, as my informant noted, those in the susthān ranked the emigrants lower because "they were away and could easily camouflage their actual traditional rank." Only a sizeable dowry could allure susthān Kanya-Kubjas to marry their sons to the daughters of emigrated Kanya-Kubjas. The concern about one's location continues today, even if less severe.

Kanya-Kubja orthodoxy in marital alliances establishes a centripetal tendency towards the original locus of their concentration, mainly in western and central Uttar Pradesh. Families of Kanya-Kubjas who have emigrated search for bridegrooms geographically, from outward to inward (i.e., from Calcutta, Hyderabad, Ahmedabad toward the susthāns—Lucknow, Hardoi, and Kanpur), although some do not consider Uttar Pradesh because there are fewer prospects for finding "better class" (more prosperous) bridegrooms there. My investigations suggest, however, that there is still a preference for Uttar Pradesh. If this is the case, one would expect most of these Brahmans eventually to return to Uttar Pradesh, which would lead to their establishing a politically effective size (i.e., numerical dominance of Kanya-Kubjas at any one place) and more complex associational activities. However, the fact is that, although the centripetal tendency is preferred, it does not produce sufficient movement for political purposes, mainly because of the limited capacity of Uttar Pradesh to give appropriate employment to the educated. To get a proper job and/or to get an easier promotion the educated Uttar Pradesh Kanya-Kubjas must therefore migrate. This necessity continues to disperse these Brahmans today, even if they do prefer (and actually do establish) the marital connections "back home." Various distinct patterns are observable: First, the wealthier of the educated Kanya-Kubjas are as likely to marry their daughters to persons outside the Uttar Pradesh as they are to persons within the state. Second, the less wealthy among the educated are more likely to marry their sons outside the state than they are their daughters. Third, the rural Kanya-Kubjas, unless they are wealthy, most often marry both their sons and their daughters within the state. The rich are more dispersed in their marital alliances, a fact which imposes an important organizational limitation on the sabhas.

Thus the greater the geographic distance and the longer the absence of a Kanya-Kubja from his original place of concentration, the greater is the "suspicion" regarding his rank, unless there are both some agnates and affines who can vouch for his "claims" by their own relationships with him. With rapid improvements in communication and transportation, the modern Kanya-Kubja finds it much easier (and for proper affinity most important) to maintain contacts with his kin in or near the susthān. As we will discover later this contact is so important for the emigrants that their local sabha organizations may help them in maintaining it. Modern facilities of communication have strengthened rather than weakened the kinship network and the importance of traditional geographical locations. Whereas the present locations of kin are far more dispersed than they were ever before, the "mythical" susthāns that are enunciated in genealogies continue to constitute an important element of the internal ranking system (see chapter 5).

The above rank indicators (gotra, āspad, ānk, purushā, and susthān) are further combined with another hierarchical element called the *Biswā* scale. This consists of twenty equal divisions within which all the sixteen gotras, along with their numerous ānks, āspads, and susthāns, are ranked. In other words, all the rank indicators together help ascertain this controversial, but most crucial, ranking scale. (For how it happens, see chapter 5.) For the Kanya-Kubja the highest rank is 20 Biswās, and the lowest is 1. It is considered to be of relatively recent origin (of the Muhammadan period—i.e., 300 to 400 years old).

Debate and denunciation go hand in hand with the awareness today that the Biswās are the chief bases for asking a sizeable dowry from a girl's father. "Undoubtedly, it is the Biswā scale," emphasized my informants, "which initiated, as it were, the capillary processes in the caste group for registering a rise on this scale even by coercion, fraud, and concealment, leading to *banuān* [artificially risen] Kanya-Kubjas." The Biswā scheme, of course, is the main basis for practicing intracaste hypergamy (and sometimes even hypogamy) in this group (Khare 1968).

The association of those of higher Biswā with those who are wealthy (rather than orthodox and poor) is as old as the scale itself. It is thought to have "originated" in the basis of one's achieved economic status rather than traditional ascription; and it originally formed, according to my informants, a part of one's positional rank in the society (see Khare 1960, pp. 361–64). However, very soon after (approximately within one hundred years), my informants contend, this scheme became ascribed and appeared in various genealogies of the caste group, first inconsistently, but later as a fixed and exhaustive numerical rating of all the agnatic groups (ānks) of the caste group. In modern times, the rich but low Biswā rank (e.g., of 4 Biswā) marry their daughters either to those: (a) rich as well as high on the Biswā rank (e.g., 19), (b) poor but high on the Biswā rank, and (c) rich but equal on the Biswā rank (e.g., 4 or 6). The transaction of dowry gifts becomes the emphatic theme of such marriages: the greater the size of dowry available the lesser are the objections, it is generally contended, against incorporating a lower Biswā family (e.g., of 6) into a higher one (e.g., of 19) by a hypergamous affinal bond. The repetitive occurrence of such alliances paves the way for claiming a new Biswā rank. The latter is acquired with the help of kin and by a corresponding change in ānk, gotra, and susthān.

The effect of Biswā is to heavily underscore the importance of dowry, or, indirectly, of one's economic status. "The rigidity of internally elaborate Biswā ranking is most binding and most demanding for those who are high on Biswās but low on economic status, while it is a matter of strengthening positional rank with the rich," observed a railway clerk of 20 Biswā facing the problem of marrying his three teen-age daughters. As an orthodox Brahman he cannot "step down" to marry his daughter into a family of 7 or 10 Biswā; as a clerk he cannot hope to enter into the "class of 20 Biswā aristocrats," primarily because he cannot meet their "demands" in a marriage; however, as a socially respectable, honor-seeking Kanya-Kubja father, he must marry his daughter into an appropriate rank, and to a man of higher economic status so that his daughter may have a comfortable life.

Against this background, the great "push" for achievement among the Kanya-Kubjas may be more clearly understood. Their argument is that without economic status one can neither keep up his ascriptive rank nor can he be a "traditionalist" in these days. They see secular and economic positions as a means of reestablishing and stabilizing the Brahmanic traditions. It is the only way, they contend, to have the most of the two "worlds" (the sacred and the secular), and they do not find either scriptural or religious norms to contradict this approach.

The achievement motive exists in the secular as well as the sacred world.[18] All that is socially sacred is not ascribed by the caste system, although it has been the most common extension of caste ascription on the entire world of tradition. For example, for the Kanya-Kubja Brahmans the traditional concept of *kulīntā* (a sacred property) is *not* bounded entirely by the above-mentioned elements of their ascriptive hierarchy. Their Brahmanic system of ideals, like any other Brahman group, lies in *acquiring* and *choosing* certain modes of behavior that are consistent with the values prescribed by the scriptures for a Brahman. The Kanya-Kubja informants and almost all of their genealogies that I have come across emphasize these attainments as the "real" indicators of Brahmanhood, although they almost as readily concede that these values, like all ideals, are continuously attempted but only imperfectly reached. Nevertheless, as a cultural norm, they are uniformly emphasized.

The problem of ascription and achievement blends most crucially in a Kanya-Kubja marriage. The "ordeal" of finding a

18. Evidently, such a statement will be an oversimplification of the inherent strain that does exist between the profane economic status and the sacred ascriptive and achieved counterpart. However, what is more significant is the Kanya-Kubja viewpoint underlying such rationalization about the "confrontation." Through these rationalizations they seem to acquire added psychological support for pursuing secular achievement goals, and in freeing themselves from certain ritualistic dogma. Yet those who achieve secular status do not conceive it antipodal to further their entry into the ritualistic or traditional world at a later time. Thus a Kanya-Kubja elite may start with a flexible approach to tradition and emphasize achievement in the secular world, but, in his forties and fifties he may come back to regain his sacred world. Even their attitude towards tradition and the gods may change with their age (Khare 1966).

24

"same-caste-and-same-class" groom (*samkaksh var*) can be facilitated, the Kanya-Kubjas realize, only by keeping up connections with their "kin back home," on the one hand, and by enhancing one's economic status, on the other. It also follows that this kinship web be kept strengthened by appropriate gift exchanges, and that this may often cut across economic "class" lines found within the caste group.

THE MODERN COMPLEX: ELITES AND ORGANIZATION

Bottomore (1964, p. 8) notes that "elites" refer "to functional, mainly, occupational groups, which have high status (for whatever reason) in a society." Henceforth, although I shall use the term "elite" for those who have high status or more power and influence in a group, I want to stipulate certain conceptual emphases suitable for the Indian material. First, I do not intend to use the term "elite" for occupational *groups* and their status; instead, I shall emphasize individual achievements of the members of a caste group. Hence, an elite is a "high achiever," who may or may not have had a share of ancestral wealth, property, or fame. Thus, while in a more traditional sense a Brahman caste in India is an elite caste by occupation and by social privileges, it is not so simply viewed here. Only those of its members will be called elites who have during their lifetime acquired certain properties of social eminence and influence, either with or without the support of their ancestral inheritance. Second, this conception also postulates an "equal" importance to traditional and modern achievements, although the two may be unequally functional in contemporary Indian society. Accordingly, both a Kanya-Kubja pundit of astrology and a Kanya-Kubja in the Indian Administrative Service are elites. Third, these elites are conceived in terms of either some referent group or category, depending upon the context. Thus, I shall speak of a Kanya-Kubja elite as a "caste elite" in one context, an "elite kin" in another, and a traditional, a social, or a civic elite in still others. To be an elite one has to be eminent in any one of them, although some may be outstanding in several references. Multiple reference systems of elitist behavior are crucial for understanding the dynamics of modern social reality of a caste group. Fourth, as a consequence of the above, I have to somehow conceptually differentiate between those who are elites and those who are not.

25

Customarily, elites are differentiated in terms of "masses," but caste group membership is restricted enough by the unalterable facts of birth and kinship to prevent applying this general scheme to those "who could not achieve in the same degree to which the elites did." In order to emphasize the *relative* absence of achievements, I shall call these people "non-elites"—apparently an incautious way of presenting the contrast. Further in this field study, who is an elite and who is a non-elite is decided mostly by my field informants in their numerous evaluative biographic accounts of their own caste members. I shall therefore take frequent recourse to social or cultural contexts in dealing with an elite vis-à-vis a non-elite.

However we classify them, the modern Kanya-Kubjas invariably seek some kind of achieved position, whether through a secular prestigious occupation or a specialization in the sacred tradition. The former has definitely been preferred in this caste group for about a century now, and the group exhibits familiarity with complex urban life and occupational demands. They went where their job took them, making their distribution geographically diverse. They show a kind of "ingenuity" in handling the "office-home" dichotomy as coexistent, yet covariant.

This brings us to yet another operational concept of central interest to this study. Although I have briefly indicated it in the earlier pages, the terms "organization" and "bureaucracy" are used here as neutral sociological concepts. Thus "bureaucratic organization" is another label for a "formal or modern organization," and a "bureaucrat" simply means an "officer" or holder of a position in any formal organization. "Bureaucracy" conveys a set of ideal characteristics attempted in practice in specific interpersonal situations among the participants of a modern office, and between certain elites and non-elites. All this is seen in the context of the Kanya-Kubja caste group and its members. The modern Kanya-Kubjas have conceptions of "ideal" as well as actual bureaucracy. The ideal model for bureaucracy is provided by Weber, and like all ideals it has its heuristic value irrespective of whether or not it is actualized. The bureaucratic reality may therefore be notably divergent from the idea. My aim is to deal with this reality in reference to the ideal, especially as it is found in a Kanya-Kubja sabha organization.

The latter organization, as we shall see, presents peculiar dynamics of the ascriptive and achieved, formal and informal, and kinship and modern organizational elements. Fuller grasp of this flux will be made through an understanding of actual situations, especially through behavioral styles and standards of modern Kanya-Kubja elites and non-elites in "offices" and in home. The sabhas provide a significant middle ground from which one can explore either way meaningfully.

This study, then, will begin (part I) by presenting the case details of several dispersed caste associations of the Kanya-Kubja Brahmans, within and outside of Uttar Pradesh, mainly in terms of their formal aims, organization, and achievements, as well as informal, culturally patterned behavioral styles and institutionalized purposes. Available published or unpublished caste documents, including vamshāvalis and journals, will be suitably analyzed to help trace some historical circumstances of the caste group for explication of specific modernization tendencies. The second and third parts of the book will extend this discussion along two major but overlapping axes simultaneously: one will be concerned with the crucial organizational elements of the Kanya-Kubja caste association that become apparent in part I, and the other will deal with the issues of tradition and modernity.[19] The first axis will most often provide occasions for the study of the second. Whereas both the second and third parts will deal with the organizational commonalities of the Kanya-Kubja associations, part II will present a detailed discussion of status stratification, traditional and modern, along with its standard indicators and styles, rigidities and flexibilities. As became evident early in my field work, status and rank stood out as the most

19. It should be noted that part II of the book will not restrict itself to the organizational aspects of the sabhas alone; it will go outside the sabha contexts to describe some behavioral and cultural characteristics of the Kanya-Kubja sabha member as a caste member, as a Brahman, and as a modern achiever, facilitating thereby the evaluation of the organization and function of sabha organization in part III of the book. Moreover, although I shall note the "interjacency" of tradition and modernity within as well as outside of the sabha contexts, the two may not always be identical in meaning and expression. Thus the interjacent function of the sabhas (voluntary and honorary offices) and of the Kanya-Kubja's house and his bread-winning "office" may stand on different levels of cultural significance.

I thank Professor Milton Singer for pointing out the necessity of the above clarifications.

prized and elaborated features in a Kanya-Kubja's traditional as well as modern life. Since they also appeared significantly in the sabha roles and relationships, such a consideration will be, I hope, both appropriate and clarifying. Part III will present an analysis of the "formalized" end of the Kanya-Kubja associations, assessing its strengths and weaknesses and appropriate functional significance. As in the preceding two parts, the discussion of tradition and modernity will reappear here along the lines of bureaucratic ideals, cultural values, and institutionally patterned styles of behavior. This part of the book will also review and reformulate the findings of the study against a comparative as well as a general background.

Instead of generating a series of "less-precise" hypotheses first, and "testing" and making them "more precise" later at the end of the study, I find the above, less-rigid frame of reference more useful for this study, especially with the present state of social inquiry in this area.

I The Kanya-Kubja Associations

2 History and Distribution

In 1884 the Lucknow Kanya-Kubja Brahmans, especially under the initiative of two Kanya-Kubja justices and a learned priest, established the first association, the Khatkul Hitaishini Sabha. Representing what was later considered by them to be an extremely conservative position, this sabha was concerned only with the six highest-ranked gotras (i.e., the Khatkul),[1] and thus did not admit all the Kanya-Kubjas. It survived for only four years.

In 1897 Kanpur became the site of a sabha founded through the particular efforts of Pt. Ram Dularey Misra, in the house of one Pt. Brahmadin. Less conservative, it allowed all Kanya-Kubja Brahmans to become members. A lawyer was its first secretary, and with time this sabha grew into a "central body" having several local and distant branches. Nandi (1965, pp. 84–88), however, dates the existence of the first association in Kanpur from 1915 until 1938, when it was dissolved for the "lack of unity and unanimity in regard to their [Kanya-Kubjas'] organization." He reports that its membership dropped from a maximum of sixty in 1920 to only five during its last year. He also refers to another organization, Kanya-Kubja Education Trust, which was founded in the same year (1938) in which the Kanya-Kubja sabha was dissolved. The trust "had an initial membership of 15 persons. After twenty-two years of disturbed existence, it had the same number of members in 1960."

However, this estimation of the role of the Kanpur sabha did not correspond with the version provided by the caste members. They accorded the greater significance to the original Kanpur sabha for initiating and intensifying caste awareness.

1. The Khatkul cluster of the Kanya-Kubja Brahmans is comprised of the Kashyap, Shandilya, Kātyayan, Bharadwāj, Upmanyu, and Sānkrat gotras. This cluster is succeeded by another ten gotras, comprising the middle tier of these Brahmans.

Because of the success achieved by the initial sabha at Kanpur, with branches as far as Neemuch, Calcutta, Ajmer, and Jabalpur, there arose the question of founding an all-Indian Kanya-Kubja sabha. However, before such a body could be organized, a local organization in Ajmer adopted a radical position on social reforms and professed the abolition of Kanya-Kubja commensal rules. The Kanpur sabha, the focus of Kanya-Kubja attention, though somewhat liberal, was not prepared to go that far. Relations between the two sabhas became cold, and the Ajmer sabha began publishing its own journal to popularize its views. Soon, however, Ajmer also saw the birth of a conservative organization led by a local physician, and by 1909 internal quarrels resulted in the discontinuation of the progressive journal and the cessation of its reformist movement.

But these two tendencies soon erupted in the all-Indian sabha, which finally was established by a resolution of a well-attended general meeting in Kanpur in 1901 under the presidency of Pt. Umavar Bajpai. The all-Indian body, officially called Akhil Bhārtiya Sri Kanya-Kubja Pratinidhi Sabha, was a victory for the reformist forces.

This organization, on the initiative of five outstanding Kanya-Kubjas (including a deputy collector, a lawyer, and a literary editor), was founded to promote and enhance the modern achievements of *all* Kanya-Kubja Brahmans and to compete with the progressive caste groups of the region, including the Kayasthas, the Banias, and other north-Indian Brahmans. But the Kanpur sabha, a representative of the conservative forces, opposed it and was supported vigorously by the rich Khatkul Kanya-Kubjas of Calcutta, who brought out the conservative journal *Kanya-Kubja Bandhu* for a few years to publicize their stand. The present editor of *Kanya-Kubja* informed me that the disputations of these two factions went on for about thirty-five years without resulting in any spectacular reform in commensal or related marriage problems. He claimed, however, that the debate did make the Kanya-Kubjas receptive to ideas of modern education and personal advancement.

Continuing elite interest and participation in the all-Indian sabha is evidenced in *Kanya-Kubja.* In 1963 the present editor enumerated the outstanding services of numerous caste elites, including high-court judges, colonels and generals, university teachers and educators, titled *Tālukdārs* (landlords under the British regime), physicians and engineers, and politicians. He emphasized their diverse and continuous contribution to sabha activities and especially highlighted their role in the twenty meetings of the general body of the all-Indian sabha, which took place between 1901 and 1936. All of these meetings were held at cities in Uttar Pradesh (earlier, the United Provinces), including—Kanpur (1901 and 1907), Farrukhabad (1905), Kannauj (1906?), Unnao (1908 and 1928), Hardoi (1909), Allahabad (1910), Etawah (1911), Bareilly (1912), Sitapur (1913), Lucknow (1916, 1927, 1931, and 1936), Shahjehanpur (1920), Barabanki (1922), and Fatehpur (1929). It was noted that the president of the last general meeting (1936) was Pt. Ravi Shankar Shukla, later the chief minister of Madhya Pradesh, and that a core of thirteen caste elites helped to bring it about.[2] Repeated efforts to hold a meeting of the general body have failed since then, although the matter is proposed almost every year.

Despite the fact that a meeting of the general body has not been convened for the last thirty-two years, the Lucknow-based sabha is considered to be the all-Indian central organization of the Kanya-Kubjas. It has never ceased functioning since 1901, has regularly elected executives, substantial financial endowments, and continues to enjoy help from numerous caste elites from all over India. The all-Indian function of this sabha, as I shall elaborate on later, has become identified with its monthly periodical *Kanya-Kubja*, which is published in Hindi.

OTHER SABHAS

Below is some preliminary information, based upon documentary evidence and personal interviews, on the presence of several other associations in various parts of India. Although this coverage may not be exhaustive, it attempts to be fairly indicative. My efforts to acquire information on distant sabhas were quite successful, primarily because of the active persuasion led by some of

2. Justice Gokaran Nath Misra; Pt. Raghubar Dayal Misra, deputy collector; Dr. Shyam Behari Misra, M.A., D.Lit.; Pt. Jai Karan Nath Misra, barrister-at-law; Pt. Guru Dayal Tiwari, advocate; Pt. Rama Narain Misra, physician; Pt. Shiva Prasad Misra, teacher; Raja Sri Krishna Dutt Dube; Raja Kali Charan Misra; Rai Bahadur Raj Narain Misra; Rai Bahadur Pt. Suka Deva Behari Misra; Pt. Ravi Shankar Shukla.

my Kanya-Kubja friends and acquaintances in Lucknow and Kanpur. Initially, however, there was some reluctance in giving detailed information, and some distant Kanya-Kubja sabhas could not be induced by mail to deliver sufficient information. For example, suspicions probably were aroused concerning the intentions of an investigator who was a member of a caste that could be competing with theirs for higher socioeconomic statuses.

Thus, undoubtedly, there exist many more associations which are not listed in table 1. For example, *Kanya-Kubja* (1966, 1967)

TABLE 1

KANYA-KUBJA ASSOCIATIONS

Association	Founding Year	Year When Last Known Functioning	Founding Place	Present Location
Khatkul Hitaishini Sabha	1884	1888	Lucknow	. . .
Kanya-Kubja Sabha	1897	1938(?)	Kanpur	. . .
All-India K.-K. Association	1901	1967	Kanpur	Lucknow
Rajasthan K.-K. Sabha	1906	1966	Ajmer	Ajmer
Rajasthan K.-K. Sabha	(?)	1966	Jaipur	Jaipur
Sri K.-K. Sewā Sangh	1910	1966	Lashkar	Lashkar (Gwalior)
Sri K.-K. Vidya Prachārini Sabha (Sri K.-K. Yuvak Mandal, its subsidiary organization)	1914	1966	Indore	Indore
K.-K. Sabha	1939	1966	Ujjain	Ujjain
Sri K.-K. Mandal	1960	1966	Amravati	Amravati
K.-K. Mandal	1961	1966	Bhopal	Bhopal
K.-K. Sabha	1964	1966	Dohad	Dohad
K.-K. Sabha	1965	1966	Jaipur	Jodhpur (branch of Jaipur in 1965 and in 1966, an independent body)
Dakshin Bhārat K.-K. Sabha (new name is Sri. K.-K. Sabha Hyderabad)	1965	1966	Hyderabad	Hyderabad
K.-K. Brahman Jila Parishad	1965(?)	1966	Sagar	Sagar

MAP 1. Geographic distribution of some Kanya-Kubja associations.

reports the existence of an old association (prior to 1930) in Ambikapur, Sarguja district (see map 1), and of plans to establish one soon in Echatu, Hazaribagh, and in other parts of southern Bihar. Bombay had one association working under the presidency of Pt. Jagdeva S. Sharma, but currently there is no detailed information available. Occasionally, there appear appeals directed to the editor of *Kanya-Kubja* from a group of remotely situated Kanya-Kubja Brahmans to help them in organizing their caste associations. Thus, there was recent mention of organizing Kanya-Kubja women's associations in Madhya Pradesh; and it is known that at least one such association has existed in Allahabad for the last thirty years. In 1967 the *Kanya-Kubja* editor published a note saying that around 1942 Madhya Pradesh alone had forty-eight sabhas. However, exact details are lacking. Many of these sabhas are presumed to exist, only because a certain region had, or still has, a concentration of the Kanya-Kubja Brahmans. Thus some informants suggest that there may be sabhas in Assam, where around 1920, there were several prominent Kanya-Kubja families. Map 1 includes some such locations to provide a general idea of spatial spread.

Since 1906, Kanya-Kubja associations have been working in Rajasthan; obviously there are more than one, for the present Jaipur branch—about which some information is available—is labeled as a *shākha* (branch) of Rajasthan Kanya-Kubja Sabha. Similarly, there is more definite information about the existence of a Kanya-Kubja sabha in Ahmedabad. In 1965 it was under the presidency of a prominent elite, Pt. Shiva Kumar Avasthi. However, further details about its executive committee, past meetings, and specific functions could not be obtained, except that this sabha, like others, "is actively serving the Kanya-Kubja Brahmans, and especially the students, by awarding scholarships, by supporting poor boys' funds, and by helping the destitute." This association, according to my informants, was established in the 1920s; however, documentary support of the date is lacking.

The relatively better-known sabhas are Sri Kanya-Kubja Vidya Prachārini Sabha (and its subsidary youth bodies), Indore; Sri Kanya-Kubja Sewā Sangh, Lashkar (Gwalior); Rajasthan Kanya-Kubja Sabha, Jaipur branch; Sri Kanya-Kubja Mandal, Amravati; Kanya-Kubja Sabha, Dohad; and Kanya-Kubja Mandal, Bhopal (see table 1 and map 1).

More than half (8) of the better-reported associations existed before Indian Independence, and the first seven associations in table 1 were functioning before 1920. However, the establishment of the last six associations in the 1960s may be partly understood in the context of the post-Independence (i.e., the 1950s) migration of Uttar Pradesh Kanya-Kubja officers to several new state capitals (e.g., Bhopal and Jaipur) or to metropolitan centers of adjoining states in search of better job opportunities, less competition, and easier rank-salary promotions. Further, this table suggests that certain famed individuals, when acting as leaders, paved the way for the establishment of a new sabha. For example, in 1964 in Dohad a renowned physician of Indian Railways and a learned traditionalist started an association "for Kanya-Kubja improvement and solidarity," with only one hundred families. Similarly another caste elite, Mr. S———, originally of Ujjain Kanya-Kubja Sabha (1939–43), when transferred to Bhopal around 1960, established a new association there "for accomplishing radical social reforms among the Brahmans," and became its secretary. Bhopal, as a new administrative and political center, attracted hundreds of educated Kanya-Kubja Brahmans from Uttar Pradesh, and this new association undertook the work of forging "solidarity among the Kanya-Kubjas of different lands and places" (Mr. Shukla). The Amravati association (1960) started with sixty subscribing members and only sixty-five urban Kanya-Kubja families.[3] This sabha, which was led by three Kanya-Kubja elites (two of them successful local lawyers) since 1960, hoped to consolidate the scattered rural Kanya-Kubja population surrounding Amravati.

After the Lucknow and Kanpur complexes (1884–1910), the Lashkar (Gwalior) (1910) and Indore (1914) sabhas are regarded as the oldest ones. However, the first is least known, except for the controversy described earlier. But the other two have been able to enjoy considerable economic stability, have worked and prospered under strong caste-elite patronage, and have never ceased functioning. They are regarded as the Madhya Pradesh "centers" of the Kanya-Kubja Brahmans; hence the associations of Dohad, Bhopal, and Amravati may tend to look to Indore and Lashkar (Gwalior) for help as well as for models to emulate.

THE KANYA-KUBJA PERIODICALS

The first caste journal, *Kanya-Kubja Bhāskar*, was published in 1885 in Lucknow and lasted for about four years. Other journals followed, namely: *Kanya-Kubja Hitkāri* (1899–1929) from Kanpur; *Kanya-Kubja Sudhārak* (1906–9) from Ajmer; *Kanya-Kubja Nav-yuvak Samāj* from Bombay; *Kanya-Kubja Bandhu* from Calcutta; and *Kanya-Kubja Nāyak* from Jabalpur. None survive today.

According to the *Press in India* (1966), the annual report of the Registrar of Newspapers, the Kanya-Kubja Brahmans are

3. There are some indications, however, that this association is a continuation of an older unit, but I could not succeed either in getting definite details about it or in establishing that there were some continuing members of the older body. Hence, I decided to categorize this sabha as a new one.

reported to have two journals: the *Kanya-Kubja*, dealt with in detail in this study, and the *Kanya-Kubja Samāj*, another Hindi monthly published in Calcutta and having a circulation of 215. Since I did not have access to the latter during the time I was collecting data on the subject, I am not aware of its contents or exact organizational functions. However, it is apparently a publication serving only the local or regional Kanya-Kubja Brahmans. There is also mention of *Māheshwari*, another caste periodical from Hyderabad, which is edited by a past editor of the *Kanya-Kubja*, Lucknow.

Although *Kanya-Kubja* did not bloom into a voluminous periodical, it has, however, never ceased functioning for a long period of time. As the details in chapter 4 bear out, it had—and still has—problems, but so far it has faced them successfully. Now, it is the most important single spokesman of almost all the scattered Kanya-Kubja associations. As a Hindi monthly, it publishes news, proceedings of meetings, elite biographies, budgets, and problems of numerous Kanya-Kubja associations, including the one at Lucknow.

Kanya-Kubja was born with the passage of a resolution moved by Pt. Raghubar Dayal Misra, a founding member of the All-Indian Kanya-Kubja Sabha, during its annual meeting of 1905 in Farrukhabad. Its first issue was published in Lucknow in January 1906 under the editorship of Pt. Devi Prasad Shukla. Unfortunately, the history of the journal is vague up to 1933, because the back files are incomplete. The present editor is in possession, however, of a few numbers from 1908, 1914, 1917, 1919, 1920, 1921, and 1926, which do give a rough idea of the journal's history. It was published successively from Lucknow, Kanpur, Fatehgarh, Banaras, Allahabad, and finally again from Lucknow, but the exact dates are unknown. For the last thirty-five years the journal has been published in Lucknow. Although several outstanding Kanya-Kubja Hindi writers are known to have edited the journal in various periods, again, the exact details are unknown.

The journal was brought to Lucknow in 1933 from Allahabad where it ran up a debt of Rs. 1,000. Since then it has been published under the organization of the present editor, Pt. Rama Shankar Misra "Sripati Ji," except for a few short breaks owing to some temporary financial problems. But in 1958, the periodical ran into prolonged financial trouble and was discontinued for about a year—long enough to require fresh permissions from local authorities and from the Registrar of Newspapers, New Delhi, to publish *Kanya-Kubja* as a registered magazine. However, since the publication backlog was soon caught up and the volume serialization was not affected, the present editor attained his cherished goal of "uninterrupted" publication. In 1963 the editor was again apprehensive of a similar situation, because the periodical started the year with a total loss of Rs. 1,617, but substantial donations from two prosperous Kanya-Kubjas of Calcutta staved off the crisis. We will turn to the nature and magnitude of this periodical's problems in chapter 4.

THE EDUCATIONAL INSTITUTIONS

The educational institutions that had Kanya-Kubja sponsorship were started through the efforts of various eminent Kanya-Kubjas present a history of continuous, but not easy development (see table 2). These bodies were originally established as institutions "for serving the Kanya-Kubja community." However, now they do not, as far as is known, refuse admission to any student on the basis of caste or religion—a precondition for becoming eligible for state recognition and financial support. Thus, although predominantly caste-managed and caste-financed, these institutions are now "open" educational forums but with a bias favorable to Kanya-Kubja Brahmans.

Lucknow saw the foundation being laid of the first—and still the largest—Kanya-Kubja institution in 1917, when Kanya-Kubja Anglo-Sanskrit Mahājani Pāthshāla was established under the management of a prominent Kanya-Kubja contractor, A——. In the absence of a building of its own, it had a few rented cubicles for classrooms. In 1920 Kanya-Kubja Pt. Din Dayal Misra donated to this institution his entire estate of over Rs. 80,000, which went a long way towards the building program. In 1921 a renowned Kanya-Kubja justice brought high school classes to this institution "by using his influence in the appropriate quarters of the government"; and in 1923 when the question of making it an intermediate college crucially hinged on meeting the government condition that there must be made more teaching space available, another Kanya-Kubja contractor, the younger brother of A——, volunteered to construct enough classrooms (costing

TABLE 2

KANYA-KUBJA EDUCATIONAL INSTITUTIONS

Name and Location	Founding Year	Founding Persons	Enrollment	Some Dates of Expansion
Sri K.-K. Degree College, Lucknow	1917	Sri Narain Misra Pt. Krishna Dutta Dube (Raja Sahab of Jaunpur) Pt. Kali Charan Misra, (Raja Sahab Bareilly) Kardaha Rajya-ki-Rani	4,522	1917—6th to 8th class 1920—High School 1923—Intermediate (Arts) 1936—Intermediate (Science) 1942—Intermediate (Commerce) 1946—B.Sc. (Biology) 1947—B.Sc. (Mathematics) 1954—B.A. and B. Com.
Sri K.-K. Vocational Degree College, Lucknow	1936(?)	Pt. Sri Narain Misra	3,000+	From kindergarten to degree classes
Sri K.-K. College, Kanpur	1915	Raja of Jaunpur, Sri Krishna Dutta Dube	. . .	1915—Primary section 1917—High School 1940—Intermediate
Sri K.-K. College, Bhagwant Nagar	1925	Pt. Durga Prasad Bajpai	. . .	1925—1st to 8th class 1926—English Education 1926—Govt. recognized school 1945—High School
Sri K.-K. High School Vidya Prachārini Sabha, Indore	1914	Pt. Deen Dayal Misra	. . .	1914—High School
Sri K.-K. Sewā Sangh, Lashkar (Gwalior)	1963	Pt. Rameshwar Shastri, Shukla	. . .	(?)—Student Hostel

Rs. 55,000) to enable the institution to begin this advanced instruction without further delay.

The institution has always been administered by Kanya-Kubja principals "who significantly helped in the expansion programs launched by the management committee." Good administration is held responsible for the recognition it received in 1946 for opening the Bachelor of Science courses of Lucknow University. In 1965 this college was the largest affiliated college of Lucknow University with 4,522 students on its rolls, including 1,577 in undergraduate classes in the arts, science, and commerce divisions. It was then continuously expanding its physical plant, involving a yearly expenditure of Rs. 100,000 on building construction alone. The younger brother of A—— (for long the secretary-manager of the college)[4] was again noted in the *Annual Report* of 1965 as donating Rs. 10,000 every year to the institution.

More difficulty was involved in establishing its twin institution, the Kanya-Kubja Vocational Degree College. This college, which now stands in the same compound in which the Kanya-Kubja College does, and which mostly replicates the educational facilities that the bigger college has, had its unofficial beginning in 1936, when contractor A—— felt that those students who were educated in rural vernacular "middle" schools, confronted great language difficulties when entering an English institution. He planned on opening a "special class" which would help these students to make up the language deficiencies and which would also prepare them for some special technical or industrial skill.

4. As an upshot of internal political maneuverings of almost three years duration (1963–66), the meeting of the general body of the college in August 1966 ousted its secretary-manager of long-standing and elected a new management committee composed of twelve members and office-holders. The new president was a barrister-at-law and the new secretary-manager, a locally famous physician. Other members included two other physicians, four rich erstwhile Tālukdārs, one magistrate, one press proprietor, one retired audit officer, and one banker. The new committee includes *three non-Brahman members* (a Thakur, a Kayastha, and a Sikh). Further, it does not include any longstanding members of the earlier committee—an indication of the shift from the old regime and its policies.

This committee is elected every five years by members of the general body who have donated at least Rs. 500 to the college. The secretary-editor of the Lucknow association is also a member of the general body of the college, and he reported the formation of the new committee in *Kanya-Kubja* (1966).

41

His proposal was turned down by the education division of the state government, but he, against the advice of his own colleagues, went ahead and "informally opened" with a class of thirty-two students by using the space and furniture of the preexisting Kanya-Kubja College.

The plan, now with a clear emphasis on vocational training, was resubmitted to the government after a few years. This time the administration yielded, and the new institution opened under the name Kanya-Kubja Vocational Institute with eighty-five students in grades five through eight enrolled in vocational training classes. Its existence was felt to be threatened, however, because it was a duplicate of an institution in the same place.

A longer struggle followed the proposal to develop it into a high school. At one time the government stipulated that the college must invest Rs. 20,000 in facilities before the development could be approved. Although this was done, in the end the "recognition committee" did not agree on the high school's necessity and the proposal fell through. Then there followed several unsuccessful negotiations with higher educational officials, including the Education Minister of the Congress ministry. Finally, the recognition came after complying with the request for another commitment of Rs. 5,000, and the institution became the Kanya-Kubja Vocational High School around 1942 when the Independence movement was at its climax; the school pioneered as a platform for nationalist spokesmen. It thus got added publicity, and collected funds to open basic and nursery classes. At the junior high school level it gave instruction in agriculture, sewing, textiles, carpentry, bookbinding, and publishing. In 1957 its "basic section" alone had some 2,000 children on its rolls.

In 1947–48 the institution was recognized for its intermediate classes, as a result of the donation by the younger brother of A—— of about twenty acres for agricultural instruction. By 1957, the college was recognized by Lucknow University for undergraduate instruction in liberal arts, and by 1965 it had also extended its instruction to selected science subjects.

The fact that A—— nurtured this enterprise almost singlehanded made him a de facto "owner" of the institution. He was an octogenarian when the college was recognized for undergraduate instruction, and he was still active in 1965. Whether this institution (also said to be a product of fraternal rivalry between the two contractors) will remain independent or will merge with the bigger unit after his death is a favorite topic of speculation among the Kanya-Kubjas. However else the other castes may look at it, the Kanya-Kubjas pride themselves for bringing about these institutions of "public service."

Closely related to the above schools is the Kanya-Kubja College in Bhagwantnagar (Hardoi district), established in 1925 as a middle school and opened primarily through the efforts of Pt. Sri Narain Misra. The following year a chief justice and a Tālukdār used their respective influence in the government to get the institution recognized as a middle school (1926); and after a long struggle it became a high school (1945). It was raised to an intermediate college in 1950 through the efforts of a past-principal of Lucknow Kanya-Kubja College and a Kanya-Kubja colonel of the Second World War.

Financial support was primarily obtained, again, through donations from the Kanya-Kubjas. For example, the contractor-brothers of Lucknow, referred to earlier, donated an acre of land; six rich Kanya-Kubjas of Bhagwantnagar financed the construction of seven classrooms; deeds and wills of two local landlords brought Rs. 17,000 in capital to the college (plus some income for scholarships); and there was a donation of Rs. 13,000 from a rich Kanya-Kubja of Jaipur plus Rs. 1,000 annual income from his Jaipur trust. In 1963 a group of eleven members of various Kanya-Kubja associations again donated Rs. 16,801.

Kanpur also has a Kanya-Kubja Intermediate College (officially recognized in 1940) for boys, founded in 1915 as a primary school by the late Kanya-Kubja Raja of Jaunpur, who donated Rs. 10,000 to the institution. A Kanya-Kubja vaidya brought another Rs. 10,000 and a building to the institution, both of which he had received for curing one of his Muslim patients. Nandi (1965) reported that in 1948 the Kanya-Kubja Educational Trust opened a girls' High School as well as evening and night classes for embroidery and musical training for women. However, progress was regarded as slow, prompting the editor of *Kanya-Kubja* (1965) to exhort the Kanpur Kanya-Kubjas to come out and help this institution because "it was enigmatic that in a city of the rich, an old 'fortress' of the Kanya-Kubja Brahmans, the latter could not make the boys' institution even into a degree college."

Vidya Pracharini Sabha of Indore provides another caste-founded high school, a library, and a number of student scholarships (amounting to Rs. 2,000 annually) awarded only to caste students. It was reported to own three different buildings in the city, accounting for its property valued at over Rs. 150,000. (Recently the organization bought 14,600 square feet of land.) In 1965 the whole institutional complex was run by a trust presided by a Kanya-Kubja Supreme Court lawyer.

Lashkar (Gwalior) association was reported in 1963, and again 1965, to be constructing a Kanya-Kubja hostel (to cost over Rs. 100,000) for the Kanya-Kubja students, and had spent already Rs. 16,000 towards that end. More monetary donations were solicited by the association in 1963 and in 1966.

Since 1960, the Amravati association began helping Kanya-Kubja students by finding and financing lodging and boarding facilities for them and by paying their tuition fees. In 1963 it was trying to have a building of its own, and had bought a piece of land. Financial difficulties were also reported and the association issued a general appeal (through *Kanya-Kubja*) to the Kanya-Kubja Brahmans to subscribe generously "for the sacred cause of serving the Kanya-Kubja *Samāj* [society] and Kanya-Kubja *bhāi* [brothers]."

An Overview

The preceding chronological developments, along with the leads found in the back issues of *Kanya-Kubja*, allow us to note some rough tendencies concerning the proliferation of the sabhas and their activities in the last one hundred years (see figure 1). First, there was a continuous rise in their numbers, from the 1880s to the 1930s. The reasons for this spurt are found largely in the historical and social circumstances that the Kanya-Kubjas faced during this period. With increasing education and the lure of modern occupations, these Brahmans moved to distant locations, thus facing social isolation and psychological insecurity. Moreover, they also encountered the growing fact of intercaste competition for the same secular ends. These factors prompted them to organize their caste sabhas wherever they were and whatever their numerical size. Caste organization brought them social security for marriage and a sense of psychological interdependence "among people of the same kind." Accordingly,

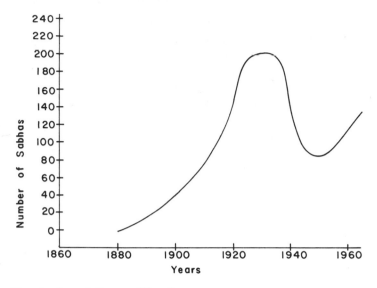

Fɪɢ. 1. Association proliferation curve.

during this period, as a report in *Kanya-Kubja* (1937) indicates, central India alone had "some 100 small sabhas."[5] Some of them had as few as ten families at one place.

The period 1940–55 saw a reduction in their proliferation; and again there are several reasons. One was that the Kanya-Kubja youth heavily enlisted in the services during the Second World War on the one hand, and became involved in the Congress movement, on the other. While the latter discouraged caste organization, the former took the organizers away from their homes. Since the Kanya-Kubja pride themselves upon being patriotic as well as brave, they are quick to produce "evidence" for their heavy enlistment in the various armies: "In 1799, we went as a Brahman regiment to fight Tipu Sultan; and as a result, even today there remain some 18,000 Kanya-Kubjas in Mysore" (personal communication from the editor, 1968). The *Farrukhabad District Gazeteer* (1911; see also Crooke 1896, Khare 1966) also reports that these Brahmans freely enlisted as soldiers. The Con-

5. The editor of *Kanya-Kubja* again noted in 1957 that in Nāgpur, Barār, Chattisgarh, and Jabalpur alone there were some forty-eight functioning sabhas and that the most impressive convention of the Madhya Pradesh Kanya-Kubjas was held in 1938.

gress policy of a casteless society, on the other hand, created a wait-and-see attitude among the caste enthusiasts, which lasted until well into the 1950s, when expanding education, economic resources, and occupational mobility brought back the same forces that were operating in the 1930s. More and more Kanya-Kubjas became educated and were dispersed even farther upon entering the government services. Simultaneously there was the "threat" from the state protections awarded to Scheduled and Backward classes. This spurred caste sentiment again; but this time it was not only for "keeping kinship contacts back home," but also for securing and maintaining their individual and group lead in occupational and economic fields. Figure 1, accordingly, shows this increase in caste organizations again during the late 1950s and early 1960s (see also table 1).

The sabha chronology also reflects the continuous geographic dispersal of the Kanya-Kubjas. Extensive and distant emigration, in turn, created problems of cultural adjustment as well as of communication with kin groups. However, since both of these problems had to be resolved by the emigrants for the marriage of their sons and daughters into properly ranked families, local caste sabhas were organized. We shall examine this theme again in the following chapters.

3 Sabhas and Educational Bodies

FORMAL ORGANIZATION OF THE SABHAS

In March 1966 the editor of *Kanya-Kubja* published a set of aims that should be achieved by all associations for members of the caste (p. 62):

1. The education and marriage of orphan or poor girls;
2. The education of orphan or poor students;
3. The education and provision of a living for widows;
4. Employment for all the jobless;
5. The improvement of the social condition of the low-ranked;
6. The promotion of religious education among children and youth;
7. The promotion of commensalism among pure [*visuddha*] and pious [*sadāchāri*] families;
8. The collection and preparation of a roster of horoscopes of all prospective brides and bridegrooms;
9. The initiation of collective endeavors to initiate suitable marital negotiations;
10. Action to increase the annual membership of the caste journal.

This list is sufficiently comprehensive to represent all the major themes actually emphasized by various Kanya-Kubja sabhas. The aims of the all-Indian sabha were formally outlined by its treasurer (a lawyer) as follows (*Kanya-Kubja* 1957, p. 92):

1. To foster unity and participation among the sabhas and their members throughout India.
2. To help promote education of the Kanya-Kubjas in science and religion and to promote the study of Sanskrit.
3. To render aid to needy Kanya-Kubjas.
4. To establish a "caste fund" [*jātiya kosh*] for helping and educating poor and handicapped Kanya-Kubjas.

47

5. To reform the prevalent social evils in Kanya-Kubja society.

Similar aims are pursued by various local sabhas. For example, the Bhopal sabha aimed to "stop caste discrimination by abolishing subcastes [*upjāti*] and by strengthening such divisions [actually, *varna*] as Brahman, Kshatriya, Vaishya, Sudra. All subgroupings of Brahmans such as *varga* and *upvarga* [ritual groupings], gotra [clan], and āspad [title] must be abolished" (*Kanya-Kubja* 1964). Accordingly, the Bhopal sabha announced that "all those who proclaim to be Kanya-Kubja can become members of this organization if they will give up the internal ritual hierarchy, the practice of dowry, etc." By 1964 the association had worked out a formal program to give shape to ideas that would promote marriage and dining across the subgroups of the caste. (But the plans were not enacted in any organized manner until 1968.) On the other hand, Dohad sabha (founded in 1964) aimed to consolidate the Kanya-Kubjas in its region to cure social evils and to help in arranging marriages. Amravati association (established in 1960) emphasized educational aims for the caste.

The Kanya-Kubja sabhas also wish to promote "brotherhood" by arranging social gatherings on Holi, Shrāvani, and Diwali (annual festivals falling in the months of March, August, and October, respectively). The Amravati association mentions an annual *sahbhoj* (community dinner) for social unity, although it is not clear if it is specifically for the abolition of internal commensal divisions. The Indore association promotes community get-togethers through its library and reading rooms, in which the Kanya-Kubjas meet for social ceremonies.

Various sabhas now tend to emphasize that their aims of caste welfare are for promoting the "social welfare" of the entire nation, because after all, as a writer (*Kanya-Kubja* 1957) put it, "our nation is, whether we believe it or not, an aggregate of numerous caste groups."

The detailed interrelationships of multiple sabha aims and themes are shown in figure 2, in which proposed themes or aims are differentiated from those actually pursued. Horizontal solidarity, reform, and community welfare constitute three mutually reinforcing themes. Although there had been several sabha proposals for establishing an active all-Indian macroorganization of the Kanya-Kubjas, nothing occurred in reality. Sabha aims

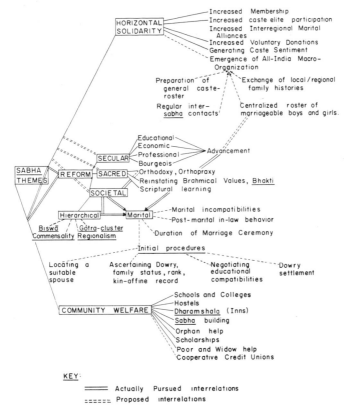

FIG. 2. Kanja-Kubja sabha aims.

are therefore local, in which individualized secular, positional advancement is emphasized alongside that of caste orthodoxy and religiosity.

Secular advancement is now directly related to societal, especially marital, problems and their solutions. This is evidenced by their dominance in the caste journal (1963–66): during this period there were eighteen articles, thirteen letters, 459 advertisements, four special editorials, and sixty-two wedding announcements under the category of "marital affairs." Comparatively, "sabha affairs" drew three caste welfare notices, twenty-nine letters, twenty-six financial notes (usually as an expression of concern for depleting resources), and twenty-three reports and editorials. The year 1963 drew 150 marital advertisements, while in 1966 there were only eighty-eight. Likewise, 1963 saw sixteen wedding announcements in the journal, while in 1966 there were only ten. These fluctuations cannot be attributed to a specific cause because there seem to be a number of interacting factors (including the editor's physical condition, the journal's financial status, and the "urgency" of individual marital cases) that might indirectly control the variations in a specified period of time. However, when examined for an extended period, marital and caste sabha affairs stand out as the most enduring themes of emphasis.

Comparatively, other aims of the sabhas are recessive. A related problem to marriage is that of the traditional hierarchy —another area needing reform, especially the rules of interdining and Biswā rank. The Kanya-Kubjas consider hierarchical-marital problems to be serious, and the latter are accordingly emphasized in all their sabhas. Figure 2 shows this emphasis by the convergence of various sacred, secular, and societal inter-relations. In practice, sacred, secular, and societal positions relate directly to one's capacity to solve marital problems at the level of individual families. The sabha efforts have so far been insignificant in achieving any "collective" solution to these problems. The only regular effort that I could find was the publication of marital advertisements of the prospective Kanya-Kubjas in the caste journal, and the extensive, though informal, consultations with the journal's editor, who has considerable knowledge about who is who, who is where, and who is related to whom.

In a personal communication (1968) the editor informed me that he was practically "swamped" by the parties who were in search of a suitable groom. He devoted over five hours daily to this work. A proposal was made for forming a central roster of marriageable boys and girls of the caste group; although nothing has actually been done. Another unacted-upon proposal suggested setting a "cooperative credit union" for taking loans for paying the dowry demands.

Organizational Structure

All of these sabhas limit their membership to Kanya-Kubja Brahmans. Among them, only those paying their annual dues (usually not more than Rs. 10) are considered to be members of the general body. Fee-paying members alone receive the right to nominate and to vote; they alone can run for an office. The all-Indian Kanya-Kubja association of Lucknow provides an elaborate constitution, and I shall describe it here in some detail.

A distinctive feature of caste sabhas that has uniformly been noted is their formal organization. And this produces an important question: why should a traditionally ascriptive group find it necessary to organize around the elements of voluntary complex organizations? We shall seek to understand the circumstances in which the first Kanya-Kubja sabha adopted them, providing us with at least a group-specific answer. The highly conservative Khatkul Hitaishini Sabha chose to have a formal organization in 1884. Did these Brahmans have any alternative ways of organization available to them? In answer to the last question, caste councils or traditional caste panchāyats come to our mind, but this high-caste group never entertained them as a possibility "because they are prevalent in lower castes and are meant only for the management of individual breaches of conduct in these castes. We never had any need for such an organization in the past, and we certainly did not want to imitate lower caste groups in organizing ourselves," said an old Kanya-Kubja sabha member. Moreover, as this informant further suggested, their organization was for a different purpose: first, it was to preserve their traditional identity in the face of increasing occupational diversity and geographic dispersal; and second, to consolidate and enhance their secular achievements through the then recently introduced Western educational system. (These two divergent purposes typify a sabha even today.) Adoption of formal organization was definitely novel, prestigious (and thus something to imitate), and "in step with the times" for those who already had achieved success through Western educational processes. All of these factors were operating, recall some of my old informants, when the all-Indian Kanya-Kubja sabha was founded.

Formal organization of a sabha is now a legal prerequisite for obtaining recognition from the state. The latter views a sabha not as a traditional corporate unit of kinship with ascriptive membership but as any other social service corporation, initiated and administered by a private group for public welfare. It deals with public funds, and it must meet certain state requirements: it must be registered and it must have a governing body of elected representatives with clearly defined duties and responsibilities for every office holder; it must have records of all financial transactions available for inspection at any time.

The formalities of a caste organization are (cf. Weberian ideal types for bureaucracy; see Etzioni 1965; and chapter 8 this volume) official functions bound by *rules;* a clear-cut division of responsibilities and rights; an official hierarchy; some laid-down rules for personal conduct; separation of the property of the organization and the officials; absence of monopoly by any single official (i.e., by resorting to elections); and a record in writing of the administrative acts, decisions, and rules. All of these ideals are basically followed when forming an executive committee of a caste association.

Formally, every Kanya-Kubja association, without exception, has an office composed of a number of formally designated officers who administer its affairs. A typical Kanya-Kubja hierarchy of officers invariably includes the following (from the top): president (one), vice-president (usually plural), honorary secretary and/or honorary treasurer (usually plural), joint secretaries (usually plural, and for specified purposes like publicity, ceremonies, and specified projects), and members of the executive committee. The latter are representatives of the "general body" (meaning the caste group); hence if the members of the executive committee are n, then the general body is always $n + 1$. Most of the Kanya-Kubja sabhas also employ "expert help," usually a lawyer and an auditor. Both may usually enjoy the de facto rank of joint secretaries in the sabha office. However, of the two, the auditor is more formal, distant, and strict, especially if he has to interact with the appropriate state offices annually. He is charged with the responsibility of keeping the sabha financial records "straight."

This typical plan may be elaborated or simplified by a particular sabha. Under the former emphasis, "complexity" and formality of a bigger sabha may be emphasized to remain appropriately answerable to the state requirements (on voluntary organizations) from time to time. However, if a sabha is smaller in size and finances, its executive body may tend to simplify and reduce the number of formal offices by having a single instead of a plural number of offices for the various ranked categories noted above. But they never break the "basic" hierarchy of president, vice-president, secretary, treasurer, and executive-committee members.

A survey of the reports in *Kanya-Kubja* (1963–66) forms the basis of above observations. For example, the sabhas of Lashkar (Gwalior) (as reported in *Kanya-Kubja* 1965), Amravati (1963), Indore (1965), Dohad (1965), Lucknow (1965), Jaipur (Jodhpur branch 1965), Hyderabad (1965), and Sagar (1965) uniformly followed the above basic organization of offices but with the following variations: every sabha had only one president; with the exception of Dohad and Jodhpur, all had plural (two to four) vice-presidents; every sabha had only one secretary; Dohad and Lucknow did not have any joint secretaries, Hyderabad had only one, the rest had two, except for Jodhpur, which had three; every sabha had only one treasurer, except for Jodhpur, which had a joint-treasurer; only three sabhas (Lashkar [Gwalior], Indore, and Hyderabad) had publicity secretaries; and only two (Lashkar [Gwalior] and Lucknow) disclosed that they had legal advisors and auditors. (But I suspect my enumeration is incomplete in these categories because I might have had access to only incomplete information through the pieces of published executive committee proceedings.) Every sabha had executive committee members ranging anywhere from between five to twenty-one (e.g., Lashkar [Gwalior], nine; Amravati, ten; Dohad, eleven; Lucknow, five; Jodhpur, eight; Hyderabad, thirteen; and Sagar, twenty-one).

The above information about the actual organization of the sabhas underscores the point that these bodies are answerable to the state bureaucratic rules as applicable to any voluntary (welfare) organization and that they are, legally speaking, constrained "para-communities that enable members of castes to pursue social mobility, political power, and economic advantage" (Rudolph and Rudolph 1967, pp. 29 ff.). They are legally "valid" social welfare, nonprofit organizations which handle "public" money in the same way as does any nonprofit academic organization or society for the abolition of untouchability. Accordingly, a sabha has to register itself and its publications with the appropriate state office. But these necessities of modern times are often the occasion rather than the cause for bureaucratization of various sabhas. This is important to remember because, as we shall see below, a Kanya-Kubja sabha is most often a small-sized organization, heavily dependent on individual support of caste members and deeply steeped in informal relations. Formal elements of organization therefore appear as a strategic overlay rather than as a culturally organizational element. We shall return to this later.

Here we shall continue to note other formal (ideal as against actual) provisions that exist with the sabhas. Most elaborate "constitutional" rules are found with the all-Indian Kanya-Kubja sabha in Lucknow. Its constitution emphasizes its all-Indian character and elaborates on the schemes of honorary offices and maximum representation. The rules for the latter ordain that there will be one representative for every ten "local sabhas," that all past presidents and secretaries of the general assembly be represented, that Kanya-Kubja College in Lucknow shall have two representatives, that the Kanya-Kubja colleges of Kanpur and Bhagwantnagar shall have one representative each, that the president shall select three representatives, that during the annual convention the Kanya-Kubja *juntā* (general body) shall elect ten representatives, that the reception committee will send fifteen representatives, and that all those who are life members (fee Rs. 100) and those who had paid Rs. 5 as their annual dues to the Kanya-Kubja associations shall be considered as representatives. This general body of representatives elects an executive committee composed of twenty-three members and the following officers: a president, three vice-presidents, three secretaries, and one treasurer (cf. the actual situation described above).

The all-Indian sabha constitution also specifies the geographic places or regions that should supply these twenty-three members: from Uttar Pradesh alone should come sixteen members with Lucknow, Allahabad, and Kanpur providing two each, and with Unnao, Rae Bareilly, Sitapur, Hardoi, Kheri, Barabanki, Shahjehanpur, Fatehpur, Farrukhabad, and Etawah-Agra-Etah providing one each. Madhya Pradesh is supposed to send four members, from the Nagpur-Raipur, Jabalpur-Khandva, Hoshangabad-Bilaspur-Harda, and Gwalior-Indore geographic areas. Delhi-Punjab, Bengal (West) and Bihar, and Maharashtra are required to send another three delegates, one each from their respective regions.

Further, the executive committee should include five members from the place where the head office of the all-Indian association happens to be situated.

In 1957, however, the treasurer noted the following geographic distribution of twenty-three members of the all-Indian executive committee: Lucknow (eleven), Allahabad (two), Agra (one), Farrukhabad (one), Barabanki (one), Sitapur (one), Rae Bareilly (one), Gaya (one), Jabalpur (one), Dhulia (one), Bilaspur (one), and Lashkar (Gwalior) (one). This indicates the extent of variation that is found in different accounts of these so-called constitutional rules.

The all-Indian body should also maintain a current, fixed bank account (called *jātiya kosh*); and under the rules adopted in 1938, the principal amount of the fixed deposit cannot be spent. Although most of the old financial records have been lost, the central sabha's present secretary informed me about a "cash book" covering the period from October 1905 to December 1911. He also noted that on 28 December 1911 the sabha had a balance of Rs. 11,146.75; that at the end of 1920, Rs. 13,500 had been invested in government loans; and that Rs. 3,000 deposited with the Kanya-Kubja Bank, Kanpur, were lost with the liquidation of the bank. Such occurrences called for a revision of the financial rules of the sabha, and with the active efforts of a Kanya-Kubja lawyer the new rules were formulated in 1938. These provided that the sabha money could be invested in government loans or deposited in either the Reserve Bank of India, the State Bank of India, or the Allahabad Bank. These rules also provided that the interest of the fixed deposit should be spent only on awarding scholarships to needy caste students. At present the sabha maintains a fixed deposit account for a term of nine years. According to the report of an executive committee of October 1964, this account is operated under the joint signatures of the sabha secretary and treasurer.

In the above context it may be necessary to clarify the position of all-Indian Kanya-Kubja sabha vis-à-vis the Lucknow association. The two are synonymous for all practical purposes now, as they have been for the last thirty years. Lucknow has only one sabha and that is the all-Indian body. But actually it is now much more limited in its activities. It has been unable to call an all-Indian convention since 1936, although it aims to do so every year, including in 1968, when *Kanya-Kubja* reported the decision to hold the convention at Shahjehanpur at the invitation of the local body. It has obviously no actually operative "rights" as a central body over the various local sabhas; there are no definite channels of communication between them. The only continuing indicator of its all-Indian function, beside its name, are the efforts of the *Kanya-Kubja* editor (also the secretary of the all-Indian body) to exhort, to cajole, and to induce the Kanya-Kubjas all over India to unite to share and promote the welfare of their fellow caste members. However, in case the office of the central sabha moved from Lucknow to elsewhere (as it has moved in the past), the Lucknow association would "reappear" as a local sabha, according to my informants.

INFORMAL ORGANIZATION

Underlying the above formality is a whole traditional system of conceptions, social relations, and organizations which significantly permeate the expression of formalized behavior. The latter is approached with culturally appropriate styles and purposes. The following actual behavioral accounts on varied aspects of sabha organization and function will help us understand how now, as before, the informal organization of sabhas constitutes the culturally important content, while formality is a necessary safeguard today for certain legal, financial, and administrative purposes.

Some of the relevant traditional characteristics of the Kanya-Kubjas' sabha activities described in *Kanya-Kubja* (1957) will be presented below.

Founding a Sabha

A sabha was founded in Banaras around 1930. The initiative was taken by half-a-dozen Kanya-Kubja youths who began to gather in the courtyard of a big temple in Godaulia under the guidance of Gurdin Bābā, an old Kanya-Kubja "of old Nawabi disposition, conscious of self-prestige." He acceded to the young men's request when told that he was a valued ancestor, a rich man, a wise man, and would be a "natural president" for the sabha-in-making. During the meetings, this old Kanya-Kubja entertained the youths with *pān-supāri* (betel and areca nuts presented as symbols of welcome). The writer recalls how the Bābā used to sit on the floor with a long, round pillow (*masnad* or *girdā*) at his back and how his pillow became the symbol of the sabha "presidency." He did not speak until he had his pillow with him.

After several such meetings, the youths began to bring in "res-

56

olutions" for discussion and adoption, but this simply seemed "superfluous" to the Bābā. He disliked procedural ostentations because, as the youths said, he wanted them to accept whatever he said, without discussion (*Kanya-Kubja* 1957, p. 38).

The narrator (a school principal) of the above story became the successor to the presidency of this sabha when the youths decided to replace the Bābā.

Another example is provided by the erstwhile Karnatak Kanya-Kubja Samāj which was again started in the temple of Tungabhadreshwar, built in the late nineteenth century by five rich Kanya-Kubjas of that area. The meetings took place whenever Brahmans gathered there for social ceremonies or festivals. However, this samāj was short-lived and the temple (and its well) did not attract attention again until 1942 "when it was being taken over by other local caste groups." A Kanya-Kubja filed a court case to prevent this, and won it by the support of Hindi-speaking Rajputs. Until 1942 the samāj was known as Pardesi Samāj (emigrants' sabha), afterwards it became the South Indian Kanya-Kubja Brahman and Rajput Samāj, and finally in 1946 it became the Karnatak Kanya-Kubja Brahman and Rajput Samāj. Now the sabha members meet during special worship of the temple gods. (This is the only hint available that indicates intercaste cooperation solicited by the Kanya-Kubja Brahman. But it is significant as much for its organizational aim as for its success.)

Raising Funds

In 1905 when the annual convention of the all-Indian association took place in Farrukhabad, a "caste fund" (jātiya kosh) was initiated by a *brahmachāri* (celibate saint) of this caste with a deposit of Rs. 0.25. This propitious beginning, as believed, led to a cash collection of Rs. 600 and pledges amounting to Rs. 7,000. It was recorded as an auspicious start for the collection of the sabha fund, which grew to Rs. 14,000 by 1914 (*Kanya-Kubja* 1957, p. 95).

Interesting cultural praxeology is exemplified by the way caste funds were collected during the 1914 meeting of the general body of the all-Indian sabha. As soon as the fund-raising resolution was presented to the assembly, "Pt. Ravi Shankar Shukla, later a Congress chief minister of Madhya Pradesh, took off his *sāfā* [turban], and the enthusiasts began filling it [i.e., its hollow] with their money. This was done very quickly, and Shukla ji had to get two more turbans to collect the money." The total collection was over Rs. 5,000 in cash (*Kanya-Kubja* 1957, p. 68).

This example underlines the traditional way a man can show his utmost dedication for a cause. Two culturally important symbolic meanings are involved here. Taking off one's headgear is a way of showing great respect to a person, a god, or a purpose. The doing so in public by a celebrity further emphasizes "sacredness of purpose" (*puṇya lakshya*). The other implied and related meaning is "of begging." Normally, any self-respecting traditionalist would not stake his prestige (symbolized by his headgear), unless he is in an extremely helpless position. (It should be recalled that a daughter in the Indian social scheme is despised partly because in marriage she makes her father place his turban at the feet of the groom and his father.) To remove one's headgear for collecting money for a sacred cause is the culturally most powerful and meaningful way of conveying the legitimacy of a need. (Such methods may be resorted to even in a political campaign.)

Acceptance of a Formal Office

One of the past editors of the journal recollects how he could not refuse the editorship when it was offered to him in Banaras by an old unknown gentleman who, barefoot, wearing a *dhotī* (loin cloth), and holding a pitcher full of the sacred water from the Ganges, suddenly appeared at his door and handed him a bunch of cloth-wrapped papers. There was no prior contact and no personal introduction. The stranger was discovered to be a famous Kanya-Kubja executive engineer, and a staunch devotee of Lord Shiva. The editor records how he was spellbound by the "sacred aura" of the stranger, including his humility and simplicity, and how he accepted the offer even though he did not have any experience in editing. The engineer went away pleased, saying, "My son! do not be puzzled, begin the caste service and Lord Vishwanath will bestow success upon you" (*Kanya-Kubja* 1957, p. 39). (Compare this cultural conception of "technical" qualifications with those of bureaucracy given in chapter 8.)

Actual Behavioral Styles of Some Sabha Executive Committees

The following pages describe the actually observed details of interpersonal behavior at sabha meetings. The case of the all-Indian Lucknow sabha was personally observed and recorded; others were obtained from Kanya-Kubja correspondents.

The members, officeholders, and ex–office members of the executive committee are informed of a meeting through a prior notice, an agenda is prepared earlier, and for any formal resolutions to be passed more than half of the committee members must be present. However, this condition may be waived if there is certain pressing business which cannot wait for another meeting, or which obviously is not controversial. Or alternatively, the pressing issue is discussed, opinions are obtained, and the original proposal is amended; but formal voting is postponed until the next meeting. But it would be very important to find out how such "formal" requirements are actually informally approached and met without conflict, for unanimity rather than consensus is the norm of such meetings, and open conflicts are extremely rare. Normally all sabha business is conducted in Hindi.

Lucknow. The following is an account of a typical executive meeting of the sabha in Lucknow, held in October 1964.

This meeting took place in the secretary's living room, which is officially described as Kanya-Kubja Kāryālaya (the Kanya-Kubja Office). Adjacent to this is a room with a sign reading "Misra Press" where the caste journal is printed; this also is owned by the secretary-editor. The living room opens directly into a narrow lane, from where one can notice two sign boards, one reading "Kanya-Kubja Kāryālaya" and the other bearing the name of the secretary-editor.

The living room–office is stacked with old files of *Kanya-Kubja* and the secretary-editor's own collection of books and writings. Several pictures of Vishnu, Rama, Krishna, and Shiva hang on the walls. Also prominent are large portraits of his illustrious ancestors, including those of his grandfather and father, each in traditional costumes (*angarkhā* and dhotī) and sitting decorously on a chair with book in hand. Their faces prominently display moustaches and beards (recalling in some respects the "Rajput style"), and their foreheads bear the sacred *tilak* (sandal-paste marks). The portrait of the editor's father was hung just above the editorial desk, interrupting the stacks of books and periodicals, many of which were in English and Sanskrit. The room was furnished with a wooden bed, several cushioned and cane chairs, and two or three small tables with tablecloths. Although occasionally used as writing surfaces during the meetings, the main purpose of these tables is for holding several small trays of *pān* (betel leaves), *tambākhu* (chewing tobacco), and *supāri* (areca-nut). One or two spittoons could also be found close at hand. (Most Kanya-Kubja Brahmans regard these as the most important elements of their intracaste culture.)

Charansparsh (touching the feet of an older caste member in respect), *āshirvāda* (blessings uttered by the seniors), circulation of the pān and tambākhu plates from person to person, and rising from one's seat when speaking or when greeting another senior member constitute some other important elements of cultural behavior which characterize official sabha meetings. Holding papers for a senior colleague on the committee, addressing him with either a nickname or the common title of "Pandit ji," instead of calling "Mr. President" or "Mr. Secretary," and hearing him respectfully (with implicit obedience) are the proper cultural modes for a "junior," even if the latter is politically, economically, and organizationally more powerful.

Nine persons (of whom six were lawyers) attended this meeting (see appendix A). These included the president, vice-president, treasurer, and secretary-editor of the association. The president was the oldest and was highly respected by all the others. His attitude was paternal, sober, and dignified; and he gave his patient attention to whatever the others had to say. The vice-president and the treasurer were more active, but their attitude towards the secretary-editor was one of mild correctitude. The latter, "who had no personal axe to grind, no gains to protect, and no favors to ask," was forthright; and his manner suggested his long-standing services and sacrifices for the association. However, he would reflect deference to the actually and potentially powerful and would accommodate their suggestions without much debate. He would introduce a topic only after informal consultations with other officeholders. The latter, in return, were respectfully considerate towards him and his proposals. Since many such personages were younger than him, he called them *bhaiyā* (a common term of address for a younger brother). They, in turn, would insist that the revered secretary-editor should not observe too many procedural formalities because they would produce physical discomfort at his age. For example, he was not expected to stand up whenever he spoke. The same prerogative could, however, be granted to any other old and respected member, although one's economic status subtly played an important role.

Since the secretary-editor carried the main operational burden of the association on his shoulders, he was the most directly and intimately connected official. The president, the vice-president, and the treasurer were more advisers and sympathizers than co-operaters on equal footing, because, as was commonly explained, these elites had more important professional or occupational affairs to look after (see chapter 8 for comparative time expenditure). For example, the treasurer, who is a prominent citizen, an outstanding lawyer, and a city celebrity, could hardly be expected to extensively share in the lonely burdens of the secretary-editor; and the same would apply for the vice-president and the president (an octogenarian Hindi journalist and Congress worker). Even limited participation by a prestigious Kanya-Kubja was regarded as a good gesture. Thus, while the executive committee members of the association could be variously characterized as forming either a bureaucratic office, a "team" with missionary zeal, or a caste-elite group directed towards caste welfare, they were exclusively neither of these. Their roles were overlapping and their aims diversified. They formed a group with multiple motivations and interests, sometimes along the caste and sometimes beyond it. The secretary-editor in this particular case was the single exception, for his life's mission had been to know and to reform his own caste. Still, his "lobbying" behind the scenes was most crucial for motivating and uniting the sabha committee members. This work often involved occasional family visits, especially where an elite's family members were respectful to the learned secretary-editor, for a family friend's, or counsellor's, or astrologer's, or preacher's, influence is on an informal, and hence more effective, level. The sabha lobbying went on almost exclusively at this level, and it was how the business was actually effectively transacted by emphasizing unanimity over consensus, agreement over open opposition, and casual inquiries over extended, formal discussion. In Lucknow sabha meetings these characteristics were emphasized primarily because of the confidence the secretary-editor enjoyed among his committee members. His integrity and intentions were thought to be above any doubt.

During the meeting under discussion five resolutions were passed without much discussion or debate (for details see appendix A). The last resolution for calling an all-Indian meeting of the general body in May 1965 evoked generous remarks on the secretary-editor's work and a discussion of the general apathy of the younger generation concerning caste affairs. The third and fourth resolutions were carefully worked out by the treasurer earlier and were adopted, let us note, in English so that there would not be any room for auditing and legal complications later on.

With interesting praxeology and informal interaction, these meetings reflect, as noted above, the subcultural (but distinct enough) ethos of the modern Brahman elite. Under the precedence of age seniority, traditional learning, sacrifice-for-one's caste, and missionary zeal, this meeting was clearly differentiated from a regular political or administrative meeting. It was neither hectic, nor prolonged, nor marked by sharp exchanges due to political antagonisms. Though personal dislikes and differences became evident, they were toned down either by the president or by the influential treasurer. Differences were procedural rather than substantive; there was no apparent clash of self-interest or power, as the association itself was thought to be low on actual, or organizational, or political power.

Since unanimity is considered to be so important in official business, it is interesting to compare the formal and informal (actual participation) rank scales to see how the two differ. The ranking is primarily true for the meeting under discussion, but it might have general validity for the Lucknow sabha (see table 3).

Resolutions 1 and 2 were routine jobs: the first related to passing the minutes of the last meeting; the second on passing a condolence motion on the death of one of the vice-presidents of the sabha. Resolutions 3, 4, and 5 (on sabha investments and the call for the all-Indian meeting) generated reminiscences, eulogies, and short speeches, and the ranking in table 3 is mainly based upon this part of the meeting, and upon the observable

TABLE 3

The Scale of Official vis-à-vis Actual Effective Participation
in the 1964 Meeting

Formal Rank Order	Actual Scale of Participation[a]
1. President (Physician)	3
2. Vice-President (Barrister-at-law)	9
3. Treasurer (Advocate)	1
4. Member (Advocate)	5
5. Member (Advocate)	2
6. Member (Advocate)	6
7. Member (Advocate)	4
8. Member (Advocate)	8
9. Secretary-Editor	7

a. Interdigital difference is obviously *not* quantitative; it is the observer's qualitative assessment. The scale postulates 1 as the most effective participant and 9 as the least.

initiatives, influences, pressures, and effective actions pursued by the nine members just before and during the meeting of 4 October. The latter elements, when plotted systematically, yield a message-communication grid (see figure 3).

This particular diagram attempts to record the general interrelations among the committee members, their informal discussions, and some traceable informal influences during the course of the meeting. The double-headed arrow between, let us say, 3 and 9 indicates some informal dimensions of cohesive interaction. First, these relationships are quite old—much more than three years—in the majority of the members, since all of them live in the same town, all of them enjoy high social prestige, and most of them pursue similar occupations. Second, these arrows symbolize not only interpersonal, inter-elite relationships, but also those at the inter-familial and at the kin-group level. Since not all lineage, ancestry, and family friendships could be included in the diagram, they are indicated only as "informal" influences in order to emphasize the meaning and the importance of a word that usually is used as an easy cover-all sociological term. The actual frequency with which the members "step down" from their official pedestal to converse on their kinship relations, far and near, was very frequent during the meetings. They would approach the secretary-editor for advice in finding suitable, same-class (*samkaksh*) brides and grooms for their marriageable sons

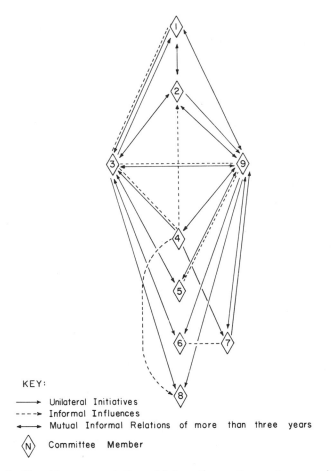

KEY:

——➤ Unilateral Initiatives
----➤ Informal Influences
◄——➤ Mutual Informal Relations of more than three years
⟨N⟩ Committee Member

FIG. 3. Graphic representation of interaction patterns at a committee meeting.

and daughters. This is one advantage that a sabha meeting can bring to the Kanya-Kubja elites.

Considering the age group of the members of the executive committee, such a concern for proper marital connections for their children was hardly unnatural. All the Lucknow committee members were over forty-five, and most of them had several unmarried children. Beyond this, during a meeting, the members could also inquire about some of those who had emigrated and were now being forgotten; that is, except by the secretary-editor who most probably had kept track of them. Thus, plurality of roles, hierarchies, and interests is not uncommon with committee members, and it is useful to indicate the content and dimensions of this plurality and how they combine to produce the particular ethos of a sabha committee.

Comparable details are added to the above description by the following material available on similar meetings held by the sabhas in Indore, Lashkar (Gwalior), and Jodhpur. However, these meetings are described only in their formal aspects as no field observation was available on them.

Indore. On 26 October 1966 a meeting was called to inaugurate a newly constructed room in the association's building and to elect a new executive committee. The room was built primarily by a donation received from a caste elite, and the ribbon was cut by a past committee president, a famous city physician, who gave a long, emotional speech in favor of caste solidarity by praising the work of the Indore association, particularly such "pious acts" as donating money for the caste building.

The secretary of the association followed him and presented the annual report—the problems and prospects—and the past budget with the report of a chartered accountant, which was *unanimously* accepted by the general body and passed. Also, ten members of the new executive committee were elected unanimously. After this official business about half-a-dozen Kanya-Kubja poets entertained the group with their compositions. The gathering was provided with refreshments; and it dispersed after the national anthem, "Jana Gaṇa Mana."

Lashkar (Gwalior). On 2 May 1965 the meeting took place in the courtyard of the new hostel that was being constructed by the Kanya-Kubja Sewa Sangh under the presidency of a retired government officer. The annual report and the budget of the association was presented, and it was unanimously approved. An amended constitution, with its associated rules and sub-rules, was passed, and it was decided that it should be registered under the rules of Madhya Pradesh. The executive committee followed this up with a proposal to set up a trust for the association's finances, and the members decided to have two physicians as its trustees. According to the rules, the meeting then elected the new executive committee, consisting of ten officeholders and ten executive committee members, most of them *pundits* (traditional scholars). The meeting endorsed the view that their association was making good progress and that this pace should be maintained.

Jodhpur. This description concerns a mid-year (1 May) meeting in 1966. It was well-attended and underlined the importance of caste welfare through concerted actions of the Rajasthan Kanya-Kubja Brahmans. The annual report traced the birth of the association in 1965 and the actions of five executive committee and thirteen general meetings which took place in this period. The important resolutions related to preparation of a roster of every Kanya-Kubja family in the state, their occupations and their family backgrounds; a separate register for a complete description of marriageable girls and boys of the caste; a children's club for fostering caste sentiment; and another important resolution related to opening a cooperative credit union for the caste members.

CASTE-SPONSORED EDUCATIONAL INSTITUTIONS: INFORMAL ASPECTS AND INTERRELATONS

Since the formal organization of an educational institution is too complex to fit the scope of this study, it will be ignored in favor of a more interesting and meaningful description of the actual cultural ethos of these institutions. They will provide some instances of how the modern organizational requirements *interjacére* with those of Kanya-Kubja behavioral styles, and how both of them are functionally interrelated. Since Kanya-Kubja College in Lucknow provides the most elaborate scene, is emulated by various other Kanya-Kubja-sponsored institutions (especially in Uttar Pradesh), and is the institution with which I am most familiar (because I taught there for almost five years), I shall present below some brief glimpses of its college life. (I shall be as brief and impersonal as possible. My prior association with the institution, and my own different caste, both qualify and disqualify me at the same time to undertake its detailed objective study.)

A College, Kanya-Kubja Style

In 1965 the college sprawled in an E-shaped building, surrounded by additional smaller structures. The larger building had a big hall bearing a man-sized white marble plaque naming the donors (the Raja of Kardaha and others) who financed its construction. This central auditorium provided glimpses of the institution's past, for on its four walls were sequentially hung numerous pictures of the chief donors, secretary-managers, and illustrious principals—all Kanya-Kubjas. It was used for Independence Day celebrations, for a visting state minister, for instruction and examination, for staff and faculty parties, for the college's annual day, and for such worship ceremonies as those during Basant Panchami or the Saraswati (Goddess of Learning) festival (in February). It was the place of spontaneous student protest as well as for student-union-arranged gymnastic, music, or variety shows. It echoed with student debates and the award of coveted prizes. Its high ceiling was ornamented, and so were the higher reaches of its walls, where the names of Lords Rama and Krishna and various mythical heroes were written in Hindi in big letters. These names were surrounded by brightly colored floral designs. On the west wall—the side towards which most of the congregations faced—was hung a large illuminated picture of Lord Rama.

Like the hall, most of the classrooms also had a white marble tablet showing the donor and his reason for giving the money—most were in commemoration of one's dead relatives. (We might note that a donation to an educational institution is an act of religious merit [punya] as well as of caste eminence. Those who are commemorated and those who commemorate are equally supposed to share the religious merit.) Of course, these classrooms housed students from the most divergent castes and communities, including Scheduled castes and Backward classes.

The teachers exhibited an understandable divergence in dress and in styles of behavior. Some wore traditional dress—a dhotī and a kurtā (a long shirt) with a long, high collared coat—and put tilak on their foreheads. These also avoided wearing calf-skin leather shoes, and each carried a metal box full of betel leaves (ready to use) in their pocket; they could take these out in the middle of their lectures and chew the leaves "to avoid the drying of their throats, while speaking." With chewing tobacco in their mouths, they would occasionally stroll to a nearby spittoon. Some teachers could restrain themselves during their lectures but ate betels soon after. The more "modernized" group,

67

on the other hand, dressed in Western style, wore leather shoes, and wore hats, but avoided free interdining and kept the betel box in their pockets.

The college undertook to perform a *havana* (sacrifice) at least once a year, marking the worship of the goddess Saraswati. The Sanskrit teachers would organize it in the "quadrangle" of the college, by erecting canopies of mango leaves, by bringing the images of gods and goddesses, and by inviting the chief administrators of the college for the occasion. They chanted Sanskrit hymns, offered oblations to the fire, and in a couple of hours they had performed an annual rite, supposed to bring progress and prosperity to the institution. On completion, they would tie *rakshā* ("protective" thread) on the wrists of the main guests, would bless them (symbolically the institution), and would distribute *prasād* (sacred offerings). Those chiefs who were absent would receive the ritual offering through a special messenger the same evening. (It might be noted that this occasion is variously celebrated by most of the "modern" institutions in Lucknow; Kanya-Kubja college does it in its own way.) On this day were also distributed sweets to each and every student, teacher, staff member, and servant of the college. The expenditure was handled through a special committee organized for the purpose.

The college, in its normal daily routine, betrayed further characteristics of its cultural ethos. Most of the teachers, including those of the undergraduate classes, were called "Pundit jis" (exceptions were the young teachers). They were greeted by *praṇām* (a salutation usually accompanied by touching the feet of the person to whom the respect is being paid). The teachers would respond variously to this salutation, depending upon the occasion and the person. Older teachers were greeted this way by the younger teachers, although those who were not students in the same institution earlier might choose to greet them by *namaskār* (a salutation which in normal usage may be comparable to "Hello," or even "Hi"). A college peon (if a Kanya-Kubja) received the same kind of salutation from his own kind (i.e., by a greeting of praṇām); he would usually greet a teacher with respect, irrespective of his caste. An office head clerk, an old teacher with years of college service, and the principal and vice-principal, among others, usually received actual "bows-to-touch-feet" (praṇām), at least once a day from numerous employees of the college. Sitting in his office, the principal might be greeted by a college employee by actually touching his feet. It was a culturally normative greeting; hence it was also socially normal between these modern Kanya-Kubja Brahmans. On the other hand, the same principal accepted the greetings of a Muslim faculty member by saying *ādābarz* (the normative mode of salutation among the Muslims performed with a bow) without any embarrassment or humiliation. (But the presentation of eatables to him would be scrupulously separated for ritual reasons, and his plates and leftovers would be suitably disposed of.)

Indicative of cultural styles of such an institution were also the college seal, the letterhead, and the language for internal use. The seal displayed an image of the goddess Saraswati riding on a peacock, with an inscription in Sanskrit in praise of learning. The letterhead carried the same seal with an emphasis on Hindi. The language for internal use was mostly Hindi, even before it became a focus of political attention and controversy on the national scale. It was therefore normal to find a faculty member replying in English to a note written by the principal in Hindi. In actual dealing, these two languages went hand in hand, depending upon the "appropriateness" of the subjects and the persons involved. But the notable use of Hindi was consistently made in communications exchanged between the college and its management committee.

Now a word about the way such "founders" as the two contractor brothers (see chapter 2) "possess" the college. It was a "paternal" possession—an "ownership" *for* the caste and community. They visited the college daily and met the on-campus principal, laborers, and other employees. They inspected and directed the pace of work, managed controversies, and conferred on an impending student crisis. But all this they did either in the early hours of morning—hours before the classes would start for the day—or late in the evening when more problems would have accumulated. During the daytime, they seldom visited, "for they did not want to distract the attention of the employees." However, on the few occasions when they did visit during class hours those Kanya-Kubja employees who saw them greeted them mostly by touching their feet and uttering "praṇām." The college principal was no exception. These "patrons" closely supervised all the crucial actions that the institution was supposed to take, whether it was with respect to the students, the faculty, the staff, the university, or the state government. It was *their* secret to successful development and a style of smooth administration of a modern complex organization.

Briefly, the above also shows the Kanya-Kubja Brahman's way of being modern in a traditionally pleasing style.

Sabhas and Educational Institutions: Some Interrelations

The educational institutions can be profitably viewed from the sabha's side, especially because almost all of them came into being through the initial efforts of the sabha officers, whether in Indore, or Bhagwantnagar, or Lucknow. For example, the present editor of the journal communicates (1968) to me that the inception of Kanya-Kubja College in Lucknow was financially supported by the all-Indian Kanya-Kubja sabha. The latter paid the rent for the school, and these financial figures are found in the old records of the all-Indian body. But these educational organizations soon outgrew their sabha protection, and became financially independent. Nonetheless, we must remember that they have remained dependent on the help that they receive from the prosperous Kanya-Kubjas and that they have always been managed predominantly by the caste elites. Still, there are several prominent Kanya-Kubjas who work for both types of organizations simultaneously, although, of late, there has been an increasing inclination to participate more freely in educational institutions than in the sabhas.

The sabhas, as expected, count these educational institutions as *their* prized achievements. They are symbols of social welfare —"the living monuments" of this caste's capacity to achieve whatever it aims at. The sabhas view these institutions as "outgrown children," fed and shaped by the sabha patronizing caste elites. Individual eminence of a Kanya-Kubja is generally regarded as a resource as well as a reward for the educational institutions.

However, if we look into the organizational complexity of the educational institutions, they present a significant change of emphases. They are significantly "deparochialized" or "decompressed" (see Rudolph and Rudolph 1967, pp. 88 ff.) in their aims and social networks. They emphasize organizational complexity and engage in diverse multicaste and multireligious participation. This makes them eligible for government financial support, which is growing larger, and hence crucial, every year, but it also prompts extracaste elites to participate. For example, we note that in 1966 the management committee of the Lucknow college included three noncaste members, a Thakur, a Kayastha, and a Sikh. But still, as can be expected, majority participation runs along caste lines, especially in the control of administration and finance and in major decision-making.

However, this "association-institution" relationship in Indore, in Gwalior, and in Amravati have still not reached the above stage. These institutions are not so developed, and the Kanya-Kubja elites supporting them are most often those who hold simultaneous positions in the sabha executive committees. For example, in Indore in 1963–64 the sabha and educational committees had seven out of every ten members in common. The Amravati case provides the closest example of a situation where the association continues to control its educational institution, while the Lucknow-Kanpur situation exemplifies the other pole —that of formally recognized separation. The Gwalior and Indore organizations represent an intermediate organizational complexity, with Indore standing nearer to the Lucknow-Kanpur situation.

4 The Caste Journal

As ALREADY NOTED, *Kanya-Kubja* is important primarily because it discharges the significant function of establishing and reinforcing contacts between widely dispersed sabhas as well as individual families. It was the most important single documentary source for this study because it describes the aspirations, achievements, and problems of the Kanya-Kubja Brahmans, recording caste history around famous happenings and personages. Precise reporting of events accounts for its continued existence: besides minutes, discussions, budgets, and annual reports of the executives of the sabhas, it brings out formally all that is considered to be relevant to caste welfare. This information has been substantially corroborated over several years by my field informants and thus leads me to accept the journal accounts as being essentially reliable.

Kanya-Kubja, issued monthly, accepts membership subscriptions for a full year only (currently Rs. 6 per annum, increased from Rs. 5 in 1966). Although there is no commercial publicity in the journal, matrimonial advertisements from members of the caste group are run at a rate of Rs. 5 per placement per person. The fee may be waived, however, for poor and old members, who are entitled to two free publications of their advertisement, and for those who enroll new members. If a person places several advertisements simultaneously, he is not permitted free publication of all of them; but one can summarize them in one short piece to receive such a concession. Acceptance of all advertisements is at the discretion of the editor, and there is an additional fee of Rs. 5 if they are to be under his care. The latter is considered helpful because the editor has a vast personal knowledge of Kanya-Kubja families and their marriageable members.

72

TITLED MEMBERSHIP

The periodical awards five types of membership according to the amount of money donated. Each carries a honorific title indicating recognition for caste services. Table 4 ranks these titles on a scale of descending importance.

TABLE 4

RANKING OF KANYA-KUBJA MEMBERSHIP TITLES

Rank	Title	Minimum Donation Required (Rs.)
1 (highest)	Kanya-Kubja-Kul-Kamal-Diwākar	1,001
2	Kanya-Kubja-Ke-Pratipālak	501
3	Kanya-Kubja-Ke-Shiroratna	251
4	Kanya-Kubja-Ke-Ājivan-Sadasya*	151
5 (lowest)	Kanya-Kubja-Ke-Sanrakshak	101

* This rank corresponds to what is commonly known as a "life member." Its rate of subscription has been changed from Rs. 100 to Rs. 151.

Every issue of the journal carries a list of current title-holders on the insides of both covers. In addition, the exterior of the back cover lists donors who have given Rs. 51 or more in memoriam (*punya smiriti*) of a dead relative.

The classification of various titled members according to occupation and geographic location is shown in tables 5 and 6 and map 2. While we will discuss occupational divergence in chapters 5 and 6, we may note here that the examples are from a zone bounded roughly by Delhi and Muradabad in the north; Bangalore in the south; Ahmedabad, Alwar, and Bombay in the west; and Bhagalpur, Gauhati, and Calcutta in the east. Map 2 shows this zone divided into four regions on the basis of Kanya-Kubja–reckoned population distribution, their marital zones (cf. Khare 1960), and on the regional organization of their social affinities. Region I contains 107 members out of a total of 165 titled members for the zone; within it, the Lucknow-Kanpur-Unnao subregion alone provides seventy-two (44 per cent) of all the titled membership. The bulk of the membership (144, about 87 per cent) is drawn from regions I and II. The overall distribution pattern of titled membership tends to follow the population concentrations of these Brahmans, and not geographic dis-

TABLE 5

DISTRIBUTION OF TITLED MEMBERS BY OCCUPATION

Occupations (not ranked)	Titles					Total
	1	2	3	4	5	
Advocates	3	...	5	7	8	23
Judges	...	1	1	5	5	12
Physicians	...	1	5	2	8	16
Engineers	...	...	...	2	1	3
Professors and Teachers	...	...	...	3	6	9
Ex-Tālukdārs (now contractors and bankers)	...	2	1	6	3	12
Businessmen	1	1	1	10	7	20
Government Administrators	...	...	2	5	5	12
Nongovernment Executives	...	1	1	...	2	4
Unknown	4	5	14	6	25	54
TOTAL	8	11	30	46	70	165

Titles: 1—Kanya-Kubja-Kul-Kamal-Diwākar; 2—Kanya-Kubja-Ke-Pratipālak; 3—Kanya-Kubja-Ke-Shiroratna; 4—Kanya-Kubja-Ke-Ājivan-Sadasya; 5—Kanya-Kubja-Ke-Sanrakshak.

TABLE 6

GEOGRAPHIC DISTRIBUTION OF TITLED MEMBERS

Titles	Geographic Regions				Total
	I	II	III	IV	
1	3	2	2	1	8
2	5	4	...	2	11
3	20	5	2	3	30
4	33	9	1	3	46
5	46	17	3	4	70
TOTAL	107	37	8	13	165

Titles: 1—Kanya-Kubja-Kul-Kamal-Diwākar; 2—Kanya-Kubja-Ke-Pratipālak; 3—Kanya-Kubja-Ke-Shiroratna; 4—Kanya-Kubja-Ke-Ājivan-Sadasya; 5—Kanya-Kubja-Ke-Sanrakshak.

Geographic regions: I—(Delhi, Aligarh, Agra, Banaras, Barabanki, Bareilly, Rae Bareilly, Basti, Allahabad, Lucknow, Kanpur, Sitapur, Lakhimpur-Kheri, Pilibhit, Shahjehanpur, Hardoi, Kannauj, Unnao, Fatehpur, Hamirpur)=Delhi plus Uttar Pradesh; II—(Alwar, Gwalior, Lashkar, Rewa, Sagar, Shajapur, Ujjain, Indore, Hoshangabad, Khandva, Nagpur, Rajnandgaon, Chanda and Raipur)=Madhya Pradesh plus Alwar; III—(Bhagalpur, Nataur, Jamshedpur, Sambalpur and Calcutta)=Bengal plus Bihar; IV—Ahmedabad, Dhulia, Nander, Bulsar, Bombay, Sangli, Poona, Secundrabad, Hyderabad and Bangalore)=South India.

MAP 2. Geographic distribution of titled journal membership (number per region given in arabic figures). See table 6 for a key to the regions (I–IV).

tance. Thus the fourth region provides a greater number of members (thirteen) than the third one (eight). One explanation offered is that the educated Kanya-Kubjas were attracted more by the princedoms and metropolitan areas of IV than by III, where occupational opportunities were thought to be relatively fewer. Further, the fourth region received emigrants mostly from I (the main locus), although it would have been easier for them to locate in II, which is contiguous. This tendency indicates the increasing pressure at home for the Kanya-Kubjas to acquire better occupational status even at the cost of dispersal.

Titled membership is obtained mostly by the aged and rich.

Age seems to be an important factor: special members in their late thirties or younger are few; most are fifty or more. This characteristic is explainable in terms of the journal's character and normative attitude towards the younger generation. The journal is considered to be an important source for finding suitable brides or bridegrooms because it regularly publishes matrimonial advertisements. It attracts, therefore, those who have sons and daughters of marriageable age and not youths, who are culturally free from this responsibility. Moreover, sons of living titled members automatically receive certain considerations: for example, their marriage announcements and biographic sketches can appear in the journal's pages. Thus, although a youth normally would not enlist as a new titled member as long as his father was alive, this is occasionally done to help the journal's finances.

FINANCIAL ASPECTS

Titled members help to stave off financial crises time and again. For example, when the periodical started 1963 with a financial crisis, the editor issued a general appeal, and thirty special members at once contributed Rs. 10 per person. A Kanya-Kubja-Ke-Pratipālak (rank 2) member from Hoshangabad, enrolled eleven new members in 1963 (and seven again the following year). Finally, donations from some seventy special members and nonmembers wiped out the deficit of over Rs. 1,000. During 1963, regular journal subscriptions brought in less revenue than donations. These donations may come as voluntary contributions or as a kind of charity offering on the occasions of birth, initiation, marriage, or death in one's family, and they often may also accompany regular subscriptions.[1]

1. *Kanya-Kubja*'s budget for 1963 shows that subscriptions provided Rs. 1,418.50 as opposed to Rs. 1,646 from donations, and matrimonial advertisements brought in only Rs. 80, bringing the total income to Rs. 3,144.50.

Expenditure was more than income—Rs. 3,355 as against Rs. 3,144.50, leaving a deficit of over two hundred rupees. It was notable that the largest amount of money (Rs. 568.45) was spent on paying the deficit of the previous year. Some other major items of expenditure were Rs. 338.79 for mailing, Rs. 459 for newsprint, Rs. 630 for art paper, and Rs. 1,207 for printing (*Kanya-Kubja*, December 1963).

The following year the journal spent Rs. 2,786.36 and had a deficit of Rs. 222.36.

In comparison, *Kanara Saraswat* of the Brahmans of Bombay spent Rs. 10,263.92 for 1964 without showing any deficit or surplus.

Since the annual budget separates subscriptions from donations to satisfy formal auditing procedures we can determine the actual size of the membership of the journal; accordingly, there were 283 members in 1963 who had paid their annual dues. In 1967 the editor noted that the journal had somewhat less than 400 members with a membership income of about Rs. 1,900 annually, but the membership figure filed with the Registrar of Newspapers (1966) was above 500. This "discrepancy" is understandable because more issues were sent out than the number carried on the active list in the hope that failing subscribers would pay if they received the journal at their doors (in 1963, however, 100 customers returned the journal, incurring a loss of about Rs. 600).

Matrimonial advertisements are a limited source of income because of the numerous cases in which the fee is waived, as noted above. Between January 1963 and February 1965, the journal published some 100 new advertisements for boys and sixty-two for girls. This figure *excludes* all duplications. The column is a source of financial problems because it attracts many temporary subscribers to the journal; however, it also raises questions of social controversy (see below).

An elaborate scheme for raising the membership enrollment of the journal came in February 1966 from a member from Sarguja, Madhya Pradesh, who dwelt upon the necessity of stimulating "Kanya-Kubjism" and who suggested three ways to bring about a regular annual income of Rs. 10,000: first, enrollment of at least 2,000 stable members by the voluntary enlisting of two or three news members by each of the old ones; second, the inculcation of a firm conviction by the caste members that their caste cannot be progressive and prosperous unless all cooperate with feeling and dedication for having ten new Kanya-Kubja-Kul-Kamal-Diwākar, twenty Kanya-Kubja-Ke-Pratipālak, forty Kanya-Kubja-Ke-Shiroratna, sixty-six Kanya-Kubja-Ke-Ājiwan Sadasya, 100 Kanya-Kubja-Ke-Sanrakshak, and, in addition, 100 "Hitaishī" and 200 "associate members" (the last two categories introduced by the author of the scheme, would have subcriptions of Rs. 51 and Rs. 25 per person, respectively). This would result in a capital of Rs. 60,000 from 536 new members, accruing an interest of Rs. 2,400 annually at the rate of 4 per cent or Rs. 3,600 annually at the rate of 6 per cent. However, in practice this scheme remains unrealized: as usual, only a few prosperous Kanya-Kubjas continue to donate.

The sentimental appeals of the journal's editor do attract the attention of eminent Kanya-Kubjas from Hyderabad, Ahmedabad, New Delhi, Calcutta, Champāran, Jabalpur, Jodhpur, Kharagpur, Gwalior, Dhulia, and Shibsāgar (Assam). (However, in one example there were only four donations from Lucknow and Kanpur.) The editor's past travels and present communications keep alive such diverse contacts, and the response to his "personal" appeals are usually generous from the distant Kanya-Kubjas. His contacts with old and new elites are diverse; and thus in effect, the journal is an elite-backed, elite-solicited enterprise.[2]

The Editor

The tasks of the seventy-two-year-old editor who publishes the journal single-handed are numerous. From acquiring newsprint and art paper from the government to editing, contributing, and printing at the "Misra Printing Press" (a chamber next to his own house), he works, as he observes, "with zeal and sacrifice to inculcate a sense of unity in a caste group which has produced numerous outstanding people in all walks of life." Whatever the odds, he wants to infuse Kanya-Kubja youth with his writings and actions. He wants them to understand who they are and what they inherit by being Kanya-Kubja Brahmans. He is known to have spent his own fortune (about Rs. 48,000, according to *Kanya-Kubja* 1967) for this cause. When the journal lacks money, he raises funds. (When printing delays became crippling in the 1940s, he bought and installed his own press.) When the journal lacks material, he publishes his own poems

---

2. Donations usually are made on sacred occasions. A typical example of this assistance was published in 1964 on the occasion of Srāvaṇi (Rakshā Bandhan), when fourteen Kanya-Kubja elites sent donations to the journal for reducing its deficit. They had occupations ranging from employment in the Indian Administrative Service to printers and shopkeepers, and were located in Kanpur, Lucknow, Hoshangabad, Dhulia, Ahmedabad, Rewa, Nander, Shivapuri, Sagar, Gorakhpur, and Sarguja. Donations ranged from Rs. 100 to Rs. 5, but twelve out of the fourteen were Rs. 15 or less. The sum received on this particular occasion totaled over Rs. 250.

The above information about donors is repeatedly listed in the pages of *Kanya-Kubja* along with editorial notes of commendation and thanks to the donors and exhortations for others to come forward and help.

and articles as "fillers." He is, as he frequently notes in the journal, a "one-man editorial office." He works late at his desk to commend those who help (or can potentially help) and exhorts those who remain passive. He deals individually with matrimonial cases, suggesting potential marriageable families to the desperate, printing free advertisements for the poor, and warning of prevalent maneuverings to the innocent, distant Kanya-Kubjas. Whenever finances do not allow the hiring of help, he also does the printing. Once the journals are ready, he dispatches them; and then, as he tells in his appeals, he waits for the caste members' refusals to accept them.

The contents of his appeals are usually constant: In late 1963 the editor complained about the rising costs of paper and about the necessity of raising the journal's membership to at least 1,000 (saying that the Kanya-Kubjas were increasingly becoming indifferent to subscription). He noted that the government was not releasing newsprint for the periodical "because it was a caste periodical." While matrimonial advertisements offered some new members every year, these were temporary, being interested only in "finding a match for their sons and daughters." He warned:

> The journal will stop functioning and this highly dispersed caste will thus lose the only medium of all-Indian communication which is so important for easing the marriage problem. The latter grows acute everyday because more and more Kanya-Kubjas, as they move in search of better occupations, become unknown to one another and narrow the zone of marriageables. Thus the *Kanya-Kubja* is justified on practical as well as ideological grounds of caste welfare. All the Kanya-Kubjas should know themselves better by reading their illustrious caste history as published in the pages of the journal. They should generously subscribe to it as a sacred personal duty and not as a charity towards a particular individual [i.e., the editor]. Since the journal symbolizes the services and the sacrifices that the Kanya-Kubja ancestors made in the last century for caste consolidation and welfare, the modern Kanya-Kubjas should help perpetuate this prized forum of expression, for their caste's problems.

Undoubtedly, last but not least, he looks upon the journal, as his own enterprise, identifying it as a quasi-personal mission.

JOURNAL FORMAT AND CONTENT

Kanya-Kubja appears in issues containing two to four monthly numbers in Hindi (rarely, a notice or minute is in English). Each number has from fifteen to twenty pages, and thus issues run from twenty-five to fifty pages, depending upon the numbers it carries.

Each publication carries a portrait of a caste-elite on its front cover and the aforementioned lists of titled members on its inside covers. In addition to a list of persons donating "in memoriam," the back cover also displays a registration number and the rules of the titled membership. The first page of every number displays a line drawing in red or green ink of either Ganesh (the god of success) or Saraswati (the goddess of learning), followed by an invocation or a patriotic poem. The body is composed of obituaries, editorials, biographic accounts, and special notices, which are set off from the other journalistic writings; and famous quotes or devotional passages frequently appear as fillers. The matrimonial advertisements are on the last pages of the issue. The journal does not carry a list of contents.

Kanya-Kubja carries diverse materials in its issues, devoting almost 50 per cent of its space to caste-related affairs (see topics 1–9 of table 7). The articles (including a few which deal with science) that fill up the rest of the space come exclusively from the Kanya-Kubja Brahmans, drawn from all the four geographic regions differentiated earlier. Although these articles do *not* deal with caste per se, they are contributed only by the Kanya-Kubjas, indicating the editorial policy of encouraging writing and journalism primarily among the younger Kanya-Kubjas. The columns of the journal are de jure open, but de facto closed for participation by noncaste members, and thus *Kanya-Kubja* is exclusively a caste journal. (However, we may note that the editor published my communications as "letters to the editor," even though I am of a different caste.) Besides caste affairs, the literary writings, which take up a sizable space in the journal every year, may discuss any other subject matter (e.g., from religion, astrology, and indigenous medicine to patriotism, politics, and contemporary literature and poetry).

As table 7 shows, only seventeen pages (out of 384) are taken up by specific discussions of caste problems during 1963–64.

TABLE 7

DISTRIBUTION OF *Kanya-Kubja* SPACE ACCORDING TO TOPIC (1963–64)

Topic	Space Per Issue (in pages)									Total	Percent
1. Caste-related articles	3	…	2¼	…	2	4¼	1	…	4½	17	4.2
2. On caste associations											
Lucknow	…	…	…	…	…	…	…	…	1	1	.3
Others	¼	…	…	1	2	…	1	…	1¾	6	1.6
3. About the journal											
Financial	1½	1	1	¾	1	½	…	2	1	8¾	2.3
Other	4	4¼	5½	5¼	5	4¼	4¼	4½	4	41	10.7
4. Editorials	…	4	…	4	1½	3	1½	…	2	16	4.2
5. Biographies	2	1	2¾	2	3½	1¼	1	3	3½	20	5.2
6. Weddings, tonsure and sacred thread ceremonies	½	1	2	6	…	3	4	2	¼	18¾	4.9
7. Obituaries	¾	1¾	1	1	2	…	½	…	1½	8½	2.2
8. Matrimonial advertisements	4	4	3½	4	5½	4	3¾	3½	4	36¼	9.4
9. Correspondence	5	3	2	…	2	…	…	1	5	18	4.6
10. Literary articles	19	20	20	24	19½	21¾	21	26	21½	192¾	50.4
TOTAL	40	40	40	48	44	42	38	42	50	384	100.0

(While the table data are computed only for the 1963–64 period, the examples in the text are also drawn from later volumes.) Among them, dowry, commensal rules, and intracaste rank-scales are discussed in detail, and are repeatedly denounced as harmful to caste solidarity. Usually these articles end with appeals, exhortation, and suggestions for further unity. In 1963 one university-educated contributor ridiculed Kanya-Kubja gatherings because the latter perpetuate rather than diminish commensal rigidity: "If one cannot accept food from his own caste-brother, what is the use of calling such social gatherings? How can we, then, foster fraternal unity and compete with other progressive groups? Actually, it is a waste of time and money, unless we discard these outmoded customs." He, therefore, suggested opening a sabha devoted to caste-fraternity in every state, with branches and subbranches in every district and village. The aims of this organization, he proposed, would be to resolve caste disputes, to abolish intracaste commensal rules, to allow marriages across various subgroups (but not within one's gotra), to abolish ranking based on geographical dispersal (e.g., Uttar Pradesh Kanya-Kubjas are regarded as superior to those of Madhya Pradesh), to prepare an exhaustive roster of Kanya-Kubjas living in a particular region, and to convert those earlier Kanya-Kubjas who had married out and had become Sarjupārin Brahmans (another collateral group in eastern Uttar Pradesh). Another member suggested an extensive network of pen friendships with far-flung Kanya-Kubja families and an up-to-date roster of families.

Here are some more examples of typical articles (*Kanya-Kubja* 1965–66): a Sanskritic-"scientific" discussion of the sacred thread ceremony (by a lawyer from Agra); on ideal marriage—traditional and modern patterns (by the editor); on the social problems of the Kanya-Kubjas (by a college teacher); a caste-solidarity appeal (by a literary figure from Rajnandgaon); a "historical" reconstruction of the Biswā ranking scheme (by a lecturer of a government Ayurvedic college in Madhya Pradesh); "Were the Sages Kashyap and Shandilya—the Two Gotra Founders—Real Brothers?"—implications on "intermarriages" between these gotras (by a Lucknow Sanskritist); on caste organization plans (by an editor of a Madhya Pradesh journal); "Was Rabindra Nath Tagore a Kanya-Kubja?" (excerpt from an all-

Indian Hindi journal); "The Aged and the Youth—A Problem of Kanya-Kubja Society" (by an anonymous author); on the problem of marriage in the six highest-ranked gotras of Kanya-Kubja (by an elite from Patna); and "On the Altar of Social Rules," a one-act play depicting the suicide of a girl married to an infirm, old widower (by a pundit from Allahabad).

The above enumeration indicates the kind of topics covered, the people who write them, and their locations. Obviously, these themes are not the only ones, although they represent some common ones. But the most outstanding problem is marriage itself, attracting attention in essays, special notices, correspondence columns, and matrimonial advertisements. According to the majority of these articles, the Kanya-Kubja Brahmans agree that they have the following marriage-related problems: the Biswā-ranking scheme, intracaste commensal rigidity, dowry, widows, abandoned women, and expensive ceremonies.

Matrimonial advertisements took up about thirty-seven pages in two years, averaging thirty-five placements (including ten to twelve repeats) in every copy of the journal (each usually incorporating two or three monthly issues). However, this figure is not truly indicative of the space and attention that this problem gets from the caste members, for information also appears in letters to the editor, special articles, editorials, one-act plays, and special notices. In 1965, for example, answering a correspondent, the editor warned the Kanya-Kubjas of the existence of "fake intermediaries" who in the name of the *Kanya-Kubja* and the sabha went about earning money for "settling" marriages of Kanya-Kubja girls. The editor quipped at such "voluntary social workers" of the Kanya-Kubja community, but still condoned them if it allowed them to earn their living. A typical situation, *reported repeatedly*, concerned those who were distantly placed (mostly in Bihar and Maharashtra), who had wealth (or were well-employed), who either had prolonged illness or were now in monetary difficulties, but had several teen-age daughters to marry. Editorial notices for helping such people appear repeatedly (on an average of eighty-five to ninety times every year), and *Kanya-Kubja* publishes their matrimonial advertisements free of cost for five times.

Discussions, suggestions, help, and editorial comments on the problems of marriage, hierarchy and commensalism appear constantly in topics 1, 2 (rarely), 4, 6, 8, and 9 of table 7. The Kanya-Kubjas are usually vigorously criticized for having such "a labyrinth of social walls," considered to be responsible for enormous marital problems. Plans and phased programs are spelled out in various caste-association resolutions (e.g., in those of the Gwalior, Hyderabad, Ujjain and Hazaribagh associations in 1964–65) and in special meetings arranged during such annual major festivals as Holi, Diwali, and Rakshā Bandhan. However, no radical reform was reported to have resulted from such meetings and resolutions; and if they had any implicit influence, it was not recognized by the association members themselves.

Those who subscribe to the journal primarily for getting their marital advertisements published are called "seasonal members" by the editor, who elaborately relates how these members involve a prolonged exchange of correspondence, postal money, marriage-bureau-type chain inquiries, and finally a refusal to subscribe to the journal for the following year. (If the journal mailed in advance is returned, it incurs a loss of Rs. 6 per copy, according to an estimate published in 1966 by the editor.) Despite such a price paid by the journal annually, the editor contends that neither can the "seasonal members" be stopped from subscribing temporarily nor can matrimonial advertisements be discontinued, because the former is the "birth-privilege" of the Kanya-Kubja and the latter should be viewed as having a much wider social function and deeper "humanitarian purpose."

It is interesting to note that the journal consumed the largest space in two years (fifty pages) to describe its own affairs— probably an indication of its unstable financial affairs. Although table 7 categorizes the journal content under the conventional terms of journalism, it must be noted that the contents of topics 4 to 9 deal explicitly with intracaste matters, as do topics 1 and 2. The biographical, marital and ceremonial articles relate mostly to Kanya-Kubja notables; and over 77 per cent of such stories deal with titled members of the journal. However, by implication, this discourages the wider and more general membership of the low-income Kanya-Kubjas. The editor's interpretation is, however, different: he thinks he presents exemplary elites of the caste group in those columns to induce the commoner to better himself.

Outside the above columns, the journal carries a vigorous correspondence on various topics of caste interest. In the order of space taken and social importance, they may be categorized as follows on a descending scale: marital affairs—problems, prospects, and needed reforms; caste solidarity—problems, plans, and perspectives; traditionalism versus modernism—deviations by the younger Brahman and their social consequences (a discussion predominantly carried on by the old and the traditionalists); editorial footnotes to the above (these are usually reformative, witty and eulogistic, but at times carping against modernism and social injustices in marital affairs); and journal-association related problems (usually the publication of those letters which are accompanied or followed by subscriptions, donations, and new memberships). The latter invariably are appended by editorial notes praising such caste-serving Kanya-Kubjas. Suggestions and plans of improvement of the journal elicit interesting comments from the editor.

A 1967 issue of *Kanya-Kubja* carries some interesting examples of editorial discussion in the correspondence column. The editor published under a pseudonym a letter (written by an intermediary), which a Kanya-Kubja lady received while searching for a suitable groom for her daughter. This letter was from a person in Hyderabad stating that the groom's party contacted by the lady had had offers from several renowned Uttar Pradesh Kanya-Kubja families with Rs. 15,000 as dowry, but the groom's father did not then favor marriage because the boy was unemployed. The letter said further that this boy was *now* employed, that the boy's father was a high-ranking officer, and that any Kanya-Kubja would consider it a great privilege to marry his daughter into such a family. The letter from the groom's party asked the lady to send a photograph of the girl, stating the size of the dowry (*lén-dén*) that she could manage. (Implicitly, as the editor noted, it must be more than the sum offered earlier as the boy was now gainfully employed.) This "intermediary" also warned the lady that she should not contact anybody else to learn details about the boy's family, or he would never correspond with her again! The editor followed it up by a page-long caustic comment, suggesting that such "social thugs" should be prosecuted under the recent antidowry legislations.

Fradulent Kanya-Kubja marriage bureaus are also reported in the same issue, some of them apparently *run by members of another caste*. In addition a letter from a librarian in Indore described the difficulties that he was facing in his own marriage due to emigration (*pravāsa*) and requested help from the editor, who promised assistance with his wide social connections.

The same issue also carries a letter from a renowned traditional scholar from Balsar, Surat, who "under God's instruction" performed a *Paumān-yajña* (a special sacrifice) as given in Rg Veda at Dhasvamédha Ghāt in Allahabad during the twelve-yearly *Kumbha* fair "for the welfare of the Kanya-Kubja jāti, for its social solidarity, and for the resolution of Kanya-Kubja social problems, especially Biswā rank and dowry." This letter brought a donation to the journal.

The correspondence column, however, lacks intensive controversy. There is no regular exchange of ideas between the old and the new generations—between the traditional and the modern. Submission to the wisdom of the aged is the theme of the old people's letters, which are the bulk of those published. There was, however, no objective way of ascertaining the rate of correspondence undertaken by modern Kanya-Kubja youth; but, according to the editor's observation, it is at a minimum, for, as he writes repeatedly, "youth is apathetic to the caste, the caste organization, and the caste journal, because he imitates foreign cultures for his economic welfare, but only at the cost of his own heritage." In his editorials, articles, and footnotes to the regular correspondence, he never fails to gibe at the younger group, but apparently with no great effect. That youth participation has not increased is evidenced by the membership list; it is constant at about 7 per cent. However, if Kanya-Kubja youth participates in the journal at all, he does so mostly by publishing a literary article. In this too, the girls outnumber the boys. Participation rises with age, especially after age forty-five, because by then a Kanya-Kubja begins to worry about the marriage of his daughters, who, he knows, can be married *properly* only by the help of someone like the editor. Participation of those who are above age sixty-five is usually for different reasons. It normally displays reverence for or friendship with the editor, and a clear emphasis on caste heritage. This last group is found to most readily help the association and the journal in times of finanical crisis.

Following the general trend of membership distribution, most of the journal materials are contributed from Uttar Pradesh (sixty-six times in 1963–64) and Madhya Pradesh (sixteen).

Thirteen Uttar Pradesh cities and towns were represented in the contributions of 1963–64; of these members from Lucknow (thirty-eight), Sitapur (ten), Etaunja (four), Bareilly (three), Fatehpur (two), and Agra (two) contributed anything from articles, poems, biographies, and devotional songs to "scientific" essays (Banda, Lakhimpur-Kheri, Unnao, Jhansi, Sesendi, Kanpur, and Lalganj appeared only once). Ten cities or towns were represented in the same period from Madhya Pradesh; for example, Hoshangabad (four), Bilaspur (two), Amravati (two), Gwalior (one), Rewa (one), Khandva (one), Sarguja (one), Bhopal (two), Dohad (one), and Indore (one). Hyderabad (Andhra Pradesh) appeared twenty-six times in the same period, owing to the close friendship between the editor and a titled couple who resided in Hyderabad. Delhi (nine), Calcutta (one), Jaipur (one), Chanda (three), and Nander also appeared. All together, in this period, the journal had 123 contributions from twenty-nine locations. (Four rural locations were not ascertainable and hence they were not included in the above list.)

As far as I could trace, except in six cases, the contributors had no *explicitly* mentioned relationship with either the journal or its editor. All contributors were of course Kanya-Kubja Brahmans, and fifteen carried professional pen names in Hindi. The following āspads were represented: Misra, Sharma, Pandey, Shukla, Bajpai, Triwedi, Dikshit, Dube, Awasthi, Tripathi, and Upādhyāya. (This information was useful in several cases in ascertaining indirectly the intracaste rank of the participants; see chapter 5.)

PHOTOGRAPHIC DISPLAY AND CULTURAL STYLES

Every issue of the journal has one photograph of a Kanya-Kubja elite on its cover page (in addition an issue usually has two or more monthly numbers in it, each normally carrying at least one photograph). A survey of the 1963–65 volumes showed that of twenty-four published photographs fifteen were displayed for biographic coverage, three for achieving outstanding success in occupations, and six were of newlyweds (an average of twelve photographs per volume). Of these there were a college principal, a vice-chancellor, an army lieutenant, two engineers, five advocates, two senior central government officers, three army captains, a lady physician, a housewife, a past sabha president, two physicians, a superintendent of police, a university teacher, and two business executives (seven were titled members and ten, brothers or sons of titled members, and the rest were of "favorable disposition towards sabha activities," according to the editor).

These facts underscore two obvious facts: first, all the Kanya-Kubjas whose portraits are displayed in the journal have prestigious occupations, and second, most of them are connected with the all-Indian sabha (this relation is either direct or indirect). This connection, most frequently through kinship because the kin of an elite receive special attention, is more clearly emphasized in figure 4. It shows the kin of those whose photographs

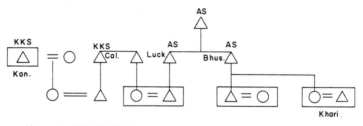

Key to abbreviations:

☐ Persons whose photographs appeared in the journal.

KKS   Kanya-Kubja Sanrakshak

AS   Ājiwan Sadasya

Kan.   Kannauj

Bhus.   Bhusāwal

Cal   Calcutta

Luck.   Lucknow

Khari.   Khariyar

FIG. 4. Prestigious relations of some of those whose photographs appeared in the journal during 1963–65.

appeared in the journal between 1963 and 1965. Though these were obviously not the only people whose photographs were published in this period, they possessed the required criteria; that is, they were kin or affines of Kanya-Kubja elites who were titled members of the all-Indian sabha. If these conditions could be met, the geographic distance was no problem. (The network was recovered from the accompanying editorial notes in the journal. It could be extended much farther, as we shall see in chapter 8.)

More than their numerical significance, these photographs provide meaningful indicators of social prestige. They illustrate modern cultural symbols of social position. Since biography and marriage are the most popular reasons for photographic display in the journal, we shall briefly describe some of their cultural meanings.

Biographic photographs, the media for conspicuous display in the journal, emphasize dress, appearance, and disposition of the honored Kanya-Kubjas. Variations in style relate most directly to age, occupation, and social position. Thus the priests and administrators, army captains and businessmen, justices and past Tālukdārs, teachers and lawyers, and Ayurvedic physicians and modern physicians of Western medicine, are all found in the pages of the journal dressed in suitable styles. Even British-regime Kanya-Kubja employees dressed differently than their modern counterparts. But some occupations are restrictive for dress. For example, a priest continues to appear in turban, kurtā, and dhotī, while a government administrator dresses Western. If the administrator was associated with the British regime, he is usually portrayed holding a walking stick, wearing a felt hat, and bow tie. On the other hand the moderns mostly wear a suit with tie, or a Jaipuri jacket (now popularly known as Nehru jacket) with slacks, or a long coat (*shérwāni*) with *churidār* (tight pajama) and Gandhi cap. These modern-dress alternatives are found among such occupationally diverse people as lawyers, physicians (modern), teachers, administrators, businessmen, past rulers, and politicians. Priests are shown, however, wearing Nehru jackets with dhotī instead of pants. When the photographs are compared over the last forty years, an outstanding change in dress is seen for past Kanya-Kubja Rajas. The swords, crowns, turbans, guilded chairs, and personal ornaments of earlier times have been replaced by Gandhi cap, long coat, and churidār.

Styles are significantly related to the age of the person. Generally, age brings conservatism in dress patterns; those who have dressed in a particular way for many years change the least—a fact borne out by past journal files. The files also show that in the last fifty years the dress of the prestigious caste members have tended to become more standardized around the alternatives already described. Now, there is no sharp contrast between the dress of rich rulers and the common caste member: quality of achievement has become the all-important factor for social prestige—a subject of the greatest editorial emphasis in the biographies.

Although their biographies are few, women, on the other hand, are found to dress uniformly through the years covered by the journal files. The latest notable display of a lady's photograph was in the golden jubilee number of the journal. She was the wife of a chief justice (whose portrait appeared on the cover of the same issue). It was published on the first page in honor of her diverse social services rendered through a dozen civic and caste welfare bodies. She was dressed in a simple sārī and a veil over her head.

The marital photographs also present subtle prestige indicators within a culturally permissible range of flexibility. Dress, pose, and the inclusion or exclusion of various relatives in a photograph are some common indications. Most distinctive is the dress of the bride: while grooms now dress mostly in the Western suit and tie, their brides wear sārīs. But within these dressing practices, there are various ways of signifying one's prestige, sophistication, orthodoxy, and modernity. Commonly, after the ceremony a formal marriage photograph is taken either in a photographer's studio or in the groom's house. Most couples prefer the former situation for its greater individual freedom (e.g., they could hold hands or the bride could change her hair style); but to satisfy the groom's parents and other relatives, a group photograph may be taken first. The two photographs provide a good and reliable index of the permissible variability of cultural emphasis. In a group photograph traditional formality comes to the fore, and, accordingly, they show the new couple to be more reserved. This consideration is most evident in the bride's appearance: she wears all of her heavy gold ornaments (symbols of family prestige), including such specific symbols of the married state as *nath* (nose ring) and *béndā* (an ornament at the parting of hair); she wears a veil over her forehead, looks down bashfully, and sits as her husband's relatives want her to.

Recently some photographs were displayed of the sophisti-

cated weddings of two Calcutta brothers (*Kanya-Kubja* 1964).
One groom dressed completely in Western style, while the other followed tradition in a long high-collared coat (*achkan* or shérvani) and cap. All other men in the photographs had on Western dress (some with neckties, others with bow ties). On the other hand, all the ladies wore sārīs, except for one unmarried girl who had on a shirt and churidār. All women were ornamented, the bride most conspicuously so, with béndā and nath. Both couples had garlands around their necks. The bride of the Western-dressed groom was at her place, and hence she did not draw the veil over her head; in the other case, the bride did so because she was at her husband's place. However, in another photograph the traditionally dressed husband is seen to have changed to Western clothes, while his wife has removed her bénda and nath, but has retained other ornaments and the sārī.

IN CONCLUSION

The preceding chapters have presented some essentially important aspects of the Kanya-Kubja Brahman sabhas, underlining their social, organizational, and cultural characteristics. Most importantly, they have been found to emphasize elite participation, individually achieved social position, and modernity in the face of traditional values and aims. The sabhas achieve the participation of Kanya-Kubjas on a moral basis, even if the organizational format of these bodies is basically "rationalistic" (or bureaucratic). Since sabha participants are modern achievers as well as traditional Brahmans, and since whatever behavioral pattern is reflected in the sabhas is in fact a part of wider sociocultural contexts and their processes of tradition and modernity, I shall seek to further analyze the interrelations between the traditional and the kinship, and the formal and the modern, *without* restricting the discussion in terms of the sabhas. In the next three chapters I shall examine the most distinctive and equally complex feature of Kanya-Kubja social organization—status stratification. By doing so, I hope to put sabha behavioral patterns against a wider, comparative background.

II Tradition and Modernity: Status Stratification and the Kanya-Kubja Achiever

5 Traditional Hierarchy

SABHA BEHAVIOR, as described in the preceding chapters, may be better understood, I think, if it is put back into the relevant sociocultural context, particularly in terms of the systems of traditional and modern hierarchy that characterize a modern sabha member. Thus one is simultaneously a Brahman, a caste member, an achiever, and a modernist. Since one plays these roles in terms of one another and not independently, a discussion of nonsabha, but directly relevant, aspects of Kanya-Kubja behavior should be instructive. Most important of all is the Kanya-Kubja's multivariate status stratification system in which the traditional and modern bases of rank and position come together and compete.

Accordingly, in this and following chapters the discussion of "status stratification" will have two basic referents that interrelate and coordinate with different levels of cultural values, usually subsumed under the label "tradition and modernity." The way the term "status stratification" is used here intends to convey these specific emphases. My meaning of this term will, therefore, be more inclusive than Weber's "caste status," yet less inclusive than his "status stratification" (1966, pp. 23–26). The latter in my usage is denotative of the dynamics between economic "class," caste "status," and cultural values. Weber (1966, pp. 27, 31–32) wrote: "whereas the genuine place of 'classes' is within the economic order, the place of 'status group' is within the social order, that is, within the sphere of the distribution of the 'honor.' From within these spheres, classes and status groups influence one another. . . . Classes are groups of people, who from the viewpoint of specific interest, have the same economic position." "Status," according to him, is expressed through

95

"a specific style of life." Accordingly, I shall also describe the "caste status" and "class" of the Kanya-Kubja Brahmans first by indicating some important elements of "ascribed" and "achieved" traditional hierarchy, followed by a closer look on their specific "class" standards and styles in the succeeding chapters. This will help us to later ascertain the nature of the relationships between formal sabha organization and the ascriptive structure of a caste group, a topic of continuing academic discussion (e.g., see Leach 1960; Srinivas 1962, 1966; Bailey 1963a, 1963b; Rudolph and Rudolph 1960, 1967, and Rudolph 1965a; and Fox 1967).

The following description of Kanya-Kubja traditional hierarchy will emphasize the actual cultural praxeology in order to explain how tradition ascribes some properties at birth at the group level and sets others for individual achievement. It also will show how the cultural *praxis* relates to practice, especially as constantly attempted by these Brahmans themselves.

ASCRIBED STATUS

The Kanya-Kubja Brahmans have, as briefly indicated in the Introduction, several elements of ascriptive ranking. They are elaborate and binding on every Kanya-Kubja by the fact of his birth. On the other hand, traditional "honor" is also acquired by achieving certain culturally desired styles of behavior. Both together determine a Kanya-Kubja's position on the traditional order.

In review, the chief elements of ascriptive hierarchy are gotras (exogamous, hierarchized groups or "clans"), āspad (a surname or title), ānk (genealogically reckoned name/s of meritorious agnatic ancestors), susthān ("original" or traditional place/s of their concentration within Uttar Pradesh), and Biswā scale (literally, a land measuring unit twenty of which equal one bigha, or one-third of an acre; Kanya-Kubja Brahmans use it to mean an ascriptive-numerical rank order of twenty equal divisions). Gotras form two hierarchized clusters: the higher Uttama or Khatkul or Kulin cluster of six gotras, and the lower or *Madhyama* or *Dhākara* of ten gotras (see table 8 for a listing of the gotras). Ideally, there are three; but one cluster, as shown in table 8, is "empty." Thus location, kinship, proper alliance, agnatic ancestor, gotra, and Biswā rank jointly determine or

TABLE 8

Interpenetration (Conflict) of Gotra-Biswā
Hierarchy

	Gotra	Lowest Biswā	Highest Biswā	
Khatkul or *Kulin*	1. Kashyap	3	20	"six houses"
	2. Shāndilya	2	20	
	3. Kātyāyan	3	20	
	4. Bharadwāj	2	20	
	5. Upmanyu	2	20	
	6. Sānkrit	4	20	
Madhyama, Dhākara, or *Dash-gotra Wālé*	7. Kāshyap	2	10	"half house"
	8. Garg	1	8	
	9. Gautam	1	5	
	10. Bhāradwāj	2	8	
	11. Dhananjaya	2	3	
	12. Vatsa	1	7	
	13. Vashistha	1	3	
	14. Kaushika	1	3	
	15. Kavista	1	3	
	16. Pārāshara	1	4	
"56 other unknown gotras of the Kanya-Kubja"	. . .	. . .	. . .	"unknown"
	. . .	. . .	. . .	

maintain one's ascriptive caste status. Broadly speaking, the
Kanya-Kubja exhibit two main lines of hierarchy: first, the gotra
clusters, which are supposed to be endogamous (although there
is an increasing tendency to marry across them); and second,
the powerful Biswā scale which assigns numerical ranks of from
1 to 20 (the latter being highest) to all the Kanya-Kubjas of all
sixteen gotras. But for some Kanya-Kubjas Biswā may be considered to be a "disputed" ranking scale; why this is so and how
it is possible will be answered momentarily, but here it is important to note that the Biswā rank of a Kanya-Kubja must be
ascertained by knowing his gotra, susthān, and ānk, which together "verify and cross-check" his Biswā rank claim. Gotra name
tells the cluster to which one belongs; it also tells the maximum
or minimum Biswā ranks within which one must be located (see
table 8). For example, a Kashyap Kanya-Kubja is of the Khatkul
cluster and can have his Biswā rank anywhere between 3 to 20
Biswās; if he was a Pārāshara, he would have been of Madhyama

97

cluster with a Biswā range of from 1 to 4. If the name of the place of original concentration is also known, the range narrows down further, and can be fixed once ānk names are known. Ānks are reckoned by the name/s of one or more human ancestors. Āspad, or title, is a comparatively feeble indicator of ascriptive rank for a Kanya-Kubja, although the older Kanya-Kubjas remember which titles belong to a particular gotra. For example, each Khatkul gotra may have between 3 to 9 titles: Kātyayan gotra has Misra, Dube, and Agnihotri as titles, while Upmanyu has Bajpai, Awasthi, Misra, Dixit, Trivedi, Dube, Agnihotri, Pāthak, and Upādhyāya. Also, some indicators of Biswā rank are strong or feeble, unilateral or mutual. Thus gotra, susthān, and ānk constitute three main mutually verifiable indicators, which, if known, can accurately fix the Biswā rank of a Kanya-Kubja.

But Biswā scale is considered "problematic" by Kanya-Kubjas, who say it "originated" about four centuries ago during the Muhammadan rule ("hence is not authoritative") and it was, according to Kanya-Kubjas, initially achievable by personal economic advancement (i.e., it was a "class" indicator), but within two centuries it became ascribed. The old genealogies, says Narain P. Misra (1959), did not show uniform assignment of Biswās; "it became exhaustively applied to all the gotras and their ānks in the last two hundred years." Even now, the journal does not publish Biswā ranks in matrimonial advertisements. In this scheme, the dissenters argue, the rich and nearer to political centers got higher Biswā rank, while the poor and rural (but ritually orthodox) were *allotted* lower Biswā. Whatever the actual "original" source of this discrepancy, it is clear, as we shall see below, that the Biswā scale cuts across the gotra-cluster precedence. This scale assigns the highest Biswā to the Khatkul gotra cluster, but it also awards lower Biswās to some of the ānks (also called here "agnatic ancestral groups," or AAGs, because they are much smaller than gotras and more precisely related to specific, actually accountable human ancestors, but less precise than "lineages") of all the gotras belonging to this cluster (see table 8).

Accordingly, Kanya-Kubjas of from 2 to 10 Biswā ranks can be found in the high as well as the low gotra cluster; but those of from 10 to 20 Biswās can be found only in the high Khatkul group.

A gotra, whether of Khatkul or Madhyama cluster, is composed of numerous AAGs ranging from 12 to 264 in a single gotra. (My computations are based primarily on Narain P. Misra's *Vamshāvali* [1959], although several other genealogists like Bajpai 1946, Munni L. Misra 1966, and Shastri 1966 have also been compared to include diversity and variation, if any.) Similarly several AAGs (ranging from 2 to 47) are grouped together in one Biswā rank, although rarely there may be a single AAG in one particular Biswā rank.

This caste has 1,188 reported AAGs (see appendix C) distributed between the two extremes of the Biswā scale and among all the gotras. The majority of the AAGs (931, 78%) belong to the higher gotra cluster (Khatkul), and only 257 (22%) among the lower Madhyama cluster. Sixty-nine per cent of all the AAGs of the Khatkul are located between 10 and 20 Biswās, while 43 per cent are found between 15 and 20. The lower ranks of the Khatkul (between 2 to 9 Biswās) are correspondingly emptier, having about 30% (288) of the AAGs. Madhyama cluster, on the other hand, has only 257 AAGs ranked between 1 to 10 Biswās, the prescribed limits for this cluster. Although AAGs are not direct indicators of the actual population size of a gotra or of a Biswā group, they are treated here as rough pointers of how the ascriptive hierarchy of these Brahmans has functioned over the years, and what, if any, the above distributional tendencies mean for their overall social precedence. Most importantly, the above distributional data suggest "crowding" of the Khatkul cluster, especially at the top of the Biswā scale. This is accountable in terms of the hypergamous marital practices that the Kanya-Kubjas exhibit in an institutionalized form (Khare 1968). The highest Biswā rank, accordingly, contains the largest number of AAGs (161), comprising the most prosperous and influential Kanya-Kubja Brahmans. Presence and prevalence of Biswā hypergamy is another indicator how achieved economic status can influence their marital practices. The rules lay down that a girl must be married to a man of higher (preferred) or equal Biswā but never lower. The rich marry their daughters to those of higher Biswā. By doing so, the former gains entry into higher "ascriptive" ranks, and the latter gains money in the form of dowry. In this system of exchange, women and money are given to the groom's party for entering into a higher Biswā rank in a manner other than by birth. It is hence called an "artificial rise" (banuān) by these Brahmans.

As has been indicated earlier in several contexts, marriage is a crucial testing situation of their ascriptive hierarchy. It presents many "problems" because these Brahmans want not only to marry outside of their "incest zones" (i.e., outside their own gotra) but "up" on the ascriptive as well as the "class" hierarchy. The latter two criteria severely limit the choice and thus intensify competition for the selection of marriageable boys and girls. The rich of 20 Biswā rank prefer to marry their daughters to those within their own group, but may consent to the marriage of their sons to rich but low Biswā Kanya-Kubjas. The poor, of both high and low Biswā, are put under the greatest hardship in finding "suitable" grooms: poor but educated or well-employed low Biswā boys may, in practice, be offered girls from higher Biswā rich families; but this does not hold true for poor but educated or employed girls, and their parents have the most difficulty in finding grooms. A sabha tries to relieve this pressure not so much by "reforming" the practices of dowry and Biswā rank as by providing information about dispersed families of similar ritual and economic ranks. The editor of *Kanya-Kubja* renders this service every day in his office by answering mail, by publishing the matrimonial advertisements of the poor without cost, by acting as a clearing house for hundreds of horoscopes of boys and girls, and by granting numerous interviews to the desperate. Yet all of this effort is hardly adequate. Economic status continues to be increasingly emphasized, and the problem has become so severe that a writer observed (*Kanya-Kubja* 1957, p. 23):

> We tried to reform the Kanya-Kubja samāj for the last fifty or sixty years through our untiring efforts, but the result has been negative.... Take for example, the publication of matrimonial advertisements in the *Kanya-Kubja*. It is done to alleviate the problem of Biswā and dowry, but actually those who search for a "fat" (rich) party for their sons' marriages are helped most. Now there is only one way out: The "entire" caste should be "registered" in the names of those 2 to 4 per cent rich and high Biswā families who are bereft of Brahmanic values and can give and take exorbitant dowry gifts. Those who cannot compete should marry Sanādhya, Gauda, and Sarjupārin Brahmans [cognatic north Indian

Brahman groups] and should merge with them. Kanya-Kubja society is no longer for lower- and middle-class families. To be born in the latter strata is the greatest sin.

The same Hindi writer, at another place (p. 22), noted that now Biswā is insignificant and economic status is all-important. "To be a prestigious officer is worth more than 20 Biswā." He cited the case where a Kanya-Kubja administrator (of low Biswā) refused to marry his son to the girls of 18 or 19 Biswās because their fathers could not manage more than Rs. 15,000 as dowry. He quoted (in English) anonymously, "To elders marriage is a business deal, to young ones marriage is a heart's feel." On the other hand, he wondered why even the foreign-educated Kanya-Kubjas remained trapped in Biswā rank order and other ceremonial rigidities of marriage.

In a personal communication (1968), the editor of the *Kanya-Kubja* notes that today a high Biswā Kanya-Kubja employed in Indian Administrative Service, or Police Service, or Forest Service fetches as much as Rs. 50,001 as dowry, which may include or be in addition to a car and a refrigerator. (Dowry presents are always figured in odd numbers because they are considered to be auspicious.) However, if a Kanya-Kubja is in I.A.S. but of low Biswā, he may not get as much (for example, Rs. 25,001 or Rs. 30,001 depending upon the number of unmarried daughters that the bride's father still has). The next "class" consists of physicians, engineers, and officers of the state civil service. They, when of higher Biswā, can receive a dowry of as much as Rs. 25,001 and of about Rs. 17,001, if of low Biswā. A comparatively lower class is represented by university lecturers and lower state government officers, who may get dowries of Rs. 15,001. All of these "rates" of dowry also increase in relation to the ancestral property that a groom is likely to inherit. Prestigiously employed sons of rich 20-Biswā fathers are, accordingly, the most desirable grooms in the caste group.

INDICATORS OF TRADITIONALLY ACHIEVED POSITION

Gotra, āṅk, susthān, Biswā scale, and gotra-clusters are universally prescribed elements at the time of one's birth. They are immutable and unchangeable. On the other hand, references like "rich and poor" and "class and occupation" form the elements of nonuniversally achieved position. The latter has an "instrumental" value and is acquired by voluntary efforts for fulfilling certain personal and group aims. This kind of status has two interfacing dimensions in the Indian situation—traditional and modern—although both types of statuses are achieved by individual, voluntary efforts and both have instrumental value, even if in different degrees. Traditional indicators of achievement of the Kanya-Kubja Brahman along with ascriptive rank constitute what is known as the *traditional status of an individual*. Thus, a man of low ascriptive rank can be high on traditionally achieved position, and a man of high ascriptive rank can be low on traditional position. The informants often cited the examples of Vālmiki and Raidās in this connection because the former was a Brahman robber and the latter a Chamār saint. However, traditional position is predicated to ideal Brahmanic values.

The following discussion of some common indicators of a Kanya-Kubja Brahman's traditional position will only nominally refer to the textual ideological schemes but will emphasize how some nonuniversally achieved (and instrumental) indicators of traditionalism may actually appear in social reality. Briefly, I shall variously employ a series of markers of traditionalism, such as sanskritic learning, scriptural knowledge, orthodoxy in food, worship, fasts, festivals, and marital practices. I shall refer to astrological, Ayurvedic, priestly, and literary skills, appearance and behavioral styles, and philanthropic values as they are popularly thought to rank an indiivdual on the traditional scheme. I shall illustrate the meaning and function of economic fortune and social influence under the traditional scheme. How all such diverse indicators interrelate in reality will be exemplified in terms of the behavioral styles of a traditional elite.

The ideal of traditional Brahmanic behavior is repeatedly published in all Kanya-Kubja genealogies and is drawn from the Bhāgwat Purāṇa (VII, XI, 21), which lays down the following values for human conduct: nonviolence, truthfulness, celibacy, self-restraint, uprightness, purity, contentment, sacred learning, austerity, forgiveness, kindness, and devotion to God. A Kanya-Kubja noted that these are the content of a Brahman's *yama* and *niyama*, and one should follow them in practice, although he instantly remarked that they constitute ideals and can only be imperfectly reached. But how and what efforts they make now in their daily lives and how they relate these values to their over-all status are questions of greatest relevance to our discussion.

Ritual behavior concerning food preparation and consumption, marriage, worship, fasts, and festivals provide some of the most significant indicators of a Kanya-Kubja's traditional position. Those who do not eat outside their own or their relative's kitchens and who follow the rules of purity during the preparation and consumption of food are "higher" than those who eat "outside" in restaurants or at "tea-parties." Those who wear home-washed clothes, wash their feet before and after meals, and take God's name before starting to eat are "higher" or "better" (i.e., more in conformity with the ideal) Brahmans than those who do not do so.

Food and Marriage

Extreme measures of maintaining ritual purity in food has been an outstanding characteristic of the Kanya-Kubjas. They do not, as the saying goes, even use the fire lighted by an unknown Kanya-Kubja, let alone by any other caste group, for cooking (cf. Risley 1915, p. 306, who noted "three Kannaujia's and thirteen fireplaces" for their fuss over cooking). A young Kanya-Kubja lawyer noted (*Kanya-Kubja* 1957, p. 34) that his caste members are distinguished by their practice of taking food; they eat only after bathing and after worshipping their deity and wear only a home-washed dhotī. Those Kanya-Kubjas who do otherwise may *not* be the representatives of this caste, "because even those who went to England for studies did not give up the Kanya-Kubja mode of commensalism." Food, accordingly, continues to be the mainstay of daily orthodoxy and ritualism. Those who have high economic status but do not observe commensal rules may not be considered "true" Kanya-Kubjas, although the strength of this opinion varies according to age. Some Kanya-Kubjas are traditionally allowed to eat meat (see Khare 1966), and it is not in conflict with the ritual purity requirements if meat is prepared properly for a traditionally allowed purpose.

Since this is not the place for an elaboration on the topic of food and kitchen, let us simply note that the Kanya-Kubjas are still most susceptible in these areas. They do not allow the cook to move out of the kitchen or to touch others until the cooking and eating are finished. A mother has to ask her daughter, sister-in-law, or somebody to take care of her infant. If clothes are ritually impure, the cook must wear a wet dhotī or sārī throughout the preparation of the food. Although a Kanya-Kubja's kitchen is next only to his place of worship in ritual purity, the emphasis is on the former. Usually an image of a deity is brought to the kitchen for offerings before eating can be started.

Marriage is the most important occasion for an elaborate and complicated display of the rules of commensalism. For the Kanya-Kubjas food (*rotī*) and daughter (*bétī*) emphasize the same cultural principle; both tell them with certainty with whom to marry and to eat. "We eat with those to whom we can give our daughters" is the famous Kanya-Kubjas saying (cf. Lévi-Strauss 1966, where he says marriage and food are one and the same thing). Thus in a marriage (especially in the *bhāt* ceremony which involves the communal eating of boiled rice, an easily pollutable item) who can sit and eat together under the marriage canopy (*mandapa*) with the groom's relatives provides the most sensitive situation. Cases are known where disputes occurred among the members of a marriage party for this claim. On the other hand, bride's parties have used it as an occasion for humiliating the groom's side by serving them bhāt prepared by Kanya-Kubja cooks of lower Biswās. Normally, a Kanya-Kubja is most circumspect in attending a bhāt dinner at a marriage, especially if there is any doubt about the ritual rank of the bride's or groom's side.

Besides food, marriage is the other most crucial achievement for retaining and enhancing one's traditional position. Under this scheme dowry is basically a traditional gift; it is a symbol of one's traditionally achieved position. Dowry, a part of the sacred cultural concept of *kanyādān* (that is, making a sacred offering of one's daughter in front of the gods), is the gravest "debt" into which a man runs the moment a daughter is born to him. Accordingly, to be unable to marry one's daughters for any reason constitutes the gravest lapse in one's traditional position, irrespective of what one's secular achievements are. It is an important yardstick applied to all the elite biographies published in the *Kanya-Kubja*. Under the tradition daughters should not only be married, but they should be married into economically and ritually higher families. If a man's son-in-law is better employed than he himself is, he has enhanced his traditional position "because he assures the welfare of his daughter—a religious and moral duty of every parent."

Other Forms of Traditional Behavior

More observance of religious fasts, festivals, and social ceremonies invariably leads to an improvement in one's traditional position. The basic principle is the same as in modern secular achievements. More investment of time and energy leads to enhancement of one's traditional position. On this basis, a priest, an astrologer, and an orthodox Kanya-Kubja are achievers of the same order as are a Kanya-Kubja lawyer, a judge, and a politician. Both categories of Kanya-Kubjas invest time and energy for achievement, one for sacred and the other for secular ends. A Kanya-Kubja fasting on the eleventh day of every fortnight (*ekādashī vrat*) is thus considered higher on the traditional positional scale than one who does not keep such fasts. Elaboration of daily worship or ceremonial rituals is traditionally prestigious, and a commendable act. One that worships and then goes to his office every day is more Brahmanic than one who does not worship at all, or irregularly.

However, some related aspects of worship may now be regarded as superfluous. For example, daily worship by a Brahman is something expected by the caste norm, but carrying sacred sandal-paste marks on the forehead may not be so any more, although it was so in the beginning of this century. The latter is borne out by an incident reported by a Kanya-Kubja in the journal (1957, p. 37), in which a Kanya-Kubja lawyer with a prominent sandal-paste mark on his forehead went to plead in the court of a Muslim judge and drew a remark from the judge, but he promptly pointed out to the latter to look on his own forehead which had the marks of *namāz* (the prayer in course of which a Muslim touches the ground with his forehead so many times that the skin there becomes marked). The other use of an external mark that has similarly atrophied is the sacred tuft (*chotī*) of the Brahman. A Kanya-Kubja lawyer quipped (*Kanya-Kubja* 1957, p. 30) that the young generation has not lost it but has replaced it by long hair at the forehead rather than on the top of the head.

But the sacred thread which normally remains underneath one's garments is not exposed to the same selective pressures. It is a much more prized indicator of Brahmanhood and is, according to my observations, still worn by the majority of urban Kanya-Kubjas. However, the attendant rituals, for example, of lifting it over the waist whenever in toilet may be dropped or modified (e.g., some solve this problem by coiling it around the neck). In traditional situations the sacred thread is of course crucial, and even the youth, with few exceptions, keep it on. After marriage and food rituals, the sacred thread is the most explicit indicator of a Kanya-Kubja's position on the achievable traditional order. Those who delay the sacred thread ceremony for their boys are actually reprimanded by the orthodox, including the caste journal.

One's traditional position is further strengthened by achieving skill or expertise in one or more sacred crafts. These coexist with secular achievements. Sanskritic and scriptural knowledge and learning, and awareness of some principles of astrology, priest-craft, and Ayurvedic prescriptions contribute positively towards one's traditional achievements. Scores of biographies of judges, lawyers, engineers, physicians, administrators, and politicians bear out this observation (*Kanya-Kubja* 1957–68). For example: a deputy director-general of the state health services wrote a genealogy in Sanskrit "after a decade of research" on his own gotra; a secretary of finance of a state government also published a genealogy and wrote scores of articles in Hindi and Sanskrit; a deputy commissioner "wrote over two dozen books in Hindi" under a pen name (*Kanya-Kubja* 1957, p. 61); a retired judicial secretary of Lucknow spent all his time in reading and interpreting the devotional literature. Ayurvedic prescriptions, astrology, and priestcraft are not learned as consciously as are the above skills, but their preliminary awareness stems from the "family circumstance." Astrology at the domestic level may thus mean one's ability "to read and interpret the traditional calendar and constellations of stars for daily use." Priestcraft may refer to one's knoweldge of some sacred prayers and special incantations for conducting certain family rituals. Ayurvedic medicine may mean one's awareness about the medicinal properties of certain herbs and shrubs "for maintaining a balance between 'heat and cold,' and 'air and water' contents of the body." It is also the expertise of preparing certain family prescriptions for such varied diseases as cold and eczyma. Obviously some of these skills are acquired as one grows in one's family. If however one has learned them under the tutelage of a traditional expert, he becomes an expert enhancing his traditional position further.

Dress and garments, as already discussed, are the most obvious indicators of tradition and modernity of a Kanya-Kubja, although like others this is also exposed to modern influences. The dichotomy is marked between home dress and office dress. Normally, the later demands the Western clothing style from youth, the urban, and the educated. However, these same people dress differently in their homes. But the exception may be provided by urban priests and old people who dress the same way at work and at home. Thus age, occupation, education, social situation, and location influence the dress of Kanya-Kubja men. Even under British influence, one Kanya-Kubja engineer was noted for not giving up his traditional head gear (turban) and canvas shoes (*Kanya-Kubja* 1957). Many urban orthodox even now do not wear leather shoes. They put on wooden slippers at home and canvas shoes when on the street. Some of them avoid mill cloth not so much in deference to Gandhian ideals as for its ritual impurity. Those who dress traditionally, use hand-woven cloth, and do their laundry at home (even if it has already been cleaned by a washerman) are higher on the traditional scheme than those who do not do so. But if a Kanya-Kubja does so while at home and wears washerman-washed Western clothes for his office work, he is commended because he has *not* replaced one mode by another but has successfully combined the two. His traditional position is higher than the one who does not so adapt but leaves the tradition behind for the sake of secular appearance.

In this discussion of the attributes of traditional position, it is important to note that economic achievement (*artha*) comes as an *integral* dimension. The traditional scheme broadly differentiates between what one inherited as a family fortune and what one acquired himself. However, both go to determine one's economic position, except that if one excels in achieving more than what his forefathers did, he is accorded greater prestige. But the conception of economic position is different under tradition. Riches enhance one's traditional position *only if* they are spent on traditionally favored or permitted ways. Outside of this, a rich man's influence receives little traditional approval. This conception is crucial for understanding the very basis of Indian "class" within the framework of caste obligations. If wealth is successively used for fulfilling familial and kinship obligations (which include rites of passage expenses incurred for one's near and distant relatives), caste welfare, charity, and philanthropy, one's traditional position is enhanced. The first obligation is the foremost. Next is the support of caste sabhas, which are modern symbols of "caste welfare"; to do so is to discharge a traditionally *sacred* duty. Accordingly, subscription to a sabha for regular or titled membership is an act of prestige-bearing charity rather than the mere fulfillment of a condition of voluntary association. This conception is also reflected in the almost uniform use of the term *dān* (charity or donation) rather than *shulk* (subscription) in Kanya-Kubja sabha records. The formal budget separates them properly, however.

If a rich man spends on dowry gifts, it is traditionally commendable (even if now legally punishable). If a poor man incurs debt to arrange for the demanded dowry items, he is putting himself to economic strain but is gaining traditional position. To him, the latter is costly but desirable. If one of his rich brothers helps him financially in this endeavor, his brother's traditional position (but not his) is enhanced. If one builds wells, hospitals, roads, schools, and libraries where they are wanted for the caste people and/or the general public, one's traditional position becomes eminently outstanding. Such extensive references are found in the biographies of individual elites, which underline the idea that accumulating wealth for personal comforts is meaningless. To sacrifice wealth for a traditionally valuable cause is socially most desirable. For example, a famous lawyer is proudly mentioned as "bankrupt" because he gave away all he earned during each day to the needy who met him as he went between his court and his drawing room. A rich raja is said to have summoned for his wealth to show it to his mother. But when the mother happily ordered her son to keep it safe, the raja distributed it to the poor to achieve the traditional value of selflessness or detachment. One of the biggest trusts of the Kanya-Kubjas was endowed by another raja *after* he had fulfilled his obligations to his only daughter and other relatives. (All of these examples are drawn from *Kanya-Kubja* 1957, which relates these with specific dates and personages.) Under this conception of the riches expenditure on distant kin, it may be noted, is not "personal" use of the money; it is obligatory and culturally expected. Spending to display and gain recognition for one's caste and kin members is customary and is prized even by the most modernized Kanya-Kubjas. Actually, in India there is still no stable meaning of wealth independent of this traditional epistemology.

The above observations are borne out by empirical data provided by fifty-one elites of Lucknow, classified by occupational prestige and average monthly income. The purpose of presenting this information is to demonstrate the actual dimensions of the expenditures made by the modern Kanya-Kubjas in some of the most crucial ceremonies for achieving traditional prestige. My informants, in order of their earning capacity (average monthly income) were: two politicians (Rs. 1,475); seven ex-Talukdars (Rs. 1,430); ten physicians and engineers (Rs. 1,185); ten government administrators (Rs. 1,020); and twenty-two teachers, priests, and clerks (Rs. 438). The estimation (in per cent) was made by the informants themselves and hence the quantification is indicative of only a *rough* distribution as recognized by the informants for four categories of ceremonial expenditures: tonsure, sacred thread, marriage, and other miscellaneous ceremonies. It was most evident that marriage consumed between 71 and 80 per cent of the total ceremonial expenditure, that the tonsure ceremony (3% to 6.5%) was generally less expensive than the sacred thread (6.5% to 9.5%), and that in most cases the miscellaneous category involved more expenditure than the tonsure and the sacred thread ceremonies combined. Lower-income Kanya-Kubjas were found to spend a little less on marriage and a little more on other smaller ceremonies, not because they wanted to do so but because within their income they wanted to fulfill as many ceremonial obligations as possible. Among the group at the fifth income level (teachers, priests, and clerks), nine out of twenty-two individuals ran into debt either to discharge traditional obligations or to subtly enhance status through costly gift-giving. This group admitted that if they had more money, they would like to spend it "to ensure the comfort and security of our daughters." Among the higher income groups, the tonsure and sacred thread ceremonies are also thought to provide occasions for "socialization" among the elites. Such occasions allow them to invite extra-caste, civic, and political personages

109

for a "party" or a "dinner." Hence, they tend to spend more on such ceremonies too. But some of them, on the other hand, might disregard the performance of smaller ceremonies in order to be able to give more on marriage occasions so that they could earn honor in their kin and caste groups. This was usually a matter of personal decision, depending upon the circumstances.

These caste elites have not yet actually initiated, as the sabhas also admit, any significant reform in practice. They continue to follow the exacting tradition in social ceremonies. Even for the urban, modern, and occupationally Western, the "age old styles of social honor and prestige provide the desirable goals." However, the reasons for such elite response may be found in the intrafamily socialization pattern of the elites, alluded to briefly later on.

Finally, one's traditional position also varies according to one's age (Khare 1966). "A modernist becomes traditionalist in his old age" was the observation of a retired chief justice. He elaborated:

> An old man's view towards life and its events changes. He
> may foresake numerous little physical pleasures of daily liv-
> ing. He may sleep on a wooden instead of a cushion bed. He
> may try to control his speech by practicing silence [mauna],
> his taste by giving up the delicacies at the feet of his diety,
> and his eyes and ears by using them for maximum scriptural
> learning. Most of all, he may retract his "self" from the ex-
> ternal world as a turtle does so under its shell.

If ways of one's youth persist in old age, it is disliked and not appreciated. Such people are considered immature and unsuitable for traditional wisdom. Concerning this aspect, an old priest informant observed:

> What is traditionally proper behavior for one stage of life
> cannot be appropriate for the succeeding one. With time, a
> man steeps deeper in worldy affairs, and accordingly he re-
> quires profound sacred knowledge to extricate himself from
> it. For example, the behavioral ways of my youth can not be
> satisfying to me now, especially in terms of my spiritual
> needs. I must become more and more attentive to my soul's
> welfare, now that I have achieved the best that I could in
> this world. Since I have discharged my major social obli-
> gations, I must concentrate on devoting my time and thought
> to nonmundane affairs.

PRAXEOLOGY OF A TRADITIONAL ELITE

A combination of one's ascribed and achieved status on the traditional order is best reflected in one's daily living. It is a normal version of the culturally normative. Orthodox as well as modern Kanya-Kubjas exhibit it in varying degrees. Here, however, I shall briefly present the living patterns of a traditional Kanya-Kubja priest, for he is the standard-bearer of the achieved traditional position even for other modern Kanya-Kubjas, and he approaches near to the traditional ideal—or so he thinks.

The case described below relates to a well-known and respected Kanya-Kubja priest (aged 60 years) of Lucknow whose *jajmāns* (clients) were mostly Kanya-Kubjas or other high caste groups, but included no one from the lower castes. He was especially proud to serve Kanya-Kubja government administrators, who respected him. Most of them would greet him by leaving their seat, folding their hands, and uttering "Pandit ji, praṇām." The priest expected this from them, for they had risen to high positions "before his own eyes." He recalled how their parents, when alive, asked him to undertake special worship so that their sons could rise quickly under the divine blessings. Now that the priest's prayers had been answered he did not hesitate to visit their families; and he shared the joy and the pride of the progress among his own caste members. He observed:

> They are like my own children. I call them bhaiyā. Whenever they are in distress, I am worried. I worship for hours sitting in a room in their bungalows, and the God answers my prayers. When they are relieved of a trouble, I also feel lighter. This is the kind of relationship that I shall have as long as I am alive, no matter what positions they hold in their offices. And I am sure these children will not betray me, though my own son may do so once. But this relationship endures because I do not have to go to them begging for any favor. I do not expect any special favor, unless they themselves offer to help. I do not want to sound selfish and spoil my image.

However, he admitted that on occasions he had to ask for their favors, especially when his son had finished his education and was looking for a good job.

The priest rose early every morning and took his bath while chanting sacred verses, prayers, and *prabhātīs* (devotional songs

111

suited for morning worship). He observed the rules of ritual purity in answering his natural call: he wound his sacred thread on head and ears, did not speak while in toilet, and always had sufficient water with him for washing himself. He also performed some "special" purificatory acts which he would not spell out, for if he did so he would then lose some of his magico-religious powers. Once outside the latrine, he washed his hands twenty-one times with three types of mud, kept at three different places near the water tap. First, he thrice washed his left palm (used for cleaning after defecation) without the help of the right one. Then he washed the right one the same way, and finally both fifteen times. He also washed his feet three times. He could now speak, if necessary. Next came the cleaning of his teeth, gargling, and the washing of his face, all involving scripturally prescribed procedures. On occasions he would deviate from these to hurry on to some more important business, but he would never use modern tooth brush and tooth paste to clean his teeth; instead, either margosa twigs, or salt and oil, or charcoal, or ashes were used, depending upon the availability of these items. Normally, once a week he made it a point to bring the margosa twigs from the market for his and his wife's use. (His sons and their families, however, had begun using machine-manufactured Western powders or pastes.) His bath again was ritually elaborate, although he very rarely used soap. Between his bath and toilet he did not touch any other person of the family or any household object. If he did so, he would pollute them. After the bath he still could not touch any of the objects associated with day-to-day living, because he would be polluted by them. Accordingly, he took care that his hand-washed clothes be available to him right at the place where he took his bath. If not, he wore his soaked clothes to get them himself.

Worship followed next. He usually took not less than three hours to complete his daily worship, although in an emergency he could satisfy himself in half an hour. By seven in the morning he was usually ready to call on his jajmān's houses. His business depended upon the religious calendar. Months of marriages, religious fasts, and special worship were extremely busy, and he would curtail his own worship accordingly.

When his sons, college-educated and government-employed, got ready for their offices, the priest had already made his calls, finished his breakfast (sweets preponderating), and was again in his worship chamber. This time he recited sacred texts before the images of his gods and goddesses. Although he had built his own house with his earnings, he could not afford to have a full room to himself. His sons, their wives, and children required space, and he yielded. He even allowed his sons to use a shelf of his worship chamber, although he was very strict in denying entrance to all except those coming to worship when he was worshiping there. Although he did not like the boxes, English books, and some old pictures of relatives that this room contained, he allowed them to stay because he knew that the new house was small for the expanding family and that he could not add to the building. Any expansion was now his sons' responsibility.

He was most conscious of the fact that modern man had to run his life according to the clock. At nine in the morning, the children (his grandchildren) were either getting ready for school or had already left. His wife and daughters-in-law were hurrying in the kitchen to prepare food for his sons who were completing their daily worship, with an eye on the watch. Since he knew that his sons could not afford to be late in going to work, his duty was to be ready in time to offer the first plate of food to the deities. As a rule of normative culture, he was expected to eat first, but often he could not because of his delayed breakfast. In practice, therefore, his sons ate before him, except when he opted to eat early for the reasons of his own work. Since his oldest son was a senior employee in a government office, he could afford to be late by half an hour, and this had eased the pressure, somewhat.

Once this part of the day was over, the home was relatively quiet. The priest enjoyed playing with his grandchildren, who were too young to go to school or who had returned in the afternoon. His afternoon was taken up in preparing horoscopes of the children born in his client's families, in replying to his relatives' letters and in attending to some of his domestic problems, which might include a visit to a physician, or a tailor, or a grocer. He might also call on those families where his remuneration remained due. Although he would never verbally remind the client about it, his visit was sufficient to do so. If the client for some reason was unable to pay, the priest knew he would not return empty-handed. He often would be presented with some eatables (*sīdhā*). However, if he received nothing, he was neither disappointed nor disheartened. He would bless the family members and come away smiling. The priest knew this impressed his clients and raised him in their eyes. Anger, he said, was detrimental to the priest-client relationship, and an insult to Brahmanic behavior.

The priest again returned home at dusk to conduct his evening worship. However, if he was busy and would be delayed, he would instruct his wife to attend to the deities at the proper hour. Yet he had to worship in the evening before he had his evening meal and was, of course, most scrupulous in observing the commensal rules. He went to bed at half past ten.

The priest also recalled several experiences in which he had to intervene to resolve differences between traditionalist and modernist Kanya-Kubjas. For example, in the marriage of a Kanya-Kubja deputy secretary's daughter (who was herself an M.A. in Sanskrit), the groom refused to put on traditional clothes under the mandapa (sacred canopy) for the actual marriage ceremony. When the groom's old relatives failed to persuade him, the priest was called in. He resolved the problem by evolving a "strategy" with the help of the bride. The main argument made was that if a university requires its graduates to wear a special dress (gown) for receiving a degree, it is only natural that the groom should obey the rules of tradition and dress himself in *jāmā* (long flowing robe) and turban if he wants to legitimately acquire the bride. After half an hour of argument, the groom agreed. The priest conceded, however, that in this case the role of the girl was very crucial for she helped him to formulate the argument beforehand.

The above discussion introduces us to the phenomenon of interjacence that I enunciated in the Introduction (chapter 1); it will be amplified in the following chapters.

6 Modern Occupational Prestige

THIS CHAPTER seeks to examine the counterpart of traditional status, roughly called "class" status. Tradition governs the social expression of class in Indian society. It still directs and awards meaning to it, as we noted earlier, and it is in this sense that the use of the term class is kept distinct here. Normally class is most directly indicated by one's economic status, and to this degree Weber's (1966) "class" fits the Indian situation. However, there are several indicators of economic status: possession of material goods, possession of social power or influence, and possession of social skills. We may note that all three could be acquired under the traditional scheme too, except that the means would be different. Instead of orthodox ritualism, economic competition and education predominate in modern Indian class. Among the Kanya-Kubja Brahmans the most significant indicator of class is their modern occupational status. It relates with intracaste prestige, civic honors, charity, and social sophistication in terms of modern standards and styles of behavior on the one hand, and traditional uprightness, orthodoxy, and kinship brotherhood on the other. The above factors, when considered together, constitute the cultural content of Indian class and pervade the sectors of competition and individual achievement—the *sine qua non* of economic class (see also chapter 8). Economic competition is neither the sole means nor the main purpose of Indian class; it is, however, a necessary implication.

First we shall examine the background and modern pattern of Kanya-Kubja occupations and then examine the behavioral styles of those who occupy such privileged positions to explain the actual behavioral styles of those who constitute the caste sabhas and, in turn, to understand the sociological nature of these bodies.

115

The modern occupations of the Kanya-Kubjas are best understood when viewed as a result of certain historical circumstances through which this caste group has passed. Some of these circumstances were general and favorable, while others were specific and limiting.

OCCUPATIONAL HISTORY

In the first half of the last century when the British plan of education was systematically implemented, one aim was "to make the Indian officers of the Government intellectually and morally fit to perform their duties with efficiency and probity" (B. B. Misra 1961, pp. 149 ff.; the following general remarks on occupational history are based on Misra's *The Indian Middle Classes,* especially chapters 6, 7, 10, and 11).

According to Misra, by the 1930s the wealthy people of Calcutta had Westernized so much as to speak tolerably good English, to ride in carriages built in England, and to indulge in what was called the "English luxuries," including champagne. This may be taken as a rough indicator of the culture contact and culture change that was then occurring in Calcutta. While it may require intensive historical research to ascertain the situation that prevailed in Uttar Pradesh in the same period, the few unpublished Kanya-Kubja descriptions indicate little Westernization, if any at all. However, after the 1850s the awareness of "sahib" influence had enlarged, although the adoption of Western dress and language still was quite rare among those outside of the military. (These are only a few rough indications that I could gather from the old records of these Brahmans; however, it does not exhaust the possibility that more detailed records may exist on this period.) By the 1880s, English education and local, lower administrative positions were successfully achieved by the urban Kanya-Kubjas, especially in Lucknow and Kanpur; and these families later provided the reference group for imitation, emulation, and identification. The modern "occupational culture" had begun to take shape by this time, and an increasing number of records documented this tendency (*Kanya-Kubja* 1905–11, 1957).

In the later part of the last century law became the preponderant Western profession among the Kanya-Kubja Brahmans. The appearance of physicians and engineers came relatively late.

This pattern seems to tally with general historical developments. For example, the legal profession was "the most significant" of the new professions in the 1830s. Emerging from the Western constitution of courts and several legislative enactments, this profession flourished first in the cities and in higher courts (B. B. Misra 1961, pp. 170–71) and only later reached the districts. The Kanya-Kubjas, living in cities in the 1880s had, accordingly, several lawyers and revenue officers among them. With the continuous expansion of educational facilities in Uttar Pradesh towns (in 1921 it ranked third in the number of colleges), if these Brahmans of the cities had increasingly taken the positions of lawyers, public servants, doctors, engineers, writers, and scholars, it was, as Misra notes, mainly due to educational, judicial, and administrative development rather than to technological or industrial progress. This was mainly because the initiative in the latter fields remained entirely in British hands until 1911; and even in 1951 there were 382 British companies out of a total of 619.

Between 1900 and 1950 according to Misra (1961), the legal profession enjoyed maximum prestige, especially during the 1930s and the 1940s, while the medical profession slowly but continuously became better rated. Engineering got a boost in 1930s and outdid medicine in the late 1940s. Today the latter two continue to compete among themselves, but are considered much more prestigious than law. This general pattern of occupational prestige is, of course, evident among the modern Kanya-Kubjas (see figure 6 below). Physicians and engineers are supposed to earn more; they do not have to face the danger of unemployment because they can start a shop of their own; and they can have greater organizational freedom. Those who can not compete are thought to go into a profession like teaching which remains a comparatively low-prestige occupation. More and more educated youth have entered the above prestigious occupations rather than law, except as B. B. Misra (1961) notes, in the generation educated in the 1930s.

In terms of the Brahman's participation in Western occupations in India, even in 1887, 904 positions were held by the Brahmans (especially of Bombay and Madras) out of 1,866; there were 545 posts taken up by the Kayasthas. Misra (1961, p. 323) observed, therefore that "the brown bureaucracy of the British in India remained largely Brahmanical and definitely dominated by the members of a few upper castes." This was mainly owing to, as Bottomore (1964) also recognizes, the availability of proper resources and motivations among the higher castes. These general observations also seem to apply to the northern Kanya-Kubjas, as they have continuously expended a great amount of their resources in the pursuit of Western occupations.

During the last half of the nineteenth century, acquisition of Western professions by the urban Kanya-Kubjas was facilitated further by the presence of occupational mobility, stable sources of income from landholdings, urban places of "original" concentration (susthān), and a tendency to go along with the "ruler." Once they achieved success in the British-honored pursuits, they regarded the priesthood as a low-prestige profession. The Kanya-Kubja thus saw the emergence of two classes in their caste group: one emphasizing tradition, ritual, and orthodoxy; and the other modernity, secularity, and pragmatism. The former, even if urban, remained less prosperous. These tendencies are reflected in the biographical accounts of the caste elites, especially after 1880. But even before that the Kanya-Kubjas had successfully entered law, the judiciary, and the revenue services; and they were the ones who sent their children abroad for higher Western education. For example, a son (born in 1871) of a Kanya-Kubja deputy collector of Lucknow became a lawyer (Bachelor of Laws) in 1895, and a foreign-qualified justice of Oudh Chief Court in 1925. He sent his brothers to England in 1911 to become barristers-at-law. There was much social opposition to this "daring step" (involving ritual impurity from a sea voyage to a distant land). As a consequence, for some time this family was labeled as *bilaitihā* (of, or pertaining to England), and the orthodox did not propose for marriages. However, the resistence had disappeared by the 1930s when scores of Kanya-Kubjas had been educated abroad.

Simultaneously, there were other socioeconomic forces which determined certain occupational characteristics of the elites of this caste group. For example, they lacked both inclination and capital, and remained confined to small business (cf. the Kanara Saraswat Brahmans who seem to be more business oriented; see their caste journal 1963–65). They could not become business elites, so more and more they had to enter into government services and specialized professions, leading to their spatial dispersal. Because of this their local strength and organization suffered, disallowing them to form a politically powerful grouping (cf. the Tyagis of Meerut or the Sarjuparins of Deoria as described by Brass 1965), and they had only individual politicians rather than group politization. Their group logistics prevented concerted political action and interest in the military. Although there could be found some outstanding military captains, they were not many (cf. Jadavas' "militarization" as reported by Rao 1964, pp. 1439–43) despite the fact that these Brahmans reported military rationale for one of their gotras, and joined the army during the past century (see Khare 1966). In the past, they said, they took military careers to save their *dharma* from outsiders; and as one of my informants said, "we would do the same now if the country is invaded or if our dharma and karma [religious ways] were threatened. But there is now hardly any distinct effort to acquire excellence in these areas."

The Kanya-Kubja elites, therefore, have remained mostly administrative and professional elites, and most often as members of the Indian middle class ever since the 1860s. But after the introduction of industrialization around 1910, the economic and social character of the Indian middle class became more complex, according to Misra (1961). Industrial towns like Calcutta, Bombay, Jamshedpur, and Kanpur juxtaposed working-class with elites and established the primacy of earnings and higher secular ranks. With stiff educational and economic competition, a lower middle class of salaried employees appeared among the Kanya-Kubja Brahmans, especially around Kanpur and Lucknow. With Independence this competition accounted for the "downfall" of several elite families which were established by the British system of land ownership. They could not survive the "open" competition, while several new elite families appeared from the less-privileged urban or rural Kanya-Kubja strata. During the late thirties, the latter educated their children at the expense of their personal comfort. After Independence, increasing availability of educational scholarships also helped them educate their children. Today, the Kanya-Kubja must educate their boys as well as girls, to provide a means of earning a livelihood to the former and attract desirable grooms for the latter. They will now educate their children at any expense.

OCCUPATIONAL PRESTIGE PATTERNS

As we have noted above, certain historical factors have helped to greatly enhance the instrumental value of modern occupations. Sole dependence on one's ancestral property is considered to be economically risky and inadequate. The property-owning Kanya-Kubja Brahmans, thus, always try to send their sons after prestigious government positions, since, unless wealth is combined with actual prestige in the society, economic status is considered inadequate.

We may note that occupational prestige systems now tend to be cross-culturally similar. Hodge, Siegel and Rossi (1966, pp. 322–34) observed:

> Despite rather extensive searches conducted by a variety of techniques, it appears that occupational prestige hierarchies are similar from country to country including the under-developed ones and from subgroup to subgroup within a country. This stability reflects the fundamental, *but gross similarities* among occupational systems of modern nations. [Italics supplied.]

Figure 5 depicts the relative prestige position of some well-known occupations and professions, primarily under the framework of public and private sectors of the modern Indian political system. It is a schematic representation of occupation types, underlining how they are placed by the Kanya-Kubja elites on an all-Indian basis. Obviously, the scheme is not comprehensive; it tries, however, to systematize the informants' conceptual scheme around private, public, and judiciary categories. We may note how judiciary is conceived as an "independent" category interpolating between the public and the private sectors. The hierarchy present in this diagram is indicative of the general levels of modern occupational prestige. Prestige of government jobs increases in direct proportion to the control that they offer over public resources. The greater the control acquired by an elite, the more instrumental value he would have for the individuals surrounding him, and the wider the social influence he would be supposed to wield. With the latter, an occupational elite becomes a social elite and his expanding field of social influence, then, demands that he be a cosmopolitan.

Table 9 and figure 6 provide more definite grounds: they present the frequency distribution and rank order of some fifteen occupations of 182 Kanya-Kubja elites (reported at length in *Kanya-Kubja* [1963–66]). There are thirty-one (about 17%) shopkeepers, almost all from Kanpur. Judges, lawyers, physicians, engineers, and government servants constitute over fifty-three per cent of the groups of which the occupational calling is known. There are twelve erstwhile Tālukdārs, and one military officer. The Tālukdārs constitute an important wealthy group, with their descendants in prestigious government positions. It is equally important to note that there are only seven (over 3%) traditional priests in the group. It would today be perfectly safe to observe that even the priests of this caste are no more likely to keep their sons in their own profession, primarily because of low and declining economic returns. However, it would be wrong to conclude that these Brahmans thereby are becoming apathetic to the Sanskritic tradition or traditional social norms. When combined with certain other indicators of prestige (e.g., the use of English, orthodoxy, and property), as we shall see, traditionalism may be regarded as a desired quality of the elites of the 1950s and 1960s.

Figure 6 shows the relative ranking order of the fifteen occupations of table 9. This ranking is not necessarily based on one's contribution to the sabha. The referents are wider. The ranking is based on the responses of the fifty-one caste elites of Lucknow in table 9. Figure 6 represents their consensus on ranking fifteen common occupations. Any serious differences of opinion between raters were found to be explainable in terms of the informants' specific experiences and biases. As it would be beyond the scope of this discussion to present multiple rank matrices for these fifty-one raters, we may note only some qualitative characters that were significant in rating the occupations. For example, the highest place accorded to politicians could be traced to two factors: the urban Brahman raters were acutely aware of the pervasive power the politicians today have in the daily affairs in government and private sectors: and they had before them, most of the time, certain cases of illustrious Kanya-Kubja politicians.

Several other important interdependent correlates of occupational prestige could also be delineated through the responses of these raters. For example, an occupation like the Indian Ad-

LEVELS	TYPES	PUBLIC (Governmental)	JUDICIARY	PRIVATE (Non-Governmental)
I	Political elites (recruitment by election)	Central: Ministers, parliamentary secretaries, members of legislative bodies; Provincial	Supreme court judge	"Big" industrialists
II	Administrative elites (recruitment by selection/seniority)	All-Indian services (central)—e.g., administrative, judiciary, specialist, essential services (railway, postal, etc.); Provincial (state) services—e.g., administrative, judiciary, specialist	Attorney-general; Private legal advisors	*Private business groups:* e.g., Managerial establishment, specialist, supervisory; All-Indian business; Regional business
III	Professional/Technocratic/specialist elites (recruitment by selection/seniority)	All-Indian jurisdiction: Directors, planners, advisors, specialists, departmental heads (auxiliary staff ranked as I, II, III, IV graders); Provincial jurisdiction	Private legal advisors	*Private business groups:* Interstate/regional; Intrastate; Local business. *Individual/private holding or business:* Ex-Tālukdārs, rājās, rais, zamindārs; or landlords or landholders; Physicians; Lawyers; Specialist shops—e.g., ranging from dentist to goldsmith; Business shops—e.g., from commodity sales shops to money lending; Traditional family services (jajmāni)

The bureaucratic ladder may be of the same kind as that of the public sector, depending upon elaboration and complexity of the business.

IV	Intellectual elites (recruitment by selection/seniority)	(This level is managed most frequently by government-supported but privately run organizations.)	
		(a) Modern—e.g., 1. University intellectuals as well as administrators (vice-chancellors); or professors with advisory roles in the government 2. Teachers and researchers	(b) Traditional intellectuals—e.g., pundits, priests, *āchāryas*, astrologers, orthoprax sanskritists, etc.

Fig. 5. General schematic representation of elite occupations relevant for the Kanya-Kubjas. This hierarchy is conceived by my informants; and it may or may not have a "salary basis," but the status stratification is multiple and dynamic. It does, however, reflect the general political cleavage of social power.

TABLE 9

Frequency Distribution of Occupations of Elites

Occupations	Number	Percent
Judges	9	5.0
Lawyers	24	13.2
Engineers	5	2.7
Physicians	21	11.6
Traditional·physicians	3	1.6
Government (central) servants	20	11.0
Government (state) servants	17	9.3
Military officers	1	.6
Managers (business)	8	4.4
Shopkeepers	31	17.0
University teachers	6	3.3
School teachers	6	3.3
Politicians	2	1.1
Ex-Tālukdārs	12	6.6
Priests	7	3.8
Government clerks	10	5.5
TOTAL	182	100.0

SOURCE: *Kanya-Kubja* 1963–66.

Prestige Levels

I	Politicians (2)		
II	Judges (9)	Government administrators (20)	
III	Physicians (21) Engineers (5) Army Capt. (1) Lawyers (24)	Ex- Tālukdārs (12) Business Executives (8)	
IV	Provincial government (officer's cadre) servants (17)		
V	University teachers (6) School teachers (6)	Shopkeepers (31)	Government clerks (10)
VI	Traditional physicians (3) (Vaidyās)	Priests (7)	

FIG. 6. Rank and frequency of fifteen prestigious occupations as found among 182 elites participating in sabha activities.

ministrative Service may be considered more prestigious than the judiciary because the former brings increasing power and prestige right from the start. One can qualify for it any time after one is twenty-one.

Judiciary positions generally come late; now they can be competed for only after a law graduate has had three years of legal practice at the bar. However, if these occupations are compared for prestige not at the time of entry but when seniority has been acquired, the prestige gap between the two tends to level off with most of the informants. Since my list of caste-elites contains mostly senior central officers and judges, figure 6 shows the two as having equal rank. Similarly, in general, physicians are considered to be of higher prestige than engineers, because the former signify more predictable economic potential. Success in engineering is generally slow because of constraining state or central government bureaucratic rules, unless one has a position in a private firm; these opportunities are few, however, but do carry greater social prestige.

The lawyers, on the other hand, are considered to be losing their earlier social prestige. Earning potential is low and uncertain; actually it is considered as a "risky" occupation. A beginning lawyer is no competitor for prestige against an engineer or a physician. Legal practice may be generally considered as an "insufficient" means of supporting one's family, unless it is reinforced with paternal or affinal property holdings, or business interests. My elite listing is remarkably full of successful lawyers: since only exceptional individuals are considered to really prosper on their legal practice alone, it hardly seems to be representative of the common situation. Lucknow had, and continues to have, illustrious Kanya-Kubja lawyers—a point the raters were greatly conscious of. A close scrutiny of all of the twenty-four cases in figure 6 reveals that these lawyers had either extra means of economic earning or at least initial professional support by some kin lawyers or judges. Those few (four) who became outstanding on their own took a period of not less than a decade. In a more representative sample, it is supposed that they would rank much lower.

Ex-Tālukdārs and business executives rank equal to or higher than those preceding them. The ex-Tālukdārs hold large properties but pursue occupations (e.g., banking, business, and mechanized farming) as supplementary or subsidiary means of income. The nature of their social influence is mostly or only informal—a point that induces the informants to assign them a comparatively lower position in the figure; although as the earlier description of sabha activities indicated, they continue to play a very significant organizational role. Some business executives from Calcutta, Kanpur, Bombay, and Hyderabad may be of comparatively equal rank, if not higher.

Provincial government servants, who wield definite bureaucratic authority and influence, are ranked higher than university teachers, whose influence in the government can be informal or semi-official at best. Government clerks are actually rated higher than school teachers and some private small businessmen on the same basis. Their deft bureaucratic maneuverings are looked upon as a highly effective, "official" zone of influence, raising their occupational prestige, although their economic status is definitely considered to be lower than most of the small businessmen.

Even between the two traditional occupations (priesthood and Ayurvedic medicine), the latter, which is more directly useful and which is therefore coupled with more earnings, is ranked higher by the raters. Low ranking for the priesthood among the Kanya-Kubja can defintely be (historically) traced to a widely prevalent unfavorable intracaste attitude towards this profession. This attitude associates the priesthood with alms, and hence is considered to be a degrading mode of earning one's livelihood; however, it does not go against Sanskritic learning, or orthodoxy, or traditionalism. The priesthood has for long been considered a "poor" and "unbecoming" way of earning one's living, according to a Sanskritist judge, "for it corrupts one's urge to earn a living through hard work and makes one dependent on alms." Nevertheless, one finds, as I exemplified in the last chapter, several well-known priests who have gained eminence by combining astrology with spiritualism, and Sanskritic learning with austerity and orthodoxy.

In brief, in modern India an occupation is most commonly judged on the basis of (1) the kind of work it involves, (2) the amount of money it fetches, and (3) the kind of social prestige it enjoys. Thus an occupation which entails prolonged and costly preparation through formal schooling and brings both good money and social prestige is a coveted aim. Of the three indicators, the second one is most crucially important, although the other two may occasionally be looked upon as appropriate awards in themselves. Figure 6, above, orders various professions, generally speaking, along these factors. For example, a politician is highest because he ranks very well on the last two criteria, and he is also supposed to be sufficiently educated and knowledgeable. His main prestige is based on the diversity of "instrumental power" that he wields for public good under the democratic system. A judge and a high administrative officer, on the other hand, rank low on public influence but high on executive and organizational powers, and they simultaneously are considered well-paid as well as appropriately educated. A teacher, in contrast, may be very high on the first criterion, but correspondingly low on the other two; his high social prestige may be considered as a kind of nonmaterial payment to balance this deficit. The same is true of a priest, because he ranks higher on the first and third criteria, but low on the middle one. In comparison, a professional physician, an engineer, and a lawyer fare better because their callings reward them in terms of money as well as social prestige. The differential prestige gradient of various modern occupations most predominently depends upon what may be crudely called "the supply and demand" situation of a particular society. Those professions or occupations which are higher in demand and lower in supply become more prestigious and better remunerated callings. The above rank order of Kanya-Kubja occupations is therefore indicative of wider social and economic circumstances in which India finds herself today as a developing nation.

Since the Kanya-Kubjas are getting increasingly more dependent upon modern occupations for their living as well as for social prestige, the sensitivity to occupational rank is very clearly pronounced. As I have indicated earlier, the modern Kanya-Kubja considers a comfortable occupation as a prime necessity for his life; his traditional ties adjust to this concern, and can no more overlook it. This aspect will be empirically evidenced again and again in the discussion that follows. As a matter of hard reality, a "commoner" Kanya-Kubja recognizes that one's education, occupation, and economic status determines one's actual social existence, including the degree and nature of sabha participation. These executive bodies are run by those who are distinguished in the above ways, and the caste journal gives prominence to their welfare (e.g., see chapter 4 for a listing of those who received photographic display in the journal). Higher occupational and economic status is the basis of elitism. Accordingly, the following chapter will focus on the numerous prestigious attributes which characterize a Kanya-Kubja elite and which mainly depend upon one's occupational achievements.

7 Modern Class Standards and Styles

THIS CHAPTER has a two-fold purpose: first, it will complete the discussion of achieved-prestige systems initiated in chapter 5; and second, it will focus on the actual details of the standards and styles of those modern elites who are active participants in the Kanya-Kubja sabhas. The latter discussion will allow us to understand how office and home, formal and informal, and "class" and caste behavioral categories are handled by these elites. These details will later help to explain the actual organizational nature of a caste sabha.

The term "elite," as explained in the Introduction, refers mainly to high achievers of this caste group; it was seen that they are the minority which, in caste groups as well as in society at large, perform the function of guiding or influencing the community (cf. Aron 1950, p. 9). Most often they are the holders of prestigious occupations and have numerous achieved prestigious differences (cf. Aron 1950, p. 7). Many of these are high-ranking government administrators, an "unquestionably important" elite type for India (Bottomore 1967, p. 245). However, if one is a modern caste elite, it is so because he, as an achiever, belongs to a particular caste, and brings added modern prestige and services to the group.

Map 3 shows the distribution pattern of the 182 sabha participating caste elites in the various parts of India, described in *Kanya-Kubja* over the last forty years and covered in my field work in Lucknow, which constitute the basis of the following discussion.

PRESTIGE INDICATORS OF A MODERN ELITE

Evidently, these indicators overlap significantly with those described for the traditional order. However, besides occupation

129

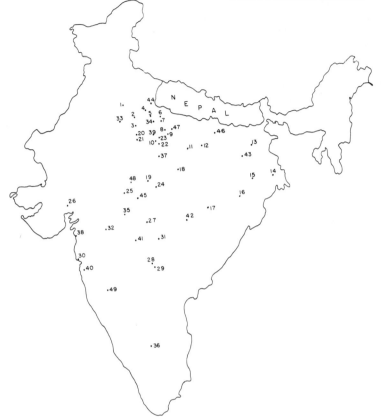

MAP. 3. Geographic distribution of 182 caste elites participating in the Kanya-Kubja sabhas (*Kanya-Kubja* 1963–66).

Map Reference No.	City	Total No. of Elites	Map Reference No.	City	Total No. of Elites
1.	Delhi	3	12.	Banaras	2
2.	Aligarh	2	13.	Bhagalpur	1
3.	Agra	3	14.	Calcutta	3
4.	Bareilly	1	15.	Jamshedpur	1
5.	Shahjehanpur	1	16.	Sambalpur	2
6.	Lakhimpur-Kheri	1	17.	Raipur	3
7.	Sitapur	2	18.	Rewa	2
8.	Lucknow	28	19.	Sagar	2
9.	Rae Bareilly	4	20.	Gwalior	2
10.	Kanpur	55	21.	Lashkar	6
11.	Allahabad	2	22.	Fatehpur	1

Map Reference No.	City	Total No. of Elites	Map Reference No.	City	Total No. of Elites
23.	Unnao	7	37.	Hamirpur	1
24.	Jabalpur	1	38.	Bulsar	1
25.	Indore	5	39.	Kannauj	3
26.	Ahmedabad	2	40.	Poona	1
27.	Nagpur	4	41.	Nander	1
28.	Secundrabad	1	42.	Rajnandgaon	1
29.	Hyderabad	2	43.	Nataur	1
30.	Bombay	2	44.	Pilibhit	2
31.	Chanda	1	45.	Hoshangabad	1
32.	Dhulia	1	46.	Basti	1
33.	Alwar	1	47.	Barabanki	2
34.	Hardoi	4	48.	Shajapur	1
35.	Khandva	6	49.	Sangli	1
36.	Bangalore	1			

and education, there are numerous secular indications of one's prestige. Most importantly, they are based on the possession of certain material objects and nonmaterial attitudes. The former refers to one's standard of life and emphasizes prestigious economic acquisitions, while the latter refers to one's styles of life which are in accordance with cultural values and individual preferences (cf. Aron 1950, p. 6). Thus a central Indian government peon may earn as much or more than a state government clerk, but their styles of life—actual conception and budgeting in terms of relevant items—may be widely different, depending upon the caste groups to which they belong to, and on the particular social circumstance in which they find themselves. An outstanding priest, as we have seen earlier, lives with a different emphasis than does an income-tax commissioner, or a government finance secretary, even if they belong to same caste group. We shall elaborate on these nonmaterial aspects later. Here, let us first briefly outline some tangible, material indicators of social prestige.

One's standard of living is reflected by the type of house he lives in—its construction, elaboration, furnishings, maintenance, and locality (i.e., whether plush or working-class neighborhood, suburb or "nerve center" of the city). A house is more prestigious if it is located in a large metropolitan area like Bombay, Calcutta, New Delhi, or Madras. In the Indian situation, if one owns a house in the "civil lines" (i.e., the place where most of the administrators live), he is more prestigious than the one who lives in a recently grown suburban colony (cf. Mehta 1968, pp. 496–508). On the other hand, an elite may also live in a colony established predominantly by his own caste members, thus producing overtones of caste-specific parochialism and "ruralism" within an urban setup (cf. Lynch 1967, pp. 143–58).

Equally important to one's standard of living in India, as in Western countries, is the type of transportation one owns. Owning a car is superior to a motor bicycle or a scooter, the latter over a horse-carriage (although its status has changed with automation), a carriage over a bicycle, and a bicycle over not having anything. However, a recent "middle class" symbol of prestige also includes one's economic capability to hire the man-drawn rickshaw for one's transportation. Underlining all these status symbols is also the principle that owning a means of private transportation is always more prestigious than using the public transportation.

Comparable to the Western scheme, Indian class prestige is also measured by the size, quality, and variety of material possessions, granting that the attitudes and values associated with them may greatly differ. Thus, possessions such as the following may be crucial material indicators: landholdings, gardens and houses; costly domestic furnishings, wardrobes, utensils, and servants; and jewelry and gold ornaments, bank balances, and business investments. By the same principle, those who daily eat more varieties of food have higher class prestige than those who can not afford to do so. However, all such material holdings are also the important items of social display, especially during important visits, festivals, and ceremonies.

More significant for us here is the way these possessions are thought of or looked at by the caste elites themselves. While all these are symbols of his success, and he prizes them, he looks at them sometimes with infatuation and at other times with renunciation. Which of the two feelings would preponderate depends much upon one's family training and the particular social circumstance, and upon age and religious dispositions. For the pleasure of their social prestige and economic status, an elite is proud to have them, especially when most others do not have access to such objects. His pleasure is doubled if he has acquired them through his independent sweat and labor; however, if he has inherited them, "he is lucky." However, for both he is thankful to his God. And this thought pulls him towards the traditional modes of showing his gratitude. He may do so by any means, ranging from extra hours of morning worship to charity to the poor, to donating to the caste sabha to vowing to remain humble, just, kind, and religious in one's daily behavior. All this has deeper significance in the religious scheme, for it gives meaning to an elite's "elitism," as it were. Thus under the widely believed *karma* (action) theory, this elite must look upon himself as a fortunate human being, for past good actions are responsible for whatever he now is. But, simultaneously, he must be aware that it is not known when this "reservoir" will become empty, and hence he must keep replenishing it through his "good" deeds, and leave the rest in the hands of God; because, as he knows, the fruits of one's karma are tricky and beyond human control. Accordingly, a Brahman elite turns to his deity on the one hand, and to his moral and social obligations, on the other, for a safe future. The former is regarded as the dispenser of personal or spiritual welfare, and the latter as a means of filling up the emptying "reservoir" of one's good karma.

This scheme applies to an elite's day-to-day behavior in his house as well as office. It may be, however, subliminal most of the time, although, when an elite takes an overview or recollects his past, he highlights these aspects, according to my field experience.

In terms of our discussion of the sabhas as an elite-managed complex of formality-informality, office-home, and modernity-tradition dimensions, we must take a closer look at the elites themselves and understand their behavioral patterns, especially outside their offices. This we shall do in two steps: first by describing a "typical" elite's biographic background, and then by a closer look at his praxeology at home. Although what is a "typical" elite is very difficult to point out, I shall rely on my informant's judgments and my own overview which I acquired through years of working with these Brahmans in "creating" a "typical version." Accordingly, the description of praxeology, unlike the one offered for a traditional elite in the last chapter, may not entirely depend on one particular case.

The generation of Kanya-Kubja elites with which I am concerned is that which was educated in the first two decades of this century, which served in high positions mostly during British rule, and which also took up the administrative task in the early years of independent India. Their forefathers were village dwellers, but their fathers were already educated urbanites. Most belonged to Khatkul gotras, to reputed agnatic ancestral groups (ānks), and to the higher Biswā ranks. Many, as far as is known, were active sabha workers at one stage or another. However, they also participated in numerous civic welfare organizations, enjoyed high economic status and possessed most of the secular prestige indicators enumerated earlier. Beyond these general features, we may do well to describe the biographic account of a particular Kanya-Kubja elite, as recorded in my field notes and as described by the *Kanya-Kubja* (1967). The elite may not be a typical achiever in some areas, while he may be so in most of the others. But, whether typical or not, his life depicts a culturally desirable, emulative, and practically attainable example for the modern Kanya-Kubja Brahmans, and hence is significant.

BIOGRAPHIC OUTLINE OF A MODERN ELITE

This description is of a Kanya-Kubja elite whose forefathers were from a village near Rae Bareilly, and who belonged to a well-known agnatic ancestral group (ānk) of a Khatkul gotra of the highest Biswā. An outstanding student, he was well-educated —in the terms of the early decades of this century—in a government college (B.A., LL.B.). The major part of his career was spent under British rule, and he was successively promoted from a teacher of mathematics to a deputy collector, to an I.C.S. (Indian Civil Service) deputy secretary of finance, to finance secretary of the state and, finally, central government. For his outstanding services he received the British-awarded title of O.B.E. (Order of the British Empire). In the all-Indian caste sabha he was a Kanya-Kubja-Kul-Kamal-Diwākar (see chapter 4), and an executive officer of several caste-run educational institutions. He also served such welfare organizations as the Red Cross and Tuberculosis Association. A good player of lawn tennis, "he lived like a British I.C.S. officer with aristocracy and affluence, but his inner courtyard was befitting an orthodox Kanya-Kubja. This was most evident in such ceremonies as the sacred thread and marriage" (*Kanya-Kubja* 1967, p. 34).

He owned a large three-storied bungalow near the state secretariat in Lucknow—a locality of the elites. This house was part of a spacious compound, including a back lawn, a garden plot, several flower beds, garages, and several servant's quarters. The front lawn had a tennis-court on one side and more flower beds on the other with a spacious well-kept lawn. The entire complex was maintained by two gardners. He had two cars and a chauffeur.

His drawing, or living, room was indicative of his achievements as well as preferences. Most prominent were life-size, garlanded pictures of his parents and illustrious ancestors above the mantelpiece. The fire-place was for decoration, only. On the mantelpiece were several British-awarded *sanads* (honorific citations), several group photographs covering his administrative career, and an old German clock, presented by a British colleague in 1933. Several souvenirs of ivory and silver dotted the small tables placed between three sofa sets, arranged in an open rectangle. A telephone was on another side table; and a radio was kept on a movable trolley, in addition to a silver box full of betel leaves, areca nuts, and tobacco. The room was also conspicuous for its exquisite carved-wood wall paneling and heavy, polished furniture with embroidered upholstery; and further elegance was added by long velvet drapes. The central carpet, though now old, was brought from Kashmir. The walls also had several glass paneled shelves of his books in English, Hindi, Sanskrit, French, German, and Persian. Although the elite had never hunted, his walls were decorated with four stuffed reindeer heads, and one, prominently displayed, head of a tiger.

He paid close attention to the maintenance of this drawing room. Everything was polished, cleaned, and properly arranged. The children of the family were not allowed to enter it without an older person at their side. In his retirement period he did not add much to it, although he kept the old things suitably replaced, the room painted yearly, and the big oil paintings of his parents frequently cleaned.

In the portrait his father, an administrator and a B.A. of late nineteenth century, is shown dressed in a closed-collar pārsi coat, with a dhotī and canvas shoes; he has a prominent full moustache, but no beard. The elite in another picture on the mantel is wearing Western dress, with thin-rimmed spectacles, very light moustaches, and a high collar shirt; he holds a gentleman's rod in his hands, and wears polished leather shoes. On the other hand, no such contrast is evidenced by the pictures of his mother and wife—in both, the traditional sārī is the dress.

The elite's style was Western when away from home, but traditional when at his residence. However, both were of costly and fine fabrics and not of *khādi* (hand-woven Gandhi-professed cloth). In his house he dressed informally in dhotī, shirt, and wooden sandals (*kharāun*). He supervised the servant's works in the same dress, although he would not step out of his compound without "dressing properly."

The elite was a staunch reformist while still being orthodox. While for the celebration of all the major ceremonies of his family (sacred thread, marriage, tonsure, etc.) he went to his village, named after his ancestors, in the Rae Bareilly district, he was very strict in not presenting or receiving dowry or any other kinds of exorbitant gifts. He, according to the *Kanya-Kubja* (1967), had a rule that a marriage be performed with gifts of not more than Rs. 11 for each ceremony. His authority commanded the respect of his relatives, and those who did not agree with his views were not invited to the ceremonies.

He was extremely punctual and regular in his daily worship, which was elaborate and prolonged in the early hours of every morning. He was equally fastidious in observing commensal rules. Whenever his official duties called for attending a British-style party or dinner, he refrained from eating anything there except fruits. He attended to his meals in the same way as the priest, described earlier: wearing dhotī, he ate the *kachchā* (boiled, not mixed with clarified butter) food in the kitchen-yard; and he would not enter the kitchen without washing his hands and feet and would not eat without offering the food to his deity. He scrupulously observed the rules during marriages, and most of his relatives took special care to prepare ritually pure food of his liking.

He built a hospital costing Rs. 100,000 in commemoration of his father and wife and later handed it over to the government for better management. He also financed the building of a guest house in the memory of his mother, which is now used for lodging marriage parties or other social functions in his ancestral village. In addition, he induced the state government to launch the construction of all-season roads around his village.

In 1964 the elite published a revised edition of the genealogy of his clan and agnatic ancestral group, extensively illustrated with photographs of his ancestors and close relatives, and folded genealogical charts. (For a summary of the achievements of several other caste elites, see appendix D.)

Table 10 shows this elite's high rating on both the traditional and modern axes.

TABLE 10

The Modern Rank Score of a Caste Elite

Class Hierarchy	Ritual Rank	Orthodoxy	Traditional Expenses	Jāti Honors	Jāti Influence
Education	(+++) +++				
Occupation		(++) +++			
Economic status			(++) +++		
Civic honors				(+++) +++	
Political influence					(+++) +

KEY: (+) = rank for traditional order; + = rank for class variables: +++ = excellent (highest); ++ = good (higher); + = average (low).

The Elite Residence: Formal and Informal Arenas

The following styles of formal and informal behavior in one's home are derived from field observations that included both elites and other urban Kanya-Kubjas. These styles are becoming standardized in the modern world of office and officers, where domestic life is increasingly differentiated from the office (cf. Fallers 1966, p. 143, who describes the same factor for an African scene), and where, especially in India, an officer's residence can be visited for official or semi-official purposes with such different motives as flattery, courtesy, personal influence, or pressure. It is proper and expected as a continuation of the British officer's idiom (e.g., see Spear 1963).

Accordingly, an elite's or administrator's house provides that arena where the informal and the unofficial come to an interface with the official and the formal. The residence can be classified into successively formal-informal levels, starting from the drawing (living) room or front lawn and ending in the kitchen. Various structures lying in between these two may show differing degrees of informal interactions. Every elite may have a somewhat different way of receiving a stranger, an official superior, an acquaintance, and an office subordinate on the one hand, and a friend, a rich and old relative, a poor but old relative, a close kin, and an affine, on the other. For the former group of visitors the general styles may be standardized across caste lines, because they originate from the modern educational and organizational ethos and not from the traditional caste-specific praxeology.

A visiting stranger may be relegated to the outer porch, verandah, or drawing room, depending upon his status. A stranger of superior or equal rank is usually received in the drawing room to make the reception more cordial as well as appropriate, although other ways of showing cordiality could vary from offering a chair to presenting the betel plate, to the offering of tea and refreshments. A visitor of inferior rank may be treated more informally. If he is an office subordinate and visits frequently, he may be accorded entry beyond the elite's drawing room, sometimes as a helper in serving the guests, and sometimes even as a performer of small domestic chores. This familiarity may affect the elite's bureaucratic insensitivity. The officially superior, on the other hand, is less likely to visit, except on special occasions like a marriage or the birth of a son, or a birthday anniversary. On these occasions one commonly observes cordiality, respect, overwhelming hospitality on the part of the host and a corresponding informality tempered with cautious familiarity, distance, and reserve on the part of the superior. Respect for one's official superior may be shown around the house without any compromise of the traditional rules of commensality. Thus, however superior the officer may be, he will not normally be led into the kitchen or the worship chamber. If he is a Kanya-Kubja of equal or superior rank, the response will be different, the visiting officer will himself observe the traditionally appropriate behavior. The same is true for the officially subordinate but ritually superior Kanya-Kubja, who may show all regard for his officer but may not compromise in kitchen and kinship matters.

Accordingly, a Kanya-Kubja house, whether of a high or low officer, may present three distinct, but not necessarily exclusive, levels of praxeology signified by the drawing or living room, the inner courtyard, and the kitchen. As one moves from the drawing room towards the kitchen, the notions of formality are successively replaced by informality, and caste and kinship considerations. Since these domestic behavioral syles are directly related to organizational formality, informality, and modernity on the one hand, and caste, kinship, and traditionalism on the other, we shall describe the typical praxeology of all three places in the order presented above.

The drawing or living room of a modern Kanya-Kubja signifies a type of interpersonal relations and cultural ethos. In terms of physical structure, this part of the house is usually a reception room best kept for receiving guests. These, as we have already seen, include many kind of people—from close relatives to the most distant and unknown strangers. We have also seen that "class" considerations further classify these people for determining the exact kind of reception that should be accorded to them. The place, the people, and the content of interpersonal relations, all combined, produce what we may call a "drawing room ethos," differentiated from that of the inner courtyard and the kitchen. These three types of ethos interrelate and overlap according to the social occasion. In summer, the drawing room ethos may move out to the front lawn. During a marriage, the other two types may overwhelm the drawing room ethos. The inner courtyard ethos is an extension of the caste-and-kinship restricted kitchen ethos.

Of all the three, the drawing room ethos of a caste elite's house is most complex but most revealing for understanding sabha formality and its place in a caste elite's world. I have already described in detail one drawing room of a Kanya-Kubja elite, which signifies the culturally common view that a drawing room is at once the "show piece" of one's achievements, traditional as well as modern. It is also an index of one's formal vis-à-vis informal behavioral styles. They may be somewhat different with every modern Kanja-Kubja, but relate roughly to occupational positions. In order to indicate this variation, I shall briefly describe, based on my field work in Lucknow, the drawing room ethos of a young administrator, a professional physician, and a priest— all Kanya-Kubjas.

The modern administrator's drawing room, although less gorgeous and smaller than that of the elite whose biographic account

I gave earlier, was full of activity before and after his office hours. The drawing room, "decorated in simplicity and modern elegance," conspicuously lacked the bold display of his parents' photographs, or the lines of coveted awards and degrees on a big mantelpiece. Actually these features were absent and the furniture in the room was clean, polished and well kept but of "new American style," as my informant put it. The room had an oil painting and a small group photograph of his immediate family on one of the corner tables. The radio, air-conditioner, and the telephone were prominently displayed, and the room wore a less-crowded look.

The administrator was busy in the mornings mostly with completing his file work with the help of a peon, a personal assistant, and a clerk. Intermittently, visitors would come, and would be asked to wait in an antechamber for their turn, but only if they had a previous appointment. If they had not secured one, the officer's staff would politely refuse an interview and would suggest another time. A visitor might, therefore, find the presence of a "miniature bureaucracy" working in the officer's drawing room. He would be required to transmit his message through the peon to the personal assistant, who, in turn, would know how to deal with the visitor, depending most clearly upon his purpose and social position. Normally, a common visitor might be required to state the purpose of his visit and to give some references, especially if he wanted quicker admittance. The latter might informally be suggested even by a sympathetic peon at the officer's residence. For such a common visitor, an officer's bureaucratic insensitivity could be as impregnable as in his office, even though the officer might be dressed in traditional attire and more informal in expression, and they might share a remark or two about each other's family welfare.

However, the response was signficantly different if the visitor happened to be a stranger but occupied an important position himself, although it was rare that such visitors would come without prior information or without an urgent task. The "link" between him and his official equals and superiors was most frequently by the telephone. Personal visits occurred only rarely and only when extremely essential. But if they did occur, this visitor's place was not in the antechamber but the officer's drawing room. The personal staff of the officer was most often ac-

quainted with such distinguished visitors and knew how to deal
with them. They would be saluted by the officer's staff and the
door curtains would be raised to facilitate their entry into the
officer's drawing room. The officer would receive them cordially
and informally in the drawing room, making their semi-official
calls into social visits. Good friends of the officer were received
in the same manner, although there was an effort to keep such
visits to the minimum, especially in the busy morning hours.

The officer had two types of working schedules for this busy
part of the day. He would either set apart some time for meeting
with his visitors or, if only a few were expected, meet them as
they came, keeping himself busy in attending to "most urgent,"
"important," and "overdue" office files. The clerk would open
these files and affix numerous tabs to indicate where the officer
has to sign or give his comments. The elite then dictated his "no-
tations" to the clerk who sat on a chair in front of him.

This officer believed in "informality" and hence, unlike his
other colleagues, did not feel the necessity of having a separate
room as his "home office." He thought the drawing-room atmosphere was more conducive to efficiency. Occasionally, the
officer ate betels from a box, which was placed early each morning on the center table of the drawing room. Sometimes his as-
sistants were requested to go to the inner courtyard (through a
hallway) and fetch something for the officer from the lady of the
house.

The officer felt that the "second office" at his home was a
necessity because of the quantity of paperwork he did every day:
"It is humanly impossible to read (let alone study) them, decide,
and then formulate a most 'noncommittal' (yet in line with the
directives of his superior) reply or notation for the files." He
observed:

> Some of these decisions may mean millions of Rupees to the
> government, and a wrong step on my behalf may conflict
> with a policy decided upon by the higher-ups. Ambiguity
> and indecision help me (that is, an officer of my bureaucratic
> rank) because if something goes wrong in a project or a
> plan, nobody can squarely blame me. It will be a team de-
> cision; most important steps being taken by the topmost ex-
> ecutive, or by us at his behest. We neither speed nor delay
> decisions, we just feel our way—the safest course—through

the maze of directives and counterdirectives coming from the top. Morning hours at home give us some extra time so essential for being cautiously judicious in our roles.

The officer, as his office time approached, had to speed up his disposal of files. Once the officer had left for the office, his drawing room again took on its role as a domestic apartment. Its cleanliness and arrangement was attended to, and normally it would be kept locked. But if an important relative visited, from out of town on a family visit, the drawing room could again be opened for his stay. It was especially appropriate to do so if the visitors came in connection with the settlement of a marriage of the officer's younger sister or his own daughter. Occasionally, the officer's wife would also use it for a meeting of a women's socal service group in which she actively participated. The latter activity would mostly be in the afternoon so that it did not conflict with her husband's morning activities.

In the evening the officer's drawing room wore a more informal look than in the morning (although during special periods of the legislature—for example, the "budget session"—the evening could also be equally formal and busy). Some visitors, however, could still come with official business in mind. At this time, his official subordinates were absent and the officer was dressed informally in *paijāmā* and kurtā, or in any other appropriate dress depending upon the occasion and season. His friends from the neighborhood, his colleagues, and his relatives visited him at this time. The betel box was more frequently used, and several servings of tea or other refreshments could be required. If a visiting relative appeared at this time, he could be invited to sit in the drawing room along with other visitors for a while. Later the officer would ask his son or some other family member to escort him to the inner courtyard where his kinship (if he was an uncle or a cousin of the officer) becomes evident. He might be invited to stay for dinner with the officer later in the evening. Being of the same ritual rank, they would eat in the same kitchen, the relative wearing a dhotī (the necessary orthodox costume for eating kachchā in the kitchen) borrowed from his officer cousin. However, affinal relatives were treated much more courteously but with a kind of formalized distance. It may be noted here that a Kanya-Kubja family priest is accorded a similar reception and entrée in the family. Almost always he came into the inner courtyard, but eating in his client's kitchen would depend strictly upon their mutual ritual ranks, and a host of other culinary considerations.

The officer's drawing room was also the venue of sabha matters. Helping to conduct its business was an "informal" and voluntary effort on the officer's part. In his conception sabha business was not evidently of the same formal order or priority as his official files, although being a sabha officer himself, he would *not* think of it as an entirely "personal" or "familial" matter. To him "it was again a matter which must be dealt with appropriately in its own place and should not be confused or mixed up with other actually official duties." (This remark of the officer is a useful indicator of his conception of the sabha organization—an aspect we shall discuss in the following chapter.) Although his drawing room was a formal place of sabha business, it sometimes could extend into the inner courtyard if the other executive officers were close friends or even relatives of the officer. On appropriate occasions, they might be also invited to a dinner or other ceremonial participation. As the officer summed it up: "The sabha is not a formal organization of the same order as my office is. The sabha participants are not official superordinates and subordinates; they are something more and nearer to us in terms of our caste and kinship. We are unpaid, honorary and voluntary workers, sharing some common welfare aims for our caste members. We are primarily motivated by a special feeling of sharing a mission and not by an official set of rights and duties."

Finally, his drawing room could also be used as a place for a sacred performance like a *kathā*, a *keertan*, or a *havana*. But this would be rare and would be so planned that the regular daily work would not be disturbed.

The inner courtyard and the kitchen were successively more limited arenas of social interaction. Not all those who were welcome in the drawing room could enter the officer's inner courtyard, although all those who could eat with him in the kitchen could easily participate in the other two zones. Between the inner courtyard and the kitchen, the latter was most restrictive. A Kanya-Kubja Brahman who visited the inner courtyard could not eat in the kitchen unless he was kinship-related to the members of the officer's family. A good friend of another caste could also be welcomed in the inner courtyard but normally he would not be eating kachchā food in the kitchen. However, he could be served his meal outside the kitchen. In comparison, a sabha executive member, if of the proper ritual rank, would not only be invited to the inner courtyard but also into the kitchen. This was a definite act of "brotherhood" (a feeling upon which the sabha based itself), even if there did not exist any kinship bond between the two. The informality of the officer's kitchen and inner courtyard was a kind of "honor" for the sabha visitor, and one would remember it with gratitude.

If we compare the above description of the three types of zonal ethos of the officer's residence with those found at the homes of, for example, a physician and a priest, the differences may be varied. The similarities in furnishings and styling would be more conspicuous between the drawing rooms of a physician and an officer (because both earn more) than that of a priest. But on the other hand the physician and the priest, strictly speaking, do not have "drawing rooms" in the same sense as an officer has. With the former it is a place only for receiving guests on social visits, with the latter it is also a place for conducting or completing some of his official duties.

If we look closely, the priest's "drawing room" is markedly different in purpose as well as furnishing styles. It is more appropriately a "man's place" in the residence, where he receives, entertains, and accommodates his male guests, and where most of the time, he himself sits and rests, except when he retires inside the house at night. (It is a setup very near to the *baithakā*s that I described for the village Gopalpur; see Khare 1962). However, it is not to say that a physician's or an officer's drawing room can not occasionally become a baithakā for rest and more informal purposes; the modern educated elites try to keep up the distinction, nonetheless. A priest's drawing room may, as expected, display greater sacred lore (through images or idols or wall pictures of gods and goddesses and sacred inscriptions), greater awareness of kinship descent (again through pictures of one's ancestors), and an absence of modern electronic appliances (e.g., a telephone or an air-conditioner). In terms of organizational formality, the officer and the priest represent two extremes, with the physician in between. In terms of traditional orthodoxy in the kitchen, the officer and the physician can be considered together, while the priest represents traditional elaboration as well as rigidity. In terms of social interrelations, the priest's kitchen and the inner courtyard stand nearer to and more exclusively secluded from his drawing room, which is conceived as a man's world (*mardānā*) and for which the effective messengers between the men and women are the family's children. The priest's inner courtyard is closed to strangers and even acquaintances. Except in crisis, it may never be opened to any person other than a relative. It is the more complete extension of the kitchen ethos, when compared with the conditions at a physician's or an officer's residence. However, in all the three cases, the kitchen is most strictly governed by kinship and commensal rules, setting off most clearly the official, occupational, secular roles and relationships that can percolate up to the inner courtyard. Accordingly, the modern Indian drawing room is socially most inclusive and the kitchen most exclusive.

The inner courtyard, whether of an officer, or a physician, or a priest, is usually a good indicator of familial ritual behavior (outside of the regular daily worship). Numerous women's fasts, festivals, and ceremonies, which occur round the year, find expression—in the courtyard or on a surrounding verandah—in the forms of a sacred *chauk* (a drawing on the floor or wall), a Tulsi (*Ocimum sanctum*) plant, a twig from a sacred tree, or a cow-dung figurine, each appearing and disappearing as the festivals come and go. If examined more closely and compared among several families, the frequency and elaboration of these ritual observances relate directly to some demands of urban living. For example, a Kanya-Kubja couple, both well-educated and employed in higher educational institutions in Lucknow, observed only two-thirds of the festivals that their parents in a village in Unnao district did. Among others, a judge's wife observed more than two-thirds; a young I.A.S. officer's wife only less than one-third; a physician's wife more than two-thirds; and a high administrative officer's wife more than one-half. However, a modern Kanya-Kubja lady did *not* forget any of those family observances that were meant for the welfare of her children or for the prolongation of her wifehood, even if she was a Ph.D. and very well employed. So far, for most of the Kanya-Kubja women, their own education, their husband's occupation, and pressure on their time have *not* kept them from observing such basic festivals as *karvācauth* (the "Pitcher Fourth" in September-October, for preserving wifehood—presiding deities Shiva and Pārvati); *batsāvitri* (the "Ficus Tree Worship" in May-June, for prolonging one's husband's life—presiding figure Sāvitri); *kajriteej* or *hartālikā* (the "Complete Fast" in August-September, for husband's life and for male progeny—presiding deities Shiva and Pārvati); *bhaiyā dūj* (the "Brother's Fast" in late October or November, for the welfare of one's brother—presiding figures Yama and Yamuna, the mythological brother and sister); *sakat* (the "Son's Fourth" in January, for the welfare of one's sons—presiding deity Gaṇesh); and *sankrānti* (the "Family Welfare Fast" in the middle of January, for the blessings of Shiva for family welfare—presiding deities Shiva and Pārvati). However, what has changed, because of urban living, in the observance of these women's fasts is the elaboration of any particular ceremony. The ritual may be performed hurriedly and in a "skeletal form" in the morning before the "officer" husband or the school children have to be provided with food from the kitchen. If other older women are present in the family (which is not rare), the traditional rituals acquire greater emphasis. Under the simpler alternatives provided by tradition and under the pressure from traditional mothers-in-law, a judge's educated wife is as anxious to observe these fasts as those of a railway clerk, or of an I.A.S. officer, or of a priest. The inner courtyards wear a festive look on almost all these occasions.

Some Social Characteristics of Modern Elitism

The most significant feature of an elite's domestic surroundings is again the interjacence between tradition and modernity, "official" formality and kinship informality, and economic "class" and socioreligious caste. This interface continues even at the extradomestic level—in neighborhoods and in distant elite-to-elite relations—and is an important consideration for completing the discussion of modern styles of elite behavior, which will lead us back to a discussion of formal organizational (bureaucratic) and traditional caste elements in sabha behavior.

There are two interdependent tendencies in elite-to-elite and elite-to-non–elite (commoner) relationships: while the elite always tries to differentiate himself from the commoners on the basis of resource-reward inequality (cf. Davis and Moore 1966), he simultaneously tends to neutralize this under the common caste and kinship bond. This is what we illustrated in the preceding discussion of domestic behavior, where an elite accepts his relative in the drawing room in a way different (i.e., by maintaining the positional distance) than he does in the kitchen (by closing the "class" or positional distance in favor of caste and kinship). This situational dynamics is essential for understanding the sociological nature of modern Indian elitism. As we shall see in the next chapter, this dynamics has some direct implications for sabha organization. On the other hand, the caste elites compete among themselves for status equalization—that is, they compete to prove themselves equal to one another in prestigious secular possessions and achievements. Yet, whenever necessary for a particular positional rise, they may underplay their "class" gap and close their caste, kin, and familial ranks for attaining a common aim. Distant and unacquainted elite families come together by creating affinal ties. This is a very strong and effective means, substantiated and analyzed in detail in the following chapter.

The nonkinship means of caste-elite cohesiveness are neighborliness and esprit de corps. Both of these properties may be promoted to some degree by modern urban or occupational conditions. Residential propinquity of modern caste elites may be due to suburban "colonies" or neighborhoods, where several officers or professionals of the same caste tend to buy or build their houses. A city like Lucknow, for example, shows old as well as new Kanya-Kubja neighborhoods. Although the old ones have declined in size and population because of occupational migration, new ones have sprung up as more and more rural Kanya-Kubjas have become educated and employed in Lucknow. An old "settlement" like Rani Katra may, accordingly, now be more heterogeneous in terms of castes than it was before. On the other hand, a new neighborhood like Krishnabagh (a pseudonym) may be dominant in Kanya-Kubja households. The latter is composed of occupationally diverse but prestigious Kanya-Kubjias, and it works as a sort of "protectorate" of caste interests. For example, a Kanya-Kubja in search of renting a house may be given preference, if the circumstances permit, by the Kanya-Kubja–dominated management committee. Moreover, the resident Kanya-Kubjas, even if unrelated, may develop close, mutually reciprocal, social relations in terms of "uncles," "aunts," "sisters," "mother's sister," and so on. These "pseudo-kinship" relations might mean mutual gift presentations or help during a daughter's marriage or for the management of a loan. Sentiments become deeper if these families have a similarity in traditional ranks, or if they happened to belong to the same ancestral village. Whatever the order of one's office duty during the day, they would share long, "exciting sessions of conversation and indoor games in the evening with their same-caste neighbors." They could discuss anything from politics to one's office problems, from one's son's problems to the management of a daughter's coming marriage, and from the rising cost of living to the Brahmanic philosophy of modern life. They could evolve a "strategy" for acquiring additional quotas of cement and steel for finishing the construction of their houses, a strategy for dealing with their official bosses, and a strategy for handling and directing their young sons' educational careers. They realized the advantages of being together in a city. Yet, their "colony" did accommodate tenants from other caste groups, ranging from Kayasthas and Baniyas to Thakurs; and there were no explosive factional differences. However, they knew that they could not expect as much from these other residents as from their own caste members.

The one-caste "colonies" may be indirectly promoted also by the esprit de corps of the Kanya-Kubja elites and by some recent government subsidy systems for house-building. Government administrators, who are preferentially treated for a state subsidy, can usually manage to get their choice of plots, which may eventually result into a concentration of several houses occupied by members of the same caste. Still it seems that a private housing enterprise, as described above, may have more pronounced caste-clustered housing patterns. However, both types of "colonies"—whether government sponsored or privately organized —can emphasize caste lines in housing patterns. In general, the first type of colony tends to emphasize elite contacts across caste lines, while the second aggregates them more freely along the caste membership. Some "older" prestigious settlements of Lucknow may also exhibit the former property, primarily because they emphasized economic "class" variables and because the elites, then, were much fewer. For example, one prestigious, nearly mile-long street of Lucknow had twenty-six spacious bungalows, ten occupied by ex-Tālukdārs and the rest by lawyers, physicians, mill owners, politicians, colonels, and judges, drawn from eleven different caste groups and representing three religious communities (i.e., Hindu, Muslim, and Sikh). This street had five Kanya-Kubjas. In such a heterogeneous neighborhood as this, a Kanya-Kubja elite underplays his parochial caste identity to emphasize the common occupational or "class" bond with his other neighbors. Mutual obligations are exchanged here too but in a different social arena: bureaucratic or organizational "favors" are exchanged on a "personal" basis; that is, neighborly professional services may be freely exchanged—a lawyer with a physician, a mill owner with a lawyer, and so on. If some elite belongs to a Scheduled caste, his ritual rank is immaterial at this level of transaction. Within these contacts, one may also discover the importance of age, occupational seniority, and sharing of professions as further factors strengthening elite behavior across caste lines. If observed over a period of time, this solidarity is used for accomplishing a specific favor for one's kin or caste member. A Kanya-Kubja elite may refer his relative's work to such an elite neighbor who can most likely perform it. Such a favor may almost always be paid back in the form of a similar "service" by the Kanya-Kubja elite.

But it is at this point that we must also note that a Kanya-Kubja elite and a Kanya-Kubja commoner are not always in the best of social terms. If standing outside one's reckonable kinship, a caste elite may practically be a "stranger". Besides, if caste and kinship generate solidarity sentiments, they can also fail to do so on many occasions for uncontrollable past or present reasons. Common kinship quarrels can cause hostility between any two relatives, sometimes for several years. In the third chapter, I described the appearance of two Kanya-Kubja colleges at one place in Lucknow. The second college came into being when two rich brothers fell out among themselves on the questions of sharing power in the older institution, and as a result the older brother had to start a new institution to prove his own capabilities to his brother. Several high government administrators as brothers or cousins, or uncles and nephews were noted to have hostile interpersonal relations for four to five years and consequently did not make mutual use of positional achievements. They neither helped each other through official influence, nor participated in smaller social ceremonies, except at marriage and death. "Animosity between brothers makes them the worst of enemies" is a popular saying among the Kanya-Kubjas. They say if once the kinship relations are spoiled, they always deteriorate with time; and if they are mended, they are never the same. With differential achievements of brothers, these differences now seem to increase in frequency. Economic inequality, geographic distance, occupational demands, and limited sharing of resources aggravate and perpetuate kin wrangles. Expectations of a relative "who could not make it" stand markedly apart from those who could. (However, as I have indicated above, these very factors may sometimes promote kinship cohesiveness, especially under the emphasis of traditional values of kin and caste welfare.) Whereas it is true that differences and quarrels between kin members undermine but cannot obliterate the kinship reciprocity, the effects of such fluctuations are significant in daily social life of caste elites as well as non-elites.

THE KANYA-KUBJAS' MODERN DILEMMA

Now, a brief allusion to Kanya-Kubja elites' conceptions about certain changes occurring during their lifetime that have influenced their behavior. In the previous pages, I have described from a close range both kinds of behavior—traditional as well as modern—and their interjacence in daily living. Here, I shall present an overview of these changes in order to underscore certain continuing cultural themes in modern behavior. For example, a Kanya-Kubja elite, in assessing the extent of changes in his lifetime, wrote (*Kanja-Kubja* 1957, pp. 30–31): "Essentially it has been a change from the emphasis on right action and right thinking [*Karmavāda* and *Buddhivāda*] to fatalism and superstitions [*Bhāgyavāda* and *Andhvishvās*]." As an example he said that the problems of Biswā, dowry, and marriage exist among the Kanya-Kubjas because the latter have not applied reason and rationale to them. If they applied these to such social problems, they could solve them as easily as they did that of the successful adaptation to modern occupations. We shall amplify this native observation below in terms of some anthropologically recognized processes of social change in India (see Srinivas

1966). But first I shall produce some more data on the old systems of values guiding elite behavior, allowing us to compare these conceptions with the new ones described earlier in this chapter.

A Kanya-Kubja engineer of British times who dressed in dhotī and remained barefoot (although rode in private carriages or on horses), or "one who lacked any kind of ostentatious behavior" (i.e., bureaucratic formality) was considered a "true" elite. An elite who observed simple living, and had integrity and unflinching devotion to religion was a truly prestigious man worthy of emulation. "Humility was an ornament of the Kanya-Kubjas." For example, another writer recalled how a British-era executive engineer used to visit his friend, Pandit Motilal Nehru, the Indian aristocrat par excellence, by hackney carriage and in old and shabby clothes. "The engineer was so honestly devoted to the government that he never charged the permissible overtime on his official trips. . . . He was so respectful toward the members of his ancestral village that even while in the company of British officers he would get down from his horse and touch their [the villagers'] feet" (*Kanya-Kubja* 1957, pp. 45–46). However, the narrative also notes that his villagers were so conscious of this endearing behavior that they would avoid appearing in his way when he was in the company of British officers, "for the latter may laugh or ridicule the engineer for touching our feet." He was also a staunch follower of his spiritual preceptor, "whom he obeyed even at the cost of his life." Another biographic account emphasizes the absence of exhibitionism by the most famous modern Hindi critic, Achārya Mahabir Prasad Diwedi. "This Kanya-Kubja again lived simply, and spoke rural Hindi, despite the fact that he was an outstanding writer and a critic of the chaste language." (*Kanya-Kubja* 1957, pp. 52–54).

These examples relate to the illustrious Kanya-Kubjas who lived either at the turn or the beginning of this century. Their progeny are now old and have their own views on how times have changed the patterns of their behavior. Whenever interviewed, they uniformly cherished the *same* values that their forefathers so scrupulously maintained. They wanted to be simple, honest, humble, and straightforward. However, they thought that their "office affairs" have become immensely complicated since then and have increasingly encroached upon their minds and actions, contracting the zone of their personal life. Yet the official and personal aspects are conceptually different for a modern Kanya-Kubja. One fifty-year-old engineer summarized the dilemma in the following words:

> While I would like to worship more in the morning, the clock, the real regulator of our lives, runs so fast that it makes us run for our office. The day is spent on files, papers, and in figuring out safe steps for making bureaucratic notes in accordance with the policies of the department, the ministry, and our immediate bosses. The evening is spent mostly either in completing the office work or in preparing for the next day. If on a field job, one's immersion in official work is more complete. The speed of our lives is controlled more by the events at our office than by those at home. Religion and rituals accordingly recede in the background, although they have grown neither less valuable nor dispensable. Whenever possible, I do break away from this bread-earning routine and slip into a spiritually exhilarating look at myself through a religious performance or a pilgrimage, or a visit to our ancestral village for meditation. When I compare myself with my *dādā* [grandfather] who was also a deputy collector, I find so many differences. He did more work more earnestly and yet remained a human being first and a bureaucrat later. Now the definitions of earnestness and efficiency have significantly changed because of the complexity of our offices. The latter control the former qualities, while earlier it was vice versa.

He was always conscious of "humanizing" his office work, although he thought he could hardly do so to the same degree that his grandfather did in his time, for it might conflict with the elaborate organizational rules and practice of his office. Within these limitations, he claimed, he was both unostentatious and humble. He thought that actions were more important than one's appearance, and accordingly, a modern administrator in Western dress can also be a practicer of humility, simplicity, honesty, and forebearance. These expressions are, he contended, subtler and less dramatic than before.

A young I.A.S. administrator viewed the problem in terms of the necessity of rationalizing change in both the traditional and the modern aspects. He found traditional values desirable, but these could not be supported, he said, either by imitating one's forefathers or by blindly following the Western concepts of office, rank, bureaucracy, and so on. He thought that change in either form should be understood in the contexts of as well as the trends for successfully integrating them in one's activities. He welcomed the bureaucratic insensitivity that would improve the efficacy and efficiency of his official actions, although he did not underrate the "larger purpose" which, according to him, was nearest to the sacred value system for the welfare of all. He thought that if he deparochialized religion and decompressed Western thought, he could handle both of them as interrelated categories. He reasoned:

> If bureaucratic impersonality is important for keeping objectivity in our office behavior, it does not mean that I should never look at my subordinate as a human being full of joys and sorrows, opinions and failings like my own. While in office, I would like to keep both aspects in front of me. It would mean neither promoting inefficiency nor religious sectarianism if I am careful enough to be just and rational in dealing with actual situations, although I admit in an office it is not at all simple, and the guiding principles can only be broad and humanistic. Understandably, they come to us through upbringing, and it is entirely a matter of our cultural training and religious background. We can not get out of this mold however secular we may claim to be, and in this basic sense my family background reflects itself in my official behavior as well. And I try to make this heritage as rational and deparochialized as possible. I do not underestimate its value for my office or home. It directs my thoughts as well as behavior.

Both the officers quoted above represent stages of modernization in an Indian situation (for a recent summary of social change in India, see Srinivas 1966), when contrasted to the picture represented by their forefathers who were also Western educated and had held prominent administrative positions. The modern Kanya-Kubjas tend to show continuities as well as discontinuities with the past. They learn to handle their Brahmanic ideal and family upbringing with educational and occupational rules and demands. As Brahmans they are obviously Sanskritized, and the modern circumstance does not stop this process in them; it only promotes a different emphasis, where neological interpretations—what the informants above called "rationality or understanding"—of the old and the sacred abound. In their scheme rationalization of the "content of tradition" is more important than its alteration or replacement. Another way of describing its continuity may be to say that tradition rides on the wheels of modernization as well as Westernization, even if in a subtle way, to influence the thought and action of the modern Kanya-Kubja. This version of tradition is pliable. It accentuates and attenuates according to the circumstance. Improvisations and alternatives retain "thought" or theme and prune ritualism. Religious thought rather than ritualism may be the sacred content in a modern Kanya-Kubja's busy schedule. He may modernize his living (i.e., open himself to more physical comforts), may talk to his convent-educated child in English (i.e., to prepare his child for better success later on), and may have lived in Western countries (i.e., for personal advancement), yet he may not view his modernity as an end in itself. Modern achievements may be his means of turning towards his religious beliefs, even if at the expense of ritual orthodoxy and elaboration. To him Sanskritization may mean rationalization and intellectualization of sacred beliefs and values.

The younger elite may begin with questioning the elements or contents of tradition. After getting married, they are found to rationalize and intellectualize at least those aspects that they find they can not do away with, especially in family and kinship. After having progeny, their attitudes settle further under the traditional fold, and become fixed by the time their children have married. However, when compared across several generations, the detailed contents of Sanskritization show fluctuations and changed emphases, according to circumstances, and no "basic conflict" or "total replacement."

The other processes of social change like Westernization and urbanization do not present a very different kind of continuity. The changes brought about by them are also rationalized and explained. They are also followed, especially when one's living depends on them. They are made a part and parcel of the intra-family socialization processes because they are the means of acquiring useful work and prestige for descendants. Hence a son talks to his father in English, and the latter encourages it, for this language has become a "passport" for higher education and certain coveted positions. These aspects of change influence tradition and also get influenced by the latter. But they are neither functionally contrarious nor disruptive; they are interjacent, as the above descriptive material tends to show.

STATUS STRATIFICATION: A CONCLUDING OVERVIEW

This and the two previous chapters described how caste and "class" status systems influence one another and how status prestige systems are variously reflected in specific standards and styles of Kanya-Kubja life. The description illustrates the *praxis* as well as practice of formality vis-à-vis informality, "office" vis-à-vis "home," and tradition vis-à-vis modernity. It demonstrates how these social categories come to interface, adjust, adapt, and integrate in actual life. It underlines the point that in reality both principles, ascription as well as achievement, regulate and direct the traditional hierarchy of a modern caste group, and that modern class competition has further amplified the arena of achievements. Numerous prestige indicators elaborate the importance of achievements, sometimes even in the face of ascriptive caste structure. But mostly one's achievements help discharge traditional obligations. Occasionally, high achievers may also use their influence to loosen certain ascriptive restrictions.

The preceding data on modern status stratification allows us to differentiate three distinct but interinfluencing dimensions: (a) the universally ascribed and institutionalized system of caste structure, (b) the nonuniversally achieved, instrumental, traditional prestige-position system, and (c) the nonuniversally achieved and most importantly instrumental "class" status. We have repeatedly shown how these elements influence one another in the life of a modern Kanya-Kubja. These elements, roughly speaking, produce the following typology of modern Kanya-Kubjas:

1. Those high on *a* are also high on *c* and *b;* e.g., the modern high-Biswā elites described earlier.
2. Those low on *a* are high on *c* and/or *b;* e.g., the modern low-Biswā elites described earlier.
3. Those high on *a* are low in *c* but high on *b;* e.g., priests.
4. Those low on *a* are low on *c* and *b;* e.g., Mahābrahmans (or those Brahmans that deal with death ceremonies).

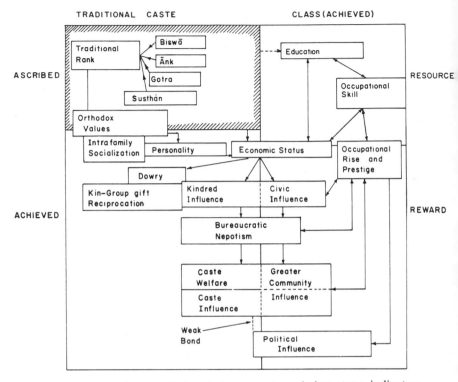

TRADITIONAL CASTE   CLASS (ACHIEVED)

FIG. 7. Interjacent relations between caste and class status indicators.

Figure 7 shows diagrammatically the interrelations, strengths, and interpenetrations of the three stratificatory dimensions discussed above. The diagram tries to indicate the comparative distribution of ascription vis-à-vis achievement, and the resources vis-à-vis the rewards as found with the modern Kanya-Kubja Brahmans. Obviously resource and reward variables exhibit a dynamic relationship; basic resources when exploited register a status rise, and the raised status then works as a resource for higher aspirational levels. Second, the diagram also intends to convey the actual limited role of ascription—a much emphasized characteristic of caste—in the modern stratificatory system. Traditionally, birth-ascribed rank plays an important role, more as a pattern of cultural values, which is socialized at the intrafamily level and produces distinct personality "poses" among these modern Brahmans. It is, as they themselves refer to it, "Kanya-

156

Kubjism." The latter refers to, as we have seen, those specific attitude styles which they find incorporated in their personalities before they enter into the processes that would make them elites or intellectuals, and they tend to stick to these peculiarities in thought and action. Family, kindred, and caste loyalties, including dowry, prestations, and economic advancement appear as parts of their style of life.

In the preceding description, I have attempted to present status and role hierarchies evoked by both the structural and cultural aspects. I have contrasted both, only to emphasize the point that modern Indian caste behavior can be understood only if both are not arbitrarily severed from each other; and I suggest that such understanding is important for the comparative sociology of intercaste behavior. The main thing in the above discussion is to *understand;* and therefore, ideas and values cannot be separated from "structure." The discussion also brings to attention a common but persistent paradox: a *holistic* account of Kanya-Kubjas in terms of the *individual.* Through individual praxeology I have struggled to convey the whole picture of the Kanya-Kubjas as a traditional-modern group. Similarly the value schemes that direct their status and prestige relations have the primary differentiation between *"that which encompasses and that which is encompassed"* —a hierarchical relation recently emphasized by Dumont (1967, p. 33) for Indian caste. A Kanya-Kubja looks at his Brahmanic status as encompassing and justifying his thrust for modern economic and social position; and of course, he is never in doubt about the instrumental value of the latter.

An implication of the above discussion for our sabha study is that a Kanya-Kubja Brahman sabha in general, displays characteristics similar to those modern Kanya-Kubja Brahmans, as its constituents, carry in other related sectors of activity. In cultural conception and function, as the first four chapters of this book describe, a caste sabha is caste-specific. In organization, however, it carries features of "universalization." The nature of the relationship between these two "contrarious" aspects in a sabha will be elaborated on in the following chapter.

III Tradition and Modernity of the Modern Kanya-Kubja Organization

8 The Sabha as an Interjacent Organization

THE PURPOSE of the preceding discussion of status stratification was to help us understand how different conceptions and inter-relations of traditional structure and modern or complex organization (e.g., see Etzioni 1962, 1965, 1967) are brought face to face in a Kanya-Kubja sabha. Sabha participants display a strongly shared sense of culture, character, and status, on the one hand, and an ability to articulate and represent the sabha purpose in ways akin to modern organizational and administrative procedures, on the other. They do not blend the two dimensions; they treat them within their logico-meaningful premises. The sabhas do not try to replace one by the other, although they deal with them within the framework of a caste group. A sabha officer may actually give greater play to the voluntary (nonkinship) modes of affiliation based on one's educational background, occupational skill, and economic status, although he is unprepared to open the sabha beyond the birth-ascriptive caste membership. This interfacing situation will be described here as it is, without bringing in the prevalent notions of "conflict," "fusion," and "replacement."

In a Kanya-Kubja sabha, traditional and modern social features interact for specific purposes and with specific consequences, *without actually* "leveling the sacred and hierarchical caste order and replacing it" (cf. Rudolph and Rudolph 1967, p. 36). In order to underscore this feature of the modern sabha, I call it an "interjacent organization." The latter admits dynamic, functional, and processual changes in *both* traditional as well as modern social factors. It may betray cultural emphasis of one factor over the other, but one can not, in terms of the present reality, do without the other. Such an interjacence is a constant feature because the people who constitute the sabha live their lives, as the preceding chapters indicate, within the two coexisting cultural worlds, which are sometimes overlapping and sometimes exclusive.

This chapter pursues the above themes further in relation to the sabha bureaucratic organization. We described its basic characteristics earlier (see chapter 3), we are now in a position to deal with its nature of cultural interjacence. This we shall do first by describing some aspects of the "incipient" bureaucracy of the sabha, followed by a discussion of some contacts it makes with kinship and caste behavior on the one hand, and with the formal office, on the other. The latter aspect will be narrowed further in terms of "bureaucratic impersonality," which will be dealt with in detail primarily to understand the organization and meaning of "formality" for the sabha.

Aspects of "Strategic" Formal Organization

When we compare the traditional structure of the Kanya-Kubja Brahmans (see the Introduction and chapter 5) with that of the modern organization of their sabha (see chapters 3 and 4), we notice those basic differences that a sociologist normally conveys by recognizing the "dichotomy" between a traditional, kinship-based, "mechanical" solidarity group, and a modern, complex, contractual one. The latter as a "formal organization" is defined (Etzioni 1965, p. 31) "as the pattern of division of tasks and power among the organizational positions, and the rules expected to guide the behavior of the participants, as defined by the management. . . ." The "informal organization," on the other hand, refers, "either to the social relations that develop among the staff or workers above and beyond the formal one determined by the organization (e.g., they not only work as a team on the same machine but are also friends), or to the actual organizational relations as they evolved as a consequence of the interaction between the organizational design and the pressures of the interpersonal relations among the participants. . ." (Etzioni 1965, p. 40).

In chapters 3 and 4, accordingly, I have described the formal as well as some informal aspects of the sabha and the journal organization. Here, however, I shall elaborate on the cultural sources of limitations and specificities of roles and relationships that accompany a caste sabha organization. This will be done by briefly comparing the "formal" and cultural conceptions of sabha roles and relationships to those bureaucratic criteria enunciated by Max Weber (e.g., see Etzioni 1965) for an "ideal type."

SABHA OFFICE AND OFFICER: ORGANIZATIONAL IDEALS AND ACTUAL LIMITATIONS

Hall, Hass, and Johnson recently discussed (1967, pp. 903–12) some of the "formalization indicators" from a sociological point of view. It may be useful to indicate them in this context, especially because unless we have information about the ideal-typical structure of a modern organization we cannot explicitly measure the "formality" of the Kanya-Kubja sabha organization. While based on the Weberian ideal scheme, these indicators are adapted for this study under the following categories: roles, authority relations, communication network, norms and sanctions, and formal procedures (with further subcategories). For example, a sabha has concrete job definitions and descriptions, has written and clear definitions of the hierarchy of authority, has regular and written channels of communication, has a number of written rules and norms with stipulation of normal legal penalties (which are sometimes written), and has rules and procedures for new entrants, *without* systematic socialization activities for them. Although most of these indicators are present in a sabha, how elaborate they are and how strictly they are followed in varying situations constitute the most crucial factors for assessing the strength of formalization, and for noting the different degrees of "refractions" the rules may present under the sabha situations.

The following, therefore, presents a summary of the "refractions" that the Weberian ideals for a bureaucratic office (indicators quoted from Etzioni 1965, pp. 53–54) and for an administrative officer (indicators quoted from Merton, Gray, Hockey, and Selvin 1952, pp. 21–22) may typically undergo under the Kanya-Kubja sabhas.

Office

1. "A continuous organization of official functions bound by rules." This is present but not exhaustive in the sabhas; informal norms dominate function, except in *financial* and *legal* matters where formal rules are binding.

2. "A specific sphere of competence . . . marked off as a systematic division of labor . . . the necessary means of compulsion are clearly defined and their use is subject to definite conditions." Formal division of labor is present in the sabhas, but the informal roles may dominate and work most of the time, formality being disfavored over missionary zeal and sacrifice.

3. "The organization of offices follows the principle of hierarchy; that is, each lower office is under the control and supervision of a higher one." Formal organization of the sabhas is parallel; but the control and supervision of subordinates is subject to the influences of kinship, age, and social status; those higher on the latter factors may also occupy a higher bureaucratic position in the sabha; no strict subordination and superordination (except on paper in limited matters); traditional values of friendship, age seniority, sacrifice, and social service provide overriding factors for creating an *effective* hierarchy *within* the framework of formal hierarchy.

4. "The rules which regulate the conduct of an office may be technical rules or norms. In both cases if their application is to be fully rational, specialized training is necessary." Such rules are present in the sabha organization, but there is no specialized training *necessary* in order to be "qualified" for a sabha position.

5. "It is a matter of principle that the members of the administrative staff should be completely separated from ownership of the means of production or administration . . . and complete separation of the property belonging to the organization . . . and the personal property of the official." Such a separation is present in a sabha but is handled on traditional moral bases; there is, however, easy expression of dominance of the "few" who happen to be chief donors or powerful caste members; instead of rational-legal bases for separating the "personal" from the "organizational" property, the reasons are moral and religious, especially as symbolized by "jāti welfare."

6. "In the rational type case, there is also a complete absence of appropriation of official position by the incumbent. Where "rights" to an office exist . . . they do not normally serve the purpose of appropriation by the official, but of securing the purely objective and independent character of the conduct of

the office so that it is oriented only to the relevant norms." A sabha organization is, as noted above, greatly subject to informal influences, and while grossly dishonest behavior may be avoided, appropriation of office "rights" is easily possible in practice (e.g., see the discussion on bureaucratic impersonality).

7. "Administrative acts, decisions, and rules are formulated and recorded in writing, even in cases where oral discussion is the rule or is even mandatory." These characteristics are present in a sabha in a legally minimum manner for keeping the record "straight" for state requirements.

Officer

The rules applicable to an administrative officer are derived from those of the office. However, Weber detailed them too (Merton et al. 1952, pp. 21–22), and I shall emphasize below those that have not been specifically covered in the above list.

Sabha officers, like administrative officers, are organized in a scheme of clearly defined hierarchical offices and have a contractual office term, but there are no formal technical qualifications set as a basis for selection (except the traditional one that one should be a born Kanya-Kubja Brahman), and they are not remunerated by "fixed salaries in money. . . ." The sabha officer holds an "honorary," subsidiary, part-time, voluntary, and missionary office. The remuneration is moral and/or religious, spoken in terms of one's jāti and varna. Hence a sabha office is *not* "treated as the sole, or at least the primary, occupation of the incumbent." It does *not* constitute a career, and there is no definite "system of 'promotion' according to seniority or achievement or both." Moral and kinship considerations of (and on) an "official" may not allow him to work "entirely separated from ownership of the means of administration and without appropriation of his position." While, according to Weber, he should be "subject to strict and systematic discipline and control in the conduct of the office," a sabha has mostly moral and kinship pressure to employ, unless the breach is so serious that it falls in the field of the state's laws and punishments.

These characteristics, therefore, suggest that a sabha organization is different on paper than in practice. Though rules are written, hierarchy of the offices is established, minutes of the meetings and verbal discussions are kept, resolutions are passed by the majority (although unanimity is preferred), and rights and obligations of officers are precisely described in a constitution, a sabha office is not formalized to the same degree and with the same rationale as a modern organization is.

If we further compare these tabulated features with the actual description of executive committee meetings given in chapter 3, the difference between the ideal and actual, and the cultural and organizational norms comes into focus. In conception, a sabha officer tries to be a caste member and a president or a secretary at the same time. In practice, depending upon the situation, he pushes one role in the background and maintains the other. For example, when a Kanya-Kubja is authorized to sign the account books, his role is of the treasurer of a modern body, and he becomes fully responsible for its financial aspects. Therefore, he makes sure, as any administrative officer in a state office will, that the accounts are legally valid and complete. He does not compromise this role with those of caste and kinship. If he does, he becomes legally punishable in much the same way as a treasurer of any other regular office. Once his official role is discharged (i.e., the sabha accounts are properly and accurately reported in writing), the sabha treasurer may act as a Kanya-Kubja as well as a prestigious caste member (influencer). He may use this combined official and social position to influence a sabha decision for awarding, for example, scholarships only to Kanya-Kubja students of a particular region. It may be "favoritism" under the strict bureaucratic rules, but it is "appropriate" for the sabha situations.

As an unpaid sabha officer, one voluntarily *donates* personal time, money, and energy, primarily in response to moral and religious appeals from one's caste members for caste welfare. However, contrary to the expectations, the modern Kanya-Kubja Brahmans *actually* devote very little amount of time to sabha affairs. This became evident when I interviewed twenty-five "active" sabha officers in Lucknow and Kanpur for finding out their estimation of time that is taken up in sabha activities (particularly management and organization) and participation. My informants came from a variety of modern occupations (i.e., there were two judges, three lawyers, three engineers, three private physicians, two central government servants, two state government servants, five business executives, two politicians, two university teachers, and the present secretary-editor of the all-Indian sabha). The informants were asked first to specify the place where the sabha affairs of an organizational nature are most usually carried out by them. They pointed out that it was either the sabha office (at the residence of the secretary-editor) or their drawing rooms. The latter was a "natural" venue for consultations, discussions, and financial management, and policy decisions prior to a formal meeting. Accordingly, I first ascertained the average time that these informants thought they spent in their drawing rooms (which would also tend to vary according to one's occupation or profession). Thus, while politicians thought they spent an average of seven hours in the drawing rooms on any one day, the rest varied between one to five hours. However, my informants readily noted that these were the best approximations that they could offer and that the "drawing room time" is a very heterogeneous social affair, as I have already noted earlier; and it is very hard to classify what precisely goes on there for a specified period of time. Caste and kinship, and office and its problems may be frequently discussed back and forth several times in one hour. However, when asked in terms of the specified sabha activities that they do perform with some regularity, they were able to offer (classified according to their occupational calling) the following estimates of average time spent biweekly on sabha affairs: ten minutes (central government servants, engineers, judges, politicians, and university teachers), fifteen minutes (business executives, private physicians, and state government servants), twenty minutes (lawyers), and over *sixty hours* (the secretary-editor of the all-Indian sabha). Obviously, the last person is an exception, providing an example of missionary zeal on a voluntary basis. It may also be noted that retired individuals may devote more time to such purposes than those employed full-time.

Actually, most caste elites do not attend to sabha business every week. The above empirical indicators may, therefore, help us to observe that if we examine the actual time, money, and energy invested in a sabha by various "active" Kanya-Kubja participants, it is insignificant, at least at this time. (For a general discussion of this procedure of discovering the "real" extent of social change, see Barth 1967, pp. 661–69.) Orally, however, the importance of the caste sabha may be grossly exaggerated by the caste members.

As a further corollary of the above discussions, it follows that a sabha office is not a specially coveted secular position for a modern Kanya-Kubja, especially since its organizational resources and capacities—economic, social, and political—are stagnant and limited. I therefore attempted to ascertain why modern achievers participate in caste sabhas. This inquiry was not limited only to "active" members, but it also included some conspicuous donors of money to the organization. However, it was conducted only among the forty Lucknow caste elites, classified according to their occupations once again. There were four categories: "high" government officers, professionals, traditional pundits, and officer clerks, each providing ten informants. They were asked what their primary and/or secondary reasons for participating in their Kanya-Kubja caste sabha(s). No informant responded that it was (primarily or secondarily) "to have monetary gain," while thirty-nine out of forty answered that it was for rendering "community" or "social" service; however, thirty-four of the forty also answered that they participated to get "help" for arranging marriages for their sisters and daughters. Three informants thought that the subsidiary aim could be to gain additional "power and authority," while seven believed that sabha participation could mean "social" (probably intracaste) prestige of some consequence. (The latter figure reflects the effect of the scattered distribution of the Kanya-Kubja Brahmans.) It may be noted that eight out of ten traditional pundits, all ten office clerks, and only four "high" government officers thought that the caste sabha is positively helpful for locating suitable grooms. Similarly, while four professionals, five clerks, and seven traditional pundits thought that sabha participation is a means of enhancing one's social prestige, no high officer thought so. For the latter, the predominant motive (for nine out of ten) was "to render social service." They said that they gave their own time, money, and energy for community and caste welfare, although the cautious ones may not expressly include caste as a referent. In contrast, the lower-income Kanya-Kubjas looked up to the sabha for prestige and for resolution of their social and financial problems.

In the light of the preceding discussion, if we do not understand the cultural conception underlying these sabhas and emphasize the "formality" disproportionately, we may miss the organizational tour de force. The Kanya-Kubjas conceive a sabha organization in terms of their caste. They serve in it voluntarily because it serves them, and them alone. Accordingly, to be a sabha member one must be a Kanya-Kubja. This conception overrides and reinterprets all aspects of Weberian formality discussed earlier. Hierarchy, offices, roles, proprieties, and competence of officers are transvalued according to purpose and occasion. They carry the titles of president, secretary, and treasurer, for the protection and perpetuation of traditional caste hierarchical rules and roles. For example, the Kanya-Kubjas do not give up commensal rules since they are sabha officers and since they should promote sabha brotherhood. They do not relax marriage rules. On the contrary, they may use the sabha organization for reinforcing such rules and for searching for a traditionally suitable bride and bridegroom for the marriage of their children.

We have already seen in chapter 3 that their actual interpersonal behavior is strongly traditionalized. Their main basis of competence is wealth and fame earned within and used for the traditional value system. If one has technical qualifications but no love for caste and tradition, he is unsuitable to be a sabha officer. Thus, the sabha officers may be "honest" not because it is a bureaucratic necessity for a modern organization, but because a sabha is one's "own," sacralized caste welfare group, which is nurtured mostly by donations and charity rather than subscriptions only. "To steal such money is like committing the theft in a temple." (Breaches, however, do occur; see chapter 3.) Thus what bureaucratic, legally inforced, rules do to separate officials from economic and administrative means in a state organization is accomplished by the sacred and moral conceptions of the sabha. Even in the role of sabha "officers," the Kanya-Kubjas primarily remain caste and kin members.

Though it is the dominant, pervasive, and persistant dimension, the sabhas do occasionally present the counterpart—the formality—as a necessary "overlay" for interactions with the state. Usually the sabha officers become maximally bureaucratized on such occasions, because as elected officers of the sabha executive body, they stand in a more accountable and responsible relationship not only to the caste but also to the state and/or legal bureaucracy. For example, strict formalization appears and specialists like auditors, lawyers, and bankers help when the all-Indian Kanya-Kubja sabha handles finances, requests the government to allot a quota of newsprint for the journal, or when the registration of the periodical is renewed, when the "caste fund" is appropriated in different private business and government investments, or when any substantial deposit or expenditure of this money is made. (It may be recalled that a Lucknow lawyer framed these elaborate rules governing the sabha finances, especially after the loss of money in a "Kanya-Kubja Bank" that went bankrupt.)

Let us now compare this sabha formality-informality to the situations obtaining to a modern office. This will allow us to know whether the above sabha conception is unique or whether it is a related variation of the wider "office ethos" in modern India. If the "informality" of a modern office also takes after the dominant cultural themes, we should infer that a formal sabha organization is only related but more caste-parochialized version of the wider pattern. Hence, the formalization of sabha business may actually reflect the twin all-Indian tendencies: to formalize the transactions on paper and to continue to keep an intensive and effective (caste-and-kinship based) network of informal communications and transactions.

THE MODERN OFFICE: A CULTURALIZED CONCEPTION

The conception of a modern office is also composed of numerous individual cultural elements, and the formal hierarchy is subject to cultural conceptions and meanings. If examined closely, the modern office carries a cultural ethos of its own. This ethos may be characterized by the "away-from-home" atmosphere regulated in terms of superordination and subordination. An officer there ranks himself to those whom he serves. He knows he has specified roles and has to maintain them by keeping appropriate interpersonal distance. If he moves too close to his boss, he is likely to be reminded of his position. On the other hand, he will do the same thing, if his subordinate approaches too near to influence his official role.

Age, seniority in rank, and administrative experience tend to increase informality in one's actual office behavior. For example, an experienced administrator may extend his drawing-room behavior to his actual office, probably as an indicator of his adeptness and ease in dealing with his official duties. He gives a "personal touch" to his office, under which familiarity with bureaucratic intricacies breeds confidence and command. His long tenure in a bureaucratic position arms him with alternative ways of blending the traditional with formal behavior, providing greater flexibility in interpersonal behavior in the office. For example, an administrator expects to have respect from his office subordinates roughly on the same basis as he would from his younger kin at home. He expects his secretarial or clerical staff to leave their seats and stand up in his honor and to sit only when he does so himself. He expects them to greet him every morning, and not vice versa. He expects them to raise the curtain of his office door if a peon is not nearby. He wants them to page through the files on his behalf and to open and point to the exact place where he is supposed to sign. He expects them to be at his beck and call for the explanation of some procedural obscurity, as well as, as I described earlier, for some occasional personal help in his domestic affairs. This administrator, in his turn, follows the same pattern of behavior when he confronts his boss. The latter's expectations may be similar, although there always remain idiosyncratic differences.

The official hierarchy of superordination and subordination is also conceived in cultural terms. Bureaucratic rank gradients seem to be consciously and unconsciously patterned along the themes of caste and kinship distance. An administrator is regarded "above," "distant," and "higher" (subtly taking after the caste order) not only in terms of his administrative power and prerogatives, but also because of his cultural "paternal" or "big brother" role. The latter may be reinforced now and then by his personal invitations to participate in a domestic ceremony, and by presentation of gifts, for example, in the marriage of a subordinate's daughter. If, however, the administrator is younger than his subordinate, he may on several occasions make culturally valued respectful references to his older subordinate either for inducing him to be more efficient in his office work or for his knowledge of office work. If the older subordinate is of his own caste group, this attitude may be expressed more frequently, but subtly.

The cultural theme may again express itself in another situation. For example, the administrator-peon relationships may very easily be found to slip into the culturally patterned "master-servant" relationships. Caste and age of a peon influence the kind of office work that he can be expected to perform. If some work is demeaning for his caste rank, he may informally approach the administrator to depute a peon of a different caste for the job. He may politely but firmly refuse to do the job. An administrator, therefore, is aware what kind of services he can expect from different caste peons. When recruiting, he may keep this factor in mind, especially if there is an applicant of his own Kanya-Kubja group. Or if he appoints him, he makes him aware of the kind of work expected of him. If the applicant agrees, the officer may appoint him. These precautions are very often necessary because of, what I called above, the "master-servant" cultural image between the administrator and the peon.

The officer expects a peon to be obedient—as obedient as he would like his domestic servant to be. He assumes the roles of master rather than an official superior. It is especially apparent when he is administratively capable of hiring or firing the peon. However, if the officer-peon relationship has remained smooth, the peon—like a good domestic servant—may pass on to earning a pseudo-kin appellation of "uncle," or "brother" from the officer's family members. In such cases, a peon's interests are "protected" by the officer and he becomes a de facto "servant" of the officer.

These remarks help us to observe that state officers and their offices also have an informal ethos conditioned by the sociocultural systems of modern India and that a Kanya-Kubja caste sabha and its officers reflect only a specific aspect of this conception. However, the difference is of the degree of elaboration of formal vis-à-vis informal dimensions, and of the emphasis of rational versus religious bases.

BUREAUCRATIC IMPERSONALITY: PROMOTING AND PREVENTING SITUATIONS

Since these aspects—especially the way they combine—are topics of continuous social anthropological discussion, and since they relate directly to the organizational nature of a modern sabha, we shall study them in detail broadly around the problem of bureaucratic impersonality. The Weberian ideal (1962, p. 5) lays down that ". . . the administrator proceeds *sine ira et studio,* not allowing personal motive or temper to influence conduct, free of arbitrariness and unpredictability; especially he proceeds 'without regard to person,' following rational rules with strict formality." However, Weber allowed for "functional" considerations of expediency for actuality. The Indian administrator tries to approach the Weberian ideal, but most often through the latter provision. His conception of "expediency" may again have important sociocultural biases.

Thus an administrator finds, consciously or unconsciously, some useful traditional behavioral elements for reinforcing his bureaucratic impersonality. Age seniority is a specially important cultural category. It signifies an increase in one's power, prestige, and privileges. An old administrator is supposed to be reserved and sober in his behavior, and effective, efficient, and strict in his official norms and duties. He inspires awe and respect. He is obeyed, and his words are taken at their face value. He avails the privilege of being curt and cold towards an unjust demand. He can reprimand a youth, even if the latter is of the same bureaucratic rank. All such prerogatives acquired through age help him if he wants to be officially impersonal in his behavior. Age brings experience and wisdom to him according to the cultural norm. He does not have to be ostentatious in his drawing room. His simplicity only enhances the age charisma, and his relatives also feel it. If the administrator happens to be old as well as religious, both aspects may reinforce his bureaucratic impersonality on religious and moral grounds. He may symbolize "integrity," which is both morally as well as administratively desirable. These two schemes may produce a functionally useful overlap, and kin and caste susceptibilities for favoritism may be minimized under this conception of age, seniority, and morality.

However, as I noted earlier, there is a related opposite conception—the other side of the same coin. One's age, seniority, and adeptness in bureaucratic intricacies may prompt him to accommodate kin and caste susceptibilities "without the infraction of a major rule." The motivation for this may again be cultural. Here, old age may be taken as a symbol of an extended "paternal" attitude towards one's caste and kin members. The latter's welfare is a concern of the administrator as a caste elite, who has acquired wealth, power, and fame only to *share* them with his people. As a part of this cultural theme may appear the erosion of his impersonality. Obviously, both of these aspects of age and seniority combine together in reality, one promoting impersonality and the other preventing it.

Young administrators, on the other hand, may reinforce their impersonality through an emphasis on their educational achievements, and by underplaying (at least initially) caste and kin influences. They may emphasize sophistication instead of simplicity, matter-of-factness instead of "personal approach," and adherence to rules rather than to alternative manipulations. However, in practice their path is not so smooth. When entering an official career, they, under the existing bureaucratic complexity, cannot do without the help of those already experienced. They are told what the official rules are, what the informal norms and normals are, and what the cultural behavioral patterns are. The young administrators are slowly but surely initiated into these three versions of the office. A successful officer must handle all three together. The older crew of the organization molds him to recognize the reality. His bureaucratic impersonality also adapts and accommodates accordingly. As an individual officer, he soon learns to formulate his own safe ways in the office; and in doing so, he acquires conceptions about it.

But young or old, an Indian administrator does inject the traditional gifts-goods-service exchange complex into his official position. Favor between officers takes after kinship reciprocity. If he received a favor from an office colleague, a family friend, or a kin, he tries to return it even if it may sometimes mean exercising his official influence (see the case study below). There is also moral pressure to comply to this norm. As a cultural ideal, humility and self-effacement are the appropriate behavioral values for a modern administrator. He must not be vocal about what he has done for others.

ORGANIZATIONAL RESOURCES AND THEIR RELATION TO BUREAUCRATIC IMPERSONALITY

The above general discussion of bureaucratic impersonality may now be examined more closely against the field data on the Kanya-Kubjas. This will help us to elaborate on their organizational resources and their relations to bureaucratic imperson-ality. The emphasis will be on actual social conditions.

We shall begin by substantiating the observation that kinship and modern administrative roles provide, at least potentially, a wide-ranging, multilateral, network of interpersonal influence. Both together provide a valuable "organizational resource" to depend on. When in need, the persons in this kinship web can approach their relatives who carry appropriate administrative influences. Hence, the greater the diversity of modern occupations pursued, the more valuable will be the resource potential of a particular caste group.

In order to illustrate this potential for the Kanya-Kubjas, see the series of genealogical figures (8 to 10) and their respective tables (11–13), representing overlapping fields of kinship influence dispersed across several states. The data for this presentation were collected through field interviews (1965 and 1966) and through a systematic plotting of kinship relations of the Kanya-Kubja families enumerated in biographic, marital, and death accounts published in the pages of *Kanya-Kubja* (chiefly 1963–67). My field data mostly corroborated the documentary evidence. The information given is mainly about prestigious families and their relatives, underscoring the point that an elite's relatives tend to occupy diverse prestigious occupations, and hence they constitute an active field of seeking and offering "favors" (see the "boxes" in figures 8 to 10). Administrative power and kinship solidarity functionally reinforce each other under this pattern. But since kinship solidarity is stronger than sabha-induced cohesiveness, a Kanya-Kubja sabha officer may frequently be found to rely on his kin administrator for a sabha work.

The purpose of these figures and tables is to present the diversity of occupations and geographic regions bridged by the overlapping extension of the kinship web; this is shown by means of various types of "boxes" (a to g) demarcating zones of family influence. These figures and tables give us an idea of the Kanya-Kubja resources and their use in a number of cases. The data also indicate the Kanya-Kubja's capacity for keeping track of their relatives and knowing who to contact for a particular type of favor and how to reciprocate it appropriately.

175

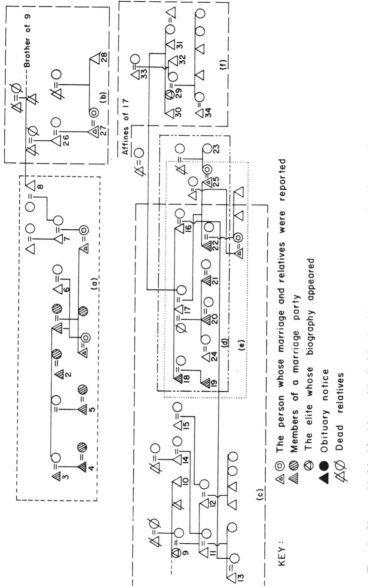

KEY:

△◎ The person whose marriage and relatives were reported

△ Members of a marriage party

⊘ The elite whose biography appeared

▲● Obituary notice

△⊘ Dead relatives

Fig. 8. Kanya-Kubja kinship and individual achievement—an overlapping modern resource.

TABLE 11

ELITES AND NON-ELITES SHOWN IN FIGURE 8

Occupation	Place
1. Sales manager (private)	Calcutta
2. Director, textile mills	Amritsar, Punjab
3. Unkn. (business inference)	Calcutta
4. Regional manager (privtae)	Delhi
5. Major	Calcutta
6. Superintendent of police	Merrut, Uttar Pradesh
7. Navy captain, ret. (now in Calcutta)	Jabalpur, Madhya Pradesh
8. Deputy collector, ret.	Lucknow
9. Barrister-at-law	Lucknow
10. Businessman	Lucknow
11. Unkn.	Lucknow
12. Unkn.	Lucknow
13. Unkn.	Lucknow
14. Unkn.	Lucknow
15. Superintendent of post offices	Lucknow
16. Managing director, cooperative bank	Shahjehanpur, Uttar Pradesh
17. Editor of *Kanya-Kubja*	Lucknow
18. Unkn.	unkn., Uttar Pradesh
19. Unkn.	unkn., Uttar Pradesh
20. Teacher	Lucknow
21. Teacher	Lucknow
22. Teacher	Lakhimpur-Kheri, Uttar Pradesh
23. Assistant editor of a journal	Bombay
24. Physician	Sitapur, Uttar Pradesh
25. Unkn.	unkn., Uttar Pradesh
26. Lieutenant colonel	Lucknow
27. Sales manager, Tata Industries	Jamshedpur, Bihar
28. Labor inspector	Kanpur
29. College professor	Kanpur
30. Physician (Ayurvedic)	Kanpur
31. Agriculturist	Banda, Uttar Pradesh
32. Physician	Aligarh, Uttar Pradesh
33. Physician	Aligarh, Uttar Pradesh
34. College professor	Gonda, Uttar Pradesh

SOURCE: biographies and reports of marriages in *Kanya-Kubja* (1964–66, vols. 57–59).

These contacts remain at the interpersonal level, and underscore the dynamics between class and kinship. They are mostly between any two caste elites or between an elite and a common caste member. However, there is some form of "alienation" between the latter pair (cf. Shils 1961, pp. 67ff.), growing out of economic status disparity (although within the continuing unity

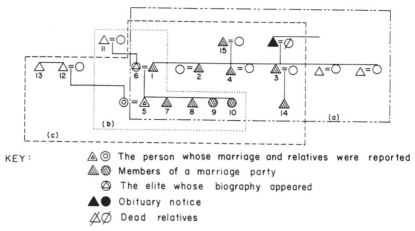

KEY:

⚐ ◎ The person whose marriage and relatives were reported
⚐ ⬟ Members of a marriage party
⬤ The elite whose biography appeared
▲ ● Obituary notice
⧄ ⊘ Dead relatives

FIG. 9. Kanya-Kubja kinship and individual achievement—an over-lapping modern resource.

TABLE 12

ELITES AND NON-ELITES SHOWN IN FIGURE 9

Occupation	Place
1. Head clerk, government	Gwalior
2. Agriculturist and trader	Radhan, Uttar Pradesh
3. Agriculturist and trader	Bedipur, Uttar Pradesh
4. Unkn.	unkn.
5. Writer	Gwalior
6. Wife of head clerk (Mahila Ratan)	Gwalior
7. Student	Gwalior
8. Student	Gwalior
9. Student	Gwalior
10. Student	Gwalior
11. Agriculturist	Bhind, Uttar Pradesh
12. Unkn.	Lakshmanpur, Uttar Pradesh
13. Unkn.	Lakshmanpur, Uttar Pradesh
14. Unkn.	unkn.
15. Unkn.	unkn.

SOURCE: biographies, obituaries, and reports of marriages in *Kanya-Kubja* (1963, vol. 56, and 1965, vol. 58).

along the kinship lines). Kanya-Kubja elites tend to cluster to-gether, maritally as well as socially, according to those inform-ants who were low on economic status and had several daughters of marriageable age. Their conceptions are somewhat substan-tiated if we examine the tables and the kinship genealogies compiled on the basis of marital accounts. Generally, the rich are found to establish marital alliances with their own kind.

This incentive is responsible for producing kinship cohesiveness along class status lines, sometimes even at the cost of intracaste ritual hierarchy. For example, a rich family of 20 Biswā established alliances with low Biswā but rich families of Raipur, Indore, Saugar, and Jabalpur in Madhya Pradesh. The family decided to establish these marital bonds because it was impossible to find comparably well-employed bridegrooms for the same size of dowry within Uttar Pradesh, where the competition is severe and the choices are limited, and hence the dowry demands are higher. The genealogical diagrams above illustrate the resultant geographic spread of the kinship network of these elites.

But economic status disparities are most often bridged by kinship rights and obligations, especially after a marital alliance is established between a rich and a poor family. For example, a rich elite of Lucknow married his son into a poor family because the girl was beautiful and his son wanted to marry her. After marriage, the elite had helped the daughter-in-law's family in several ways. Two younger brothers of the bride received their college education by residing at the elite's residence. They were helped to become employed in good jobs and were ultimately married into rich families—all owing to the contacts with the elite's family. Thus economically lower families share the resources of the rich to become rich themselves, swelling the ranks of caste elites.

Despite intracaste kinship solidarity and wide-ranging administrative resources (as shown in the previous diagrams), the appropriation of one's official position is restrained by several factors. For example, not all relatives who are officers are actually available for (or agreeable to) an appropriate administrative favor. Second, an administrator's influence is almost always incomplete for the accomplishment of a state favor. This is because a modern bureaucratic office is composed of different officers of different caste and communities, and a Kanya-Kubja officer may help complete only a fraction of the formal procedure that may be required, for example, for issuing a "newsprint permit" for the caste journal. Third, a modern officer is a subordinate and not an independent agent, he may help only par-

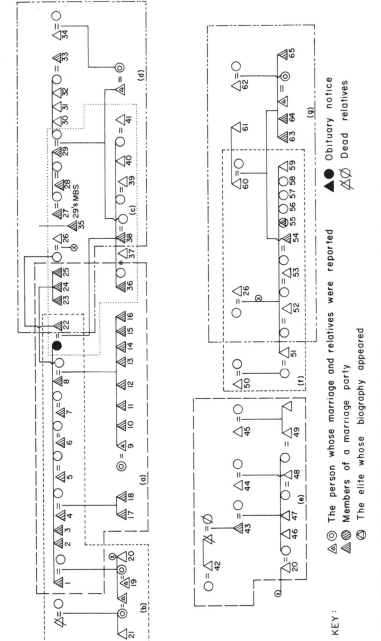

KEY:

△◎ The person whose marriage and relatives were reported

◢◣ Members of a marriage party

◉ The elite whose biography appeared

▲● Obituary notice

△∅ Dead relatives

Fig. 10. Kanya-Kubja kinship and individual achievement—an overlapping modern resource.

TABLE 13

Occupation	Place
1. Chief Justice, ret.	Lucknow
2. Additional commissioner, ret.	Lucknow
3. Additional commissioner	Lucknow
4. Advocate	Unnao, Uttar Pradesh
5. Unkn.	Lucknow
6. Unkn.	Hafizabad, Uttar Pradesh
7. Lieutenant colonel	unkn.
8. Captain	Lucknow
9. Engineer	Lucknow
10. Unkn.	Lucknow
11. Unkn.	Lucknow
12. Unkn.	Lucknow
13. Engineer	Lucknow
14. Unkn.	Lucknow
15. Engineer	Lucknow
16. Unkn.	Lucknow
17. Unkn.	Unnao, Uttar Pradesh
18. Unkn.	Unnao, Uttar Pradesh
19. Mining engineer	unkn.
20. Unkn.	Lucknow
21. Lieutenant colonel	Kanpur
22. Member of Board of Revenue, ret.	Gwalior
23. Unkn.	unkn.
24. Assistant commissioner, food and civil supply	unkn.
25. Unkn.	unkn.
26. Military physician	Lucknow
27. Unkn.	New Delhi
28. Unkn.	New Delhi
29. Labor commissioner	Jaipur, Rajasthan
30. Deputy secretary (I.A.S.)	New Delhi
31. Personnel officer, electricity	unkn.
32. College lecturer	Gwalior
33. Joint secretary (I.A.S.)	Delhi
34. Proprietor of a shop	Delhi
35. Banker	Saugar, Madhya Pradesh
36. Physician	Gwalior
37. Indian Police Service	unkn.
38. Physician	Gwalior
39. University professor	unkn.
40. Unkn.	Gwalior
41. Physician	unkn.
42. Physician	Lucknow
43. University professor	Banaras, Uttar Pradesh
44. University professor	Allahabad, Uttar Pradesh
45. Judge, ret.	unkn.
46. Working for private firm	Calcutta

TABLE 13 (Cont.)

Occupation	Place
47. Physician	Delhi
48. Unkn.	Allahabad, Uttar Pradesh
49. Unkn.	unkn.
50. Unkn.	Katni, Madhya Pradesh
51. Officer in panchāyat department	Lucknow
52. Advocate	unkn.
53. University professor	Naini Tal, Uttar Pradesh
54. Advocate	Gwalior
55. University lecturer	Lucknow
56. Woman teacher	Lucknow
57. Woman teacher	Lucknow
58. Woman teacher	Lucknow
59. Student	Lucknow
60. Physician (Ayurvedic)	Gwalior
61. Physician (Ayurvedic)	Kanpur
62. Unkn.	Kanpur
63. Engineer	Gwalior
64. Physician	Gwalior
65. Unkn.	Gwalior

SOURCE: biographies, obituaries, and reports of marriages in *Kanya-Kubja* (1963–67, vols. 56–60).

tially. Fourth, many so-called favors may be a part of one's official duty. For example, a Kanya-Kubja, instead of proceeding through the regular channels (which takes time), approached his distant nephew at a bank's teller counter and handed him his check for payment. After "paper formalities" or on the basis of "personal confidence" the nephew saw to it that his uncle got the money within minutes. Later in the same day, the nephew completed the formalities and entered the check into the bank's books.

Thus although in the tables (11–13) and figures (8–10) kinship appears as a much stronger factor within and across several families, it may only seldom override the considerations of administrative propriety. No major infraction of official duties may be allowed, especially those that can threaten one's job. No Kanya-Kubja, however devoted to his caste welfare, will jeopardize his occupational position, because it brings bread to him and his family and because it maintains his prized social prestige. Caste and culture will not back him for doing a dishonest "welfare act." As I noted elsewhere, gross favoritism would be culturally dishonest and immoral. It would not be for promoting caste solidarity.

In a recent case a Kanya-Kubja employee who misappropriated money from a Kanya-Kubja educational institution to fulfill certain kinship obligations was censured by his kith and kin, by his father-in-law as well as his own parents and brothers. The latter, who held influential positions in the administration of the educational institution, did not come to his rescue to reinstate him in his position. Even his wife did not plead with her father for an administrative favor, although being rich, her father rendered financial support to his son-in-law as long as he remained unemployed (for about two years). The favor was done, however, in another form. His case of misappropriation (the third time in one decade) did *not* lead either to his legal prosecution or arrest or his permanent dismissal from the position. He was, however, required to quietly return all of the missing money to the institution within three days of the notice. His rich father-in-law did that promptly. Moreover, he was removed from a position where he was responsible for dealing with the finances.

This case concerned a private caste-sponsored organization, yet it showed the way bureaucratic impersonality receives support from traditional sources. Legal sanctions are, however, comparatively severe when state organizations are involved. The law may take its own course, although in such cases caste and kin influences may again begin to operate to at least "soften" the punishment. Expert legal advice may be arranged by one's kin, and financial help may be rendered. But in a state case, flexibility is extremely limited, and caste and kin influences rarely succeed as much as under private enterprise. For example, in a case in 1958 Kanya-Kubja influence did keep one of them from going to the jail, although it could not prevent his transfer and demotion, once it was proved the man had taken a bribe in a state office.

The above discussion indicates the limits to which a Kanya-Kubja or any other modern caste member can safely stretch his administrative prerogatives. Bureaucratic impersonality is a necessity of the times, and a modern caste group recognizes the value and validity of it in actual life. The group submits to it in some areas, yet retains its own dominance in certain others. Marriage is the strongest zone of the latter kind, where occupation, economic status, and modern achievements are all subjugated to serve its values and meanings. Excessive kinship de-

183

mands may thus land the caste member in the most dangerous zones of bribery and corruption.

We have above examined the two extremes of "favoritism," one in the inconspicuous case of a bank interaction and the second in a most serious case of misappropriation of official funds in both a private and a state organization. Now we shall elaborate on a case that belongs to the intermediate order and is most conspicuously discussed in modern Indian life.

MODERN INTERJACENCE OF KINSHIP AND OFFICIAL ROLES:
A CASE OF ACHIEVING "STRATEGIC CONNECTIONS"

The following case was recorded as accurately as the field circumstances permitted. It is presented here as an illustration of the complexity of the social network that actually attends an interjacent strategy. Its purpose, however, is not to judge the propriety or impropriety of individual behavior.

The case concerns an urban Kanya-Kubja family of lower economic status. The family head (a common member of a sabha) was employed as a teacher and was supporting the education of his five children—three daughters and two sons. The oldest son (the chief informant) had just taken a university degree. He was considered a good student, and he wanted to study more and enter a "lucrative government job," but his father's economic status did not permit it; and therefore, he began to apply for jobs as soon as he qualified for the university degree (June 1965). His mother and father would inquire of him at least once a week if he had some success in his pursuit. His parents were anxious because they had got his older sister married a year ago (which involved an expenditure of Rs. 15,000), had run up a modest debt, and were supposed to arrange for the marriage of his next sister a year or two after. If he could begin earning in the meanwhile, he would be of some relief to them. On the other hand, he would also acquire some freedom in deciding how best to plan on his career.

As he apprehended, most of his applications were turned down by the beginning of September of 1965. Since the academic session started in July, he was late in registering for college, and thus was greatly apprehensive that he might waste a year doing nothing. He was now convinced that merely applying for a job would not assure his acceptance. At his behest his mother began to induce his father (my other informant for the case) to approach some relatives who were better placed and who could possibly help him in getting at least a temporary job. By the end of September, these approaches were intensive enough to move his father to action. Although his father thought it humiliating to appear before a younger cousin (father's sister's son), who was a district engineer, to ask for help in finding employment for his son, he decided to take a chance. But the lead failed because the engineer was in the process of getting transferred to another place; however, he suggested that he could try to help his son after a couple of months. More such hit-and-miss attempts were made, but nothing concrete happened. His father was more and more worried and disgusted, and so was he.

On 20 October 1965 the informant and his parents went to the tonsure ceremony of his young cousin (mother's brother's son). Since his mother's younger brother lived in the same town, they spent the whole day at their house. His mother's brother was a head clerk in a local government office; but, as the informant observed, he was very active and resourceful. After the ceremony when the other guests had left and when his father and maternal uncle sat down for the evening meal, his maternal aunt, who came to serve the food, mentioned "Lallā's" (a nickname of the informant) employment problem to her husband. (The informant had earlier overheard that his mother and aunt were talking about him in the kitchen.) His maternal uncle thought for a while and then suggested several names of caste and non-caste people who could be of help. His father responded by telling him whether he knew these persons or not. They talked for about fifteen minutes and then retired into the drawing room pursuing the same subject. Soon after, his maternal uncle (2a in figure 11) mentioned a caste elite who was a commissioner in the state government (and an executive committee member of a caste sabha) and who could, if properly approached, certainly do something about Lallā's unemployment. But to the informant's father it was a practically impossible suggestion because the elite was neither directly related to him nor to any of his near kin, nor could he recall that he knew any of the elite's acquaintances or close relatives. But the informant's maternal uncle counseled patience and persistence, with the assurance: "I will find a suitable link."

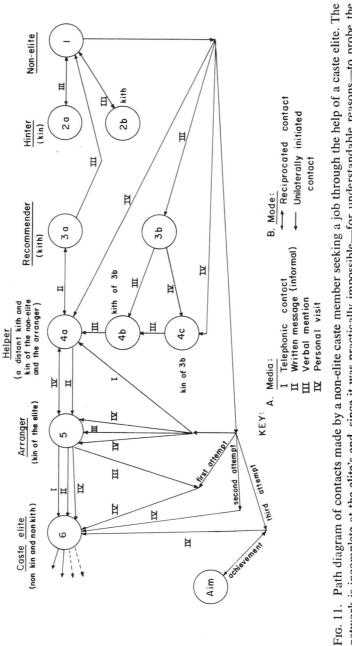

Fig. 11. Path diagram of contacts made by a non-elite caste member seeking a job through the help of a caste elite. The network is incomplete at the elite's end, since it was practically impossible—for understandable reasons—to probe the administrative elite for the communication network he used to accomplish the favor.

On 23 October his maternal uncle visited his house and brought a "lead" about a local (which he got while talking to another Kanya-Kubja in his office) prestigious Kanya-Kubja (4a) who was also an affinal relative of the commissioner's brother (5).

The informant's father, in the meantime, had independently made two contacts—both were the Kanya-Kubjas (2b and 3a) of the same *mohallā* (neighborhood), but were otherwise unrelated. The first contact was fruitless as this neighbor could not suggest any concrete "route" through which the informant's father should have proceeded. The second person (3a), a registrar in the local high court, was more useful. He agreed to send a written message to his friend (4a) explaining the nature of help that the informant's father wanted. The registrar did this because he had secured his son's school admission through the influence of the informant's father (1) and because they had been good neighbors for about a decade.

This written message, or "letter of introduction," formed the basis of the initial contact when the informant's father visited (4a) at his house personally on 27 October. But simultaneously (1) also met another unrelated caste member (3b), who put him in contact with one of his own relatives (4c), a store manager in the Railways and an acquaintance of (4a). This person (3b) did this by verbally mentioning to (4c) and a friend (4b) about the job problem of the informant. As a consequence of these initial contacts, the informant's father personally visited both (4a) and (4c). The latter contact was made on 26 October to intensify the pressure on (4a), but during the course of his visit to (4a) on 27 October, he found out that (4a) was his distant relative also: "[4a] was something like my fourth degree cousin, which we began to suspect once we discovered that our purushā [ancestors] belonged to the same susthān [geographic location]. Our great, great grandfathers were brothers; and one of them is even entered in the genealogies we possess," observed the informant's father at the time of this interview (April 1966). Once this link was discovered, the worry of dealing with (5), a successful lawyer, was almost solved. As the chart shows, the informant's father made one telephone contact with his distant relative (4a) to request him to pay a personal visit to (5), and it was done. After a fortnight (4a) also wrote a letter to (5).

Within these fifteen days, the informant and his father were also advised to meet (5) personally at his home, since personal visits carry more moral weight and since (5) was the person who would actually, as a kin of the caste elite, prepare the background and arrange the meeting between the elite and the informant's father. This preparation period lasted for about one and a half months (until the beginning of January 1966), during which the informant's father visited (5) at his home twice and once talked to him about his son's job when they met each other in the market place. During the same period, (5) made three main contacts with his elite relative for that purpose.

His first contact was by telephone and the caste elite agreed to meet the informant's father in his drawing room. When the latter first visited the elite's house, the outcome was practically nothing. Though he "was appropriately received after waiting for fifteen minutes," he was advised that his son should actually aim to compete and qualify for some all-Indian government service. Even when told about the circumstances of the family and other details, the elite did not strike a very hopeful note. He, however, suggested in passing that the son should check with his office staff whether "the department" is going to have some suitable openings and whether he (the son) would qualify for them. The informant's father returned dissatisfied, yet the informant got some line to explore by himself. Once he found out that there were going to be some suitable openings for recruitment, hope kindled further. The pressure on (5) mounted through (4a); and as consequence, he wrote a letter to the elite, telling him in detail about the informant's father, about his impressions of the informant and his father, and about the familial necessities. During their second visit to the elite, the informant recollected, "fortunately, we came to know that I should apply right away in order to be among the first for official recommendation." He applied within two days and was interviewed. When the interview notice was received, a final effort was made by both (5 and 1). Since (5) was going to visit the caste elite's house on invitation at about the same time, he thought he would mention the informant's case informally and would ascertain the elite's reaction. The talks occurred in front of the elite's family members in the inner courtyard, and the outcome was hopeful according to (5), "because the son's educational record was good enough."

On knowing this, the informant and his father paid a third home-visit to the elite. After a month's time the informant was selected for the position where he was working in April 1966, when this interview was conducted.

When asked to comment on why he thought his son was selected, the informant's father answered:

> I think it was both my son's good academic credentials and a helpful attitude of the caste elite. The latter was not spontaneously produced, it came out of the right approach and appropriate contacts. I thank God the efforts were successful, although I was unsure. Sometimes, I thought that all these connections could end in fiasco and disgrace for me. If I had an alternative, I would not have done all this. Now I stand in a series of obligations of several good friends and relatives, which must be reciprocated. For the near relatives, it is no problem; but for the distant, I will have to go out of my way to return the obligations I have taken.

The informant himself thought that both the caste elite's sympathetic attitude and his own educational performance had worked in getting him the job. Though he did not think that he stood in the same chain of obligations as his father, he did emphasize that should his father fail to return the obligations, it was his moral duty to return the favors to all those who had actually helped him (and not his father). When asked why his father took all these initiatives and obligations and not he himself, his answer was: "As long as my father is alive, it is he who is known among the kith and kin. I am known through him. My independence comes either when I have earned special fame through my achievements, or when my father is no more."

The maternal uncle, who initiated the idea was given a box of sweets on the same evening the informant received his letter of appointment. The informant's family members visited the uncle's place that evening after visiting a temple. Another box of sweets was taken to (4a). The informant's father personally went to thank him and presented the sweets.

When asked about taking help from his affinal relatives, the informant's father observed that normally one first seeks help from his agnates because one has more rights over their services. "But now I have no particular qualms over such matters, and I tell my brother-in-law the same thing. If I can help him, he comes to me; if he can help me, he never stays back. Rather, I would think that my affines care better for us because they are not expected or obligated to do so. We have wonderful relations among ourselves."

Figure 11, the path diagram showing the network of contacts, intermediaries, and consequences, examines the social relations that appear when a nonkin caste elite is approached by a non-elite for some specific favor. Though the figure shows the plotting done for a specific case, it betrays, I believe, some general characteristics that are found in such contacts. The "intermediaries," classified as hinter, recommender, helper, arranger in the figure, are most usually found in such contacts, although these roles may be taken over by one or more persons. Simplification may occur when a caste elite happens to be a fast friend or kin of the non-elite. Besides kinship, "class-fellow" friendship, or the bond of belonging to the same village, or neighborhood are the most common bases that may be recalled to strengthen the influence of an elite. (These patterns can be found to work at intercaste levels also, between an elite and a non-elite, or among the elites themselves.)

The figure also shows that, generally speaking, "verbal mention," informal written message, telephonic contact (expressing "urgency"), and personal visits are successively stronger media of exerting influence. Visiting an elite's residence is more influential than meeting him in his office or anywhere else. Repeated telephonic contact is more accepted elite technique of expressing or influencing vital decisions. It is an informal yet forceful medium for initiating as well as pursuing interpersonal links. All important contacts seem to culminate in home visits, as they are the most informal but culturally most influential means for approaching an elite.

SUMMARY AND SOME GENERAL IMPLICATIONS

Some specific and general implications of this chapter can now be summarized:

1. Since the sabhas are caste-restrictive, microcosmic, disparate, localized, and noncentralized organizations with limited and almost stagnant, economic and organizational resources, their organization is rudimentary and their contacts with state bureaucracy are as much limited as their actual formal necessi-

ties. Whatever the latter are, they are mostly satisfied by keeping their papers in order. Only rarely may the sabha organizers be required to interact directly and formally with the state offices.

2. Whenever such contacts are made, they may mostly be backed by intracaste, interpersonal recommendations. As a sabha secretary explained: "When a state office job is to be done, I approach a suitable caste or executive committee elite and leave it up to him to do it or not. Most often, he does it, or he gives a strong reference in the state office who can perform the job quickly. This saves both time and money. Without a recommendation, it takes months. Once we have the proper reference the job is done quickly, because we, of course, are not trying to do anything illegal or against the state rules."

3. Traditional structures may promote as well as prevent official impersonality—a feature which can be generalized for traditional societies. Bureaucratic impersonality is reinforced because it is conceived as culturally synonymous with "honesty." It is a matter of morals and virtue, and modern survival rather than the "mere rationality" of a modern organization, as Weber proposed. An administrator even as a caste member must establish his ethical standards of occupational behavior. The limited expression of his positional influence for a caste member (as exemplified in the above cases) is appreciated—rather, praised —but gross improprieties are denounced.

4. Therefore, caste and kinship sentiment is not a "free passport" for gaining a concrete administrative favor. Even if the relatives evoke sympathy, it may be so only for limited purposes and favorable circumstances. Normally, an administrative favor does not mean contravention of official requirements, as illustrated by the case study. One disposes "favors" mostly within rules and their alternative interpretations.

5. The discussion also suggests that at the intracaste level the feeling of "casteism" is practically confined to individuals. Among the Kanya-Kubjas there is *no* organized channelization of this feeling in any recognizable form. If the caste sabha promotes it, it is either so feeble or so diffuse that it slips back into individual cases. The overall feeling of a common Kanya-Kubja is thus different: "Our caste is most disorganized. My fellow caste member may help any other caste man, but us."

6. At the intracaste level, "caste" is cancelled out as a com-

mon denominator of all the participating members. The emphasis is, instead, on kith and kin bonds, differentiated in terms of economic status, residence, propinquity, and esprit de corps.

7. Mutatis mutandis, the Weberian characteristic of *sine ira et studio* is applicable to and maintained by the Kanya-Kubjas occupying modern occupations. But they do so in their own ways which become clear at the intensive level of analysis. Their styles emphasize their cultural background. It seems to lie in managing the caste and kinship pulls along with modern occupational demands in a way that links modernity to a system of meaning and cultural ethos. Under this system one component is always in readiness to relieve the pressure of the other when it encounters obstacles, with the consequence that there is nothing like an untractable situation, but one clearing the way for the other. This is what I mean by strategic interjacence. Without an *auto-da-fé* on the altar of modern organizations, a Kanya-Kubja remains both an administrator and a Kanya-Kubja Brahman.

8. The Kanya-Kubja elites, who actually run the caste sabhas, show both wide ranging occupational familiarity with bureaucratic organization as well as their continuing capacity to deal with sabha and office as two conceptually distinct bodies that are not to be indiscriminately transposed in actuality. In ideology, in content, and in practice, the two are appropriately kept distinct but interlinked.

9. Organizationally, therefore, a sabha is different and more formalized than any traditional or kinship group, but less than any private or state office. Although it has all the major bureaucratic characteristics represented, they are there for very limited purposes. Their expression is most usually on paper—in records, minutes, and financial books. In actuality and in Kanya-Kubja conception, a sabha is *not* a "bureaucratic organization" (for a case study proposing an opposite view, see Fox 1967). The latter is a necessary modern "overlay" on basic caste, kinship, and traditional modes of interpersonal organization.

Conclusion

9 Review
and Reformulation

IN SUMMARIZING and restating the results of this study, I should like to proceed in terms of the dimensions and dynamics of institutional and organizational behavior that I referred to briefly in chapter 1. There the possible consequences of these on the elaboration or nonelaboration of the Kanya-Kubja sabhas was noted. Following this broad framework, I presented the data for this study in two forms: one by giving the descriptive details about the organizational aims, activities, and achievements of the Kanya-Kubja sabhas, and, two, by presenting an extended discussion of their institutional-organizational dynamics, especially through such bases as status stratification, formal organization, and elite participation. This chapter will summarize and compare the main themes of this study by proceeding as follows: first, I shall briefly restate my conclusions concerning the organizational characteristics of the Kanya-Kubja sabhas. Second, since some aspects of their organization (especially stratification, bureaucracy, and caste elites) seem to be common to other such sabahs in India, and since their elaboration varies with different castes, I shall briefly compare the Kanya-Kubja data with some recent studies. This should help answer the second question that was posed in chapter 1: "Why are the sabhas as they are?" Then, finally, I shall reformulate some particular as well as general characteristics of the Kanya-Kubja sabhas as "modern" organizations.

SOME CHARACTERISTICS OF KANYA-KUBJA CASTE SABHAS

As the previous chapters have described, the Kanya-Kubja sabhas as noncentralized (i.e., with no central/peripheral administrative set-up), microcosmic (i.e., with only local influence), nonexhaustive (i.e., not each and every Kanya-Kubja belongs to a sabha), nonexclusive (i.e., one can belong simultaneously to more than one sabha), "closed" (i.e., a member can be recruited *only if* he belongs to the caste group), and mutually cooperative (i.e., the sabhas even as independent units are more inclined to cooperate than compete at the intracaste level) caste bodies. However, with reference to other caste groups they may notionally show a tendency of competition, unaccompanied by any stable or organized effort (cf. Bailey 1963a). All known sabhas have two organizational dimensions: the formalized end that is represented by a set of bureaucratic "officers," and the other, the informal or the kinship end, represented by such "networks" as have been shown in the last chapter. Both dimensions appear simultaneously and produce complementary accommodation. A sabha is, therefore, less formalized than a state office but more so than any traditional structure. All these sabhas are nonranked among themselves, but their members are ranked along a multiplex scale of ascriptive as well as achieved variables. These bodies are elite-sponsored and elite-run organizations.

These sabhas function primarily (a) to help observe the rules of marital and kinship norms, (b) to undertake caste welfare and education, and (c) to help achieve individual advancement. The first function is caste specific and is a product of particular social and historical circumstances under which this caste group has progressed over the last one hundred years. Particularly important for the continuance of their institutional interaction were improved means of communication, new economic and occupational opportunities, preexisting Kanya-Kubja groups outside Uttar Pradesh, and early, gradual, and continuous introduction to Western education. Because of these historical circumstances, these Brahmans learned to come to interface, to transvalue, and to accommodate the Western and the modern with the traditional and the ascriptive. Instead of conflict resulting, they ingeniously produced complementarity in ideas and systems of interaction. The other two functions of the Kanya-Kubja sabhas are common to the general functions of caste associations.

The organization and aims of the Kanya-Kubja sabha are shaped by certain social and historical characteristics of the caste group, most importantly its geographic dispersal for over two centuries (e.g., see Census of India 1891, and District Gazetteers

196

1903–27 of selected districts), its occupational diversity (e.g., see *Kanya-Kubja* 1957; Khare 1966, pp. 234–35; Ghurye 1961, p. 16), its early urban environs (susthāns—original places of concentration), and its early exposure to and successful familiarity with English systems of education and occupation (for a general consideration of the latter on the caste system, see Srinivas 1962, pp. 4 ff.; 1966, pp. 46–88).

As the older *Kanya-Kubja* files record, the learned Kanya-Kubja pundits came in contact with the British quite early in the last century. Their occupational flexibility and ritual orthodoxy attracted and intrigued the British. They enjoyed their confidence soon, and there was rarely negative discrimination. They were introduced to the "new culture" and were among the first in the north who received prestigious administrative, educational, and professional positions in the new British system. As the means of transportation and communication improved, they employed them to consolidate their individual achievements and channelized and expressed them by maintaining kinship cohesiveness. This "manipulation" was possible because they entered into and succeeded in the modern system not by abrupt confrontation and conflict (as lower castes did) but by slow and continuous adaptations and accommodations for what has now been over a century. As the highest Brahman group, these Kanya-Kubjas never organized for caste rank claims. Being of the north, their social status was never collectively threatened as was that of the Brahmans of the south; and they did not engage either in any "protective" or protest politics for mobility, or for modernization.

Such historical conditions help explain why the Kanya-Kubja sabhas reflect flexible emphasis on individual secular achievements on the one hand, and kinship cohesiveness, on the other. At the individual level, Kanya-Kubjas rationalized both traditional, institutionalized demands and modern socioeconomic pressures. They continue to handle them simultaneously through rationalization of modernization processes and deparochialization of Sanskritization and traditionalism. However, the latter tendency does not proceed much further, and the Kanya-Kubja sabhas still remain "involute" (i.e., their social relations are primarily turned towards intracaste kin and kith groups), parochial, and urban-based phenomenon.

Thus the Kanya-Kubja sabhas are characterized by the overlapping areas of traditional caste practices and of modern achievement organizations, but they are truly neither (cf. Rudolph and Rudolph 1960, pp. 8–9; Kothari and Maru 1965, pp. 48–50); and Rudolph 1965a, pp 982 ff.). They emphasize a system of interdependent, complementary expectations (cf. Parsons 1951, p. 15) instead of dichotomies. They emphasize individual occupational prestige and achievements; and thus, they underscore dynamic relations between home and office, and caste and voluntary organizations. The sabhas blur the process of individuation and emphasize traditional "collectivization" for marital and kinship requirements.

Thus these caste sabhas can exclusively be neither bureaucratic offices, nor traditional caste bodies, nor purely competitive economic-interest groupings, nor completely deparochialized social welfare bodies. Diversity of aims and organizational elements probably require that the sabhas behave *as* all of these together. However, one of the aspects may become a matter of contextual emphasis. And this emphasis may vary with both intracaste needs and wider socioeconomic circumstances. As we have seen, the modern Kanya-Kubja sabhas exhibit mainly two areas of such emphasis: occupation and kinship (as against others which may emphasize politics, economic status, caste rank and religion; see, e.g., Hardgrave 1964, 1965, and 1967; Nandi 1965; Rudolph 1961, 1965a, 1965b; Kothari and Maru 1965; and *The Kanara Saraswat* June 1965).

Accordingly, these sabhas are conceived as a "middle range," shifting-commitment type, interjacent organizations (see the preceding chapter). Usually the degree of commitment in an organization varies directly in proportion to the individual and/or group interest security (economic and social) that it offers to its members. As the Kanya-Kubja sabhas exist now, they are unable to offer long-range interests, and do not, accordingly, enjoy enduring commitment from their members. This is because under modern social conditions, if a sabha wants to alienate its caste members from their diverse activities so as to intensify caste cohesiveness, its sentimental appeals will have limited organizational influence, unless, basically speaking, the resource-reward capabilities of this sabha equal or exceed those of the modern occupational and/or power-acquiring systems. Thus if the Kanya-Kubja sabhas and their participants are rated on organizational complexity, the commitment is low;[1] if they are ranked in terms of mutual marital and kinship help, the commitment is definitely higher. Accordingly, the future elaboration of their sabhas is projected in the latter direction (e.g., the decisions for the creation of an all-Indian roster of Kanya-Kubja marriageables, and for a cooperative credit union for financing the dowry demands).

KANYA-KUBJA SABHAS AND THE WIDER CONTEXT

The Kanya-Kubja sabhas, as summed up in the beginning of this chapter, essentially conform to those general features that Rudolph and Rudolph (1967, p. 35) note for all modern caste sabhas:

> ... at the organizational level, the caste association abandons the latent structure of caste for the manifest structure characteristic of voluntary association. It has offices, membership, incipient bureaucratization, publications, and a quasi-legislative process expressed through conferences, delegates, and resolutions. On the other hand, the shared sense of culture, character, and status tend to create solidarity of a higher order than is usually found among more strictly voluntary associations where a multiplicity of social roles and the plurality of members' values and interests tend to dilute the intensity of commitment and identification.

To emphasize these features, the Rudolphs call caste associations "paracommunities." They then go on to find out the general function of caste associations in modern Indian scene: They contribute "to fundamental structural and cultural change by providing an adaptive institution in which traditional and modern social features can meet and fuse. The caste association, a crucial paracommunity for Indian society, is both leveling the sacred and hierarchical caste order and replacing it" (p. 35–36).

When examined against this general function, the Kanya-Kubja

1. This commitment may increase, for example, if a caste sabha was employing full-time, regularly paid, and permanent personnel. With this increase in resource-reward aspects, the sabha may be as good as a "private" social-purpose organization, although it may still not be the same as a business firm, much less a government office (the Kanara Saraswat Brahman sabha approaches this condition).

Various political organizations also tend to vary in terms of such a commitment and the attendant forces for its erosion.

sabhas provide an essentially corroborating example. They perform the function of an adaptive organization in which the tradition and modernity intensely come face to face. However, beyond this similarity, there are important differences of degree. For example, although sabhas have facilitated cultural change, the Kanya-Kubja traditional caste structure has neither been "leveled" nor "replaced" in any perceptible degree. Instead, it has become rigid and demanding because of the "link up" of the hierarchical caste order with the economic "class" status. We have seen that these interrelations are complex, pervasive, and functionally reinforcing and that they date back to pre-British periods. They early faced the conflict between Indian "status" and British contract (for a general idea, see Cohn 1961, pp. 613–28) and gradually devised their own styles of living with the Western conceptions of "work" and "office" (see chapters 5, 6, 7). They do not "fuse" in a Kanya-Kubja sabha; neither do they show a definite trend toward the replacement of one tendency by the other, nor the dispensability of either of them. They come to interface and are strategically interjacent. They are dealt with in one's priority scales (see also Singer 1968, pp. 423–52). Conflicting claims are resolved by evolving adjustment- or alternative-strategies in which both tradition and modernity are amenable to attenuation, emphasis, and accommodation. The capacity to evolve "strategies" is a product of caste history, family socialization, and wider socioeconomic contacts, including exposure to urban living, Western education, and modern occupations.

In the last eighty years, Kanya-Kubjas, with sabhas, have been unable to show any cumulative "fundamental structural" change, especially in the areas of intracaste hierarchy, marital practices, and kinship network. However, on the other hand, modern educational and occupational achievements have become in the same period an indispensable, basic means of earning livelihood and social fame. There is a definite accent on secular achievements, but not for their own sake. It is mostly to attain the prized traditional meanings of social existence.

The Kanya-Kubja Brahmans, though individually well-exposed to modern living, remain organizationally and politically rudimentary. Horizontal mobilization is almost impossible among them since they are so widely scattered and are numerically few. Their successful individual adaptation has not demanded strong political mobilization. In their progress under modernization, countervailing political powers of other castes have never seriously clashed. Accordingly, chances for the political mobilization of the caste remain extremely weak. Instead of accommodating politics with caste and kinship (for a general but useful account, see Easton 1959, pp. 210–62; for a historical account of Indian political scene, see Cohn 1962, pp. 312–20) as the Rudolphs recently (1967) describe for several caste groups, the Kanya-Kubja Brahmans have continuously tried to adjust tradition with their modern achievements of almost a century. Although there could be Kanya-Kubja politicians, there can be no politicized Kanya-Kubja caste under the present caste conditions. Although more and more of these Brahmans are becoming "modernites," they are not doing so by replacing the tradition. Their genius lies in handling these contrarious claims.

ELEMENTS OF SABHA ORGANIZATION

Organizationally, the Kanya-Kubja sabhas simultaneously employ status stratification (see chapters 5, 6, 7) and formal bureaucracy as the most important "means" of collective action. As interacting elements, they produce a range of behavioral complexity mainly owing to: first, the simultaneous employment of intracaste ascriptive hierarchical principles with those of diverse achievements; second, the presence and the simultaneous reckoning of multiple referents of various group levels, values, and relationships; and third, the situational dynamics of all of these dimensions, accommodating the "societal guidance" presented by the Kanya-Kubja elites. In order to understand their organizational specificity, we shall now summarize the three most important bases of sabha interaction: status organization, formal organization, and elite participation.

Status Stratification: A Multiple Reference System

Multiple references[2] determine the expression of status strati-

2. This, of course, covers general sociological connotations of "reference group"—that is, a group with which an individual identifies and whose values he accepts for societal guidance (cf. Etzioni 1967). But the usage here emphasizes the attendant notion of "higher" or "lower," or "superior" or "inferior," and amplifies it to include such references as local, regional, subcultural, and cultural. The latter includes references to the processes and the consequences of modernization, urbanization and Westernization, and so on.

fication for their intended as well as consequent meanings. These references constitute a dimension, which basically organizes itself around the same dichotomy of the institutionalized and the organized, but which, in practice, mostly produces diverse functionally complementary consequences. Kinship and residence, and bureaucracy and "office" are thus, among others, the recurrent, pervasive, and flexible references for the modern Kanya-Kubja positional system. The sabha is neither equivalent to one's residence, nor is it exactly an "office." It is more formal than the former and more informal than the latter. Among the Kanya-Kubjas, the emphasis is again towards informality, although the dividing line may be thin; for example, as pointed out earlier, a caste elite's drawing (living) room is formal enough, though his inner courtyard may not be, for carrying out a sabha meeting. These polarities of kinship and bureaucracy also involve a notion of high or low social prestige. Under the normal secular circumstances and for sabha participation, the bureaucratic prestige of a Kanya-Kubja is considered to be "superior," since it has higher instrumental value today.

The Kanya-Kubjas also relate their internal stratificatory status to locality, region (e.g., western or eastern Uttar Pradesh, or outside of it), "kinship conformity," and Sanskritic values. Those who are nearer to their original places of concentration are higher than those elsewhere in western Uttar Pradesh; the latter being higher to those anywhere within this state, and the last category being higher to those outside of it. Kinship conformity is most importantly reckoned through the strict adherence to marital rules, especially when arranging marriages for one's sisters or daughters. It is, in turn, closely related to, as we have already noted, the reference-set of occupational prestige, material acquisitions, educational and intellectual achievements, and social influence. Both types of reference-sets are further linked up with the systems of Sanskritic themes of karma (action), dharma (religion), and kartavya (duty), whether parochialized at local or group or subgroup levels, or universalized at that of the civilization. Such a multiple reference system operates during interpersonal sabha behavior, when Kanya-Kubja elites ingeniously evolve a system of societal guidance and a series of behavioral "strategies" for caste members for bridging the gulf between the institutional and the organizational.

Formal Sabha Organization: A Strategic Overlay

The second important element of the sabha organization is "incipient" bureaucracy. It is neither as involuntary a condition as "caste birth," nor so unnecessary as to be dispensed with. The Kanya-Kubja sabhas invariably have some kind of "office," mainly as a modern expediency. It is expedient because the sabhas, as legitimate modern organizations, are responsible to and depend upon the state bureaucratic structure. But for Kanya-Kubjas formal office is only a dimension of the organization; it is neither a sabha's raison d'être nor tour de force. Modern expediency controls the elaboration of such "bureaucracies," where the twin processes of bureaucratization and debureaucratization proceed simultaneously (see chapter 8 for examples).

I discussed the parochialization of universalistic bureaucratic rules in chapter 8 in order to underscore the danger that may lie in treating bureaucracy as the most significant, single element for the modern caste sabhas. Sabha bureaucracies are submerged in caste and kinship ethos. Rudolph and Rudolph (1967, p. 65) also note that in modern pluralistic societies "bureaucratic organizations can and often do assume familial qualities [see chapter 3 this volume] in ways that approximate the experiences of those living within transformed primary groups." As they note, blurring of lines between ascriptive and achievement organizations is characteristic not only of India but also of several modern nations.

The sabha bureaucracies are limited bureaucracies at the best. (For an opposite emphasis, see Fox 1967, pp. 575–87.) They mostly involve part-time, unpaid, voluntary, "careerless" work for limited short-range ends. If they totally remove all these "deficiencies," elaborate role differentiations, *change parochial caste aims,* and strictly enforce all the rules of bureaucratic rationality, I suggest that they will no longer be interjacent organizations, and hence no longer sabha organizations capable of evoking either caste-shared activities or sentiments,[3] whether at a local or a regional level. They will be like any special purpose modern

3. Caste sentiment, as a verbalized expression, may seem to be more pervasive and persistent. It is the "we" feeling against that of "they." It is an "expressive" rather than "instrumental" dimension of the caste system; it reflects "status anxiety" (see DeVos 1966, pp. 325–84).

organization. However, such an example of total replacement remains to be found and described in detail.

Thus the sabhas use bureaucracy as a means or resource to a number of appropriate ends. However, if the sabha can accomplish a certain aim (e.g., collecting donations) without "conflicting" bureaucracy and by stressing the traditional religious values of welfare, philanthropy, and punya (pious acts), it will readily do so.

Elite Participants: Modern Strategists of Caste Sabha

With the description of the Kanya-Kubja sabhas and the examination of status stratification and bureaucracy as organizational elements, it became evident that the elites of this caste play a significant role and that they, as expected, present resource-reward relations usually on elite-to-elite and elite-to-non–elite, "noncollective" bases. As illustrated in the last chapter, the actual commitment of these caste-elites in the sabhas must be determined against the actual time, efforts, and money that they invest in them. This alone can allow us to check the verbalization of caste sentiment against its actual conversion or convertibility into individual or group action. Actually, the Kanya-Kubja elites have not shown any significant increase in their sabha commitments. If their support is constant, it has not increased.

Besides economic support, elite participation performs the function of introducing varied incentives for evolving strategies, maneuvers, communication networks, and decision-making procedures for bridging the conceptual "gaps," and for creating an appropriate apparatus of "societal guidance" (see Etzioni 1967, pp. 173–87) for handling the institutional as well as the bureaucratic demands of the modern sabha. As modern organizers they develop and handle the sabha's contacts with complex organizations, including state offices that form a "nonkinship" type segment. (However, both must be organized through the caste sabhas so as to maximally achieve certain economic, religious, social, and political ends. Since these ends are now generally spelled out in relation to wider extra-caste societal resources, they become competing aims.) The nonkinship segment of a caste group often presents such caste members who, practically speaking, may be as much "strangers" to a particular individual in certain matters as anybody outside his caste. If these strangers are known by a previous acquaintance or friendship, they become kith, sometimes of the same order as anybody else from outside the caste. In practice, as we saw in the last chapter, these relations are not so simply expressed.

The concept of kith is not well developed in modern social anthropological studies, although it is especially useful in studying informal aspects of modern organizational behavior. A kith can be either from one's own caste or from any other, as it most generally refers to acquaintances, or friends, or neighbors, usually sharing a locality, a language, and a body of cultural and economic activities. But kith may also form an endogamous group (*Random House Dictionary* 1967). Under the latter connotation, kith may be used to mean only those who come from a single caste group. For my present needs, the restricted meaning will be followed (friends or acquaintances outside the caste, then, may not be called kith).

Conceptually, friends or acquaintances of one's own caste may be regarded as "closer" than those belonging to another group. Actually, this consideration may become so diffuse or even imperceptible that it may lose its significance for a geographically dispersed group. For the modern Kanya-Kubja Brahmans the actual situation approaches nearer to the latter condition. Distantly situated Kanya-Kubjas have to interact more with noncaste members of their locality, since there are very few caste members present. Hence most often caste sentiment is dysfunctional for them. They substitute it with their positional rank and solicit help on that basis. But if kith and kin are available, as I noted in chapters 7 and 8, as caste representatives they become competitors at intercaste levels and societal guides for the caste group. They illustrate through their behavioral styles what is traditionally "proper" for modern claims, and vice versa.

A COMPARATIVE EVALUATION

At the beginning of the discussion on the caste sabha in chapter 1, I noted the lack of published intensive studies. The existing published sources that deal directly with caste sabhas are very few, while fragmentary aspects of organizational behavior may be found in anthropologists' continuing descriptions of "caste mobility."[4] Most of such caste mobility references are quite inadequate for a systematic intensive comparison, and, accordingly, the latter must wait for further publication of intensive studies. The purpose of this section, therefore, remains limited. It is to place the major themes of this study in a roughly comparative perspective.

The following comparative account is presented in terms of what I find as recurrently discussed aspects of the Indian caste sabha organizations.[5] However, neither the uniformity nor the coverage of variations in size and complexity of the sabhas seem to be sufficiently accounted to make any general claims at the all-Indian level. Here the comparison is presented to underscore an interrelated conceptual scheme for understanding the organization of sabhas.

Levels of Organization: Panchāyat, Sabha, Federation

The modern caste sabha discussion must be explicated from a related but different level of organization—the traditional caste panchāyats (see Nandi 1965; Sangave 1962; Fox 1967). After briefly surveying the aims and activities of ten caste associations ranging from that of the Daivadnya Brahmans to the Scheduled caste of Matangs from Kolhapur city of Maharashtra, Sangave

4. The meaning and dimensions of the latter may range from specific processes or actions found responsible for maintaining or enhancing one's intra- or inter-caste ascriptive ranks to organized or collectivized politicized protest movements. However, their main concern seems to have been stratification, ascribed and achieved. And this aspect, as we have seen, overlaps also with the organizational behavior of the caste sabhas. (For a recent summary statement on "caste mobility," see Marriott 1968; Singer and Cohn 1968, pp. 189–240.)

5. I shall confine myself mostly to the following recent studies: Fox 1967 and Nandi 1965 for Uttar Pradesh or north India; Rudolph 1960, Rudolph 1961, Rudolph 1965, and Hardgrave 1964, 1965, 1966, 1967, for Kerala and south India; Kapadia 1962, Sangave 1962, and *The Kanara Saraswat* 1964 for Maharashtra; Kothari and Maru 1965 for Gujarat; Leach 1960, Ghurye 1961, Bailey 1963a and 1963b, and Srinivas 1966 for some general issues specifically related to caste associations. Rudolph and Rudolph (1967) produce a most comprehensive macrosociological survey of these bodies, primarily from political science perspectives. These have been chosen because they tell us about the details and/or the status of caste associations found today. This choice is also indicative of both the beginning stage of the specific discussion of the sabha as organizations of sociopolitical behavior, and the disparate nature of conceptual considerations they have been accorded. Naturally, no claims are made about the representativeness of available complexity or diversity in India in this area.

(1962, p. 58) concluded that "the caste *panchāyat* is preserved in a modified form by introducing the principle of election in constituting the panchāyat or the Managing Committee of the caste, as the case may be."

However, Fox (1967, p. 585), while presenting the case of Umar caste of eastern Uttar Pradesh, rigidly and "completely" differentiates a panchāyat from a modern sabha:

> Far from indicating resiliency, the history of *tāt* and *panchāyat* ["that is, the body which supervised social control within the local Umar population" (ibid., p. 583)] illustrates the complete functional demise of a traditional institution under the impact of modern social change and new political organization—the same change, be it noted, that has spurred the development of caste associations.

Hardgrave (1967, p. 21), after tracing the extensive caste history of the Nadars, describes and differentiates the emergence of "the Kshatriya Mahajana Sangam" as a caste association from other earlier ways of social control.

This study finds the situation less confusing for the Kanya-Kubja sabhas because as a sabha member from Indore wrote: "We never had *panchāyats* as the lower castes have. We did not have them because the consciousness of being the highest caste group of the Brahman worked as an effective means of social control among ourselves." This was the observation of a ninety-year-old Pundit, who had not heard about the existence of panchāyats from his forefathers. The first modern Kanya-Kubja association was established a decade earlier (1885) than those of the Nadars (1895) of the south, although it never became so highly elaborated or politicized as theirs.

Besides panchāyats and sabhas, the third type of organization may be "federations." Kothari and Maru (1965, pp. 34–35) characterize them in the following terms:

> The concept of federation refers to a grouping of a number of distinct endogamous caste groups into a single organization for common objectives. . . . A caste federation is, therefore, to be distinguished from a caste association in the range of social reality it covers, although in its search for an inclusive rather than a functional identity, it resembles the caste association. . . . In sum, it (caste federation) repre-

sents a step beyond caste association in Indian development towards a political community.

The above types of caste organizations only help to indicate the beginning of research in this area. Their descriptions are sketchy, with few exceptions; and their comparative studies are almost absent (for a recent useful general summary, see Rudolph and Rudolph 1967).

Aims and Organizational Emphases

"Caste welfare" is an omnibus term which includes all kinds of activities carried on in caste organizations. "Caste mobility" —mainly meaning shared actions for positional rank claims of various caste groups—provides the most pervasive aim of almost all the sabhas or federations covered by the studies considered here. A much extended and diverse list could be compiled, as we noted earlier, from the Census of India reports (e.g., see 1891, vol. 9 for the Brahmans; 1901 6: 373 ff.; 1911 7: 239 ff.; 1931 21: 250–58; 1931 3: 202–4; 1931 8: 379–84, especially 398– 99; 1931 14: 333 ff.; 1931 8: 267–69 and 5: 425 ff., also its appendix). It is interesting to note how the earlier census reports (1891 onward) had gradually caught on to the idea of caste mobility. Srinivas (1966, pp. 96–100) also presents some processed census data to the same effect.

Earlier I mentioned the aims of the Kanya-Kubja sabhas (chapter 2); now let us see how they compare with those of the Nadar's (Hardgrave 1967, p. 21) association functioning since 1910:

(a) To promote the social, material, and general welfare of the Nadars;
(b) To protect and to promote the interests and rights of the community;
(c) To take practical measures for the social, moral, and intellectual advancement of the Nadars;
(d) To start schools and colleges for imparting Western education to Nadar children and to help poor but deserving pupils belonging to the community with scholarships, books, fees, etc.;
(e) To encourage and promote commercial and industrial enterprise among the members of the community;

(f) The raising of funds by subscription, donation or other means for the above objects, and the doing of all such other things as are incidental and conducive to the attainment of the above objects or any of them.

It is noticeable that, except for (e) above, the sabha aims of the Kanya-Kubja and those of the Nadars are *essentially* the same; yet both of them have organized differently—with different elaboration and emphasis. Both have developed under different historical circumstances and with different initial resources. The Kanya-Kubjas have aimed to tackle their institutional problems rather than caste "mobility" claims, as the Nadars did. As a high caste group, the Kanya-Kubjas, of course, did not claim a change of their caste name (as did lower castes, e.g., from Shanans to Nadars, Pallis to Vanniyars [Rudolph and Rudolph 1967]; from Kanbi to Pattidārs [Pocock 1955]; from Chandālas to Nāmasud-rās [Dutt 1931]). In contrast to the social situation of south Indian Brahmans, since the Kanya-Kubjas never faced strong protest movements against their ritual rank, they started early on the road to modernity and secular mobility. Their problem has therefore been to change their traditions with the times. Unlike Nadars, they did not have to protest to seek participation in the British-introduced system of modernity.

Political mobilization of castes is another important aim of the modern sabhas (see Rudolph and Rudolph 1967); politization of sabha relations is most usually a means rather than an end in itself; and whenever it is emphasized, it is either for the achievement of, or in direct relation to, caste welfare aims. As far as I know there is no caste sabha reported which has democratic politics as its only or even *permanent* aim, although "power through vote" makes such emphasis common. If a sabha tried to totally supplant caste welfare with democratic politics, the sabha, according to my argument, will no longer be a caste-referring and caste-centered organization. It would be a "political party" or a Weberian "house of power" because it would, then, lose the interjacence of institutional and organizational criteria of group relations. However, since there exist many intermediate stages between depoliticized sabhas (and the Kanya-Kubjas' bodies approach this pole), and highly politicized sabhas (e.g., the Rudolph's [1967] *sabhas-cum-parties*), my argument seeks to understand them in terms of their comparative microsociology. Thus, the Nadar's case (Hardgrave 1966, 1967), when closely examined, seems to reveal phasal politization and depolitization (especially for example, after the attainment of a chief ministership by Kamraj Nadar). Hardgrave (1967, pp. 36–37) notes that "he [Kamraj Nadar] was the symbol that the community had at last 'arrived.' . . . The community continues to predominantly support the Congress, but an increasing multiplicity of interests and associations has fragmented its former unity."

If the sabhas undergo politization, it is primarily to protest as well as to level off "caste-class" type inequality. However, their resources being so limited and their political organizations always being "imperfect," the actual achievements are always incomplete, providing continued "middle range" aims for the caste sabhas.

At the macrosociological level, the purposes and consequences of "the politics of caste" have been usefully brought together by Rudolph and Rudolph (1967, pp. 36–87). Consistently aware of the likelihood of underestimation of the powerful "natural associations" of India, they recognize that political aspirations of castes are not the same as of those of "established political communities." Political aspirations of castes are transvalued and integrated by wider political structures, although the strength of their political actions may depend upon numerous factors, including those of numerical size and distributional pattern, political sensitization and its social and economic resource concomitants, and the presence of crosscutting power organizations. As I indicated with regard to Kanya-Kubja sabhas, historical antecedents help to explain the political potentialities as well as limitations of a modern caste. For example, the Rudolphs describe regional caste profiles and how they seem to relate to political action (1967, pp. 76 ff.), noting especially the contextual differences of castes between the Gangetic heartland and the south.

Set against the contextual features discussed earlier, it may be easier to ascertain why the Kanya-Kubja Brahmans and their sabhas practically show the *absence* of political mobilization, horizontal or vertical. Thus, unlike the Jāts of Uttar Pradesh, Rajasthan, and Punjab who are sufficiently numerous (see Schwartzberg 1965, pp. 477–95; 1968, pp. 81–113) and geographically widely distributed, the Kanya-Kubja Brahmans are fewer (according to 1891 census, which alone enumerates them

210

in sufficient detail, they were 1,303,348) and geographically extremely scattered (see chapters 1 to 4). Unlike the Jāts who possess a political record, the Kanya-Kubja Brahmans have never been involved in any caste-organized protest. They have been landholders, educators, administrators, priests, and soldiers, even under the Muhammadan rule. With the advent of British education, they further consolidated their economic, educational, and modern occupational resources, but at the cost of their areal concentration in Uttar Pradesh. They moved where their occupations took them. While they used their improved resources to attend to the claims of ascriptive solidarities, they found political mobilization unnecessary under the British rule and logically unmanageable after Independence. Distance and size both ran against it. Though they were never a numerically dominant caste, they vertically integrated with cognatic Brahman and other caste groups. Without politicizing their caste, they produced elected union and state ministers, chief ministers, and legislators, and continue to do so. They may easily integrate with the regional castes because, as the Rudolphs (1967, p. 78) note for northern India, Brahman and non-Brahman cleavage is toned down due to more sharing of economic, educational, and professional resources. Further, their jajmāni relations, urban living, and rural landholdings have kept up their communication with Thakurs and Kayasthas on the one hand, and Ahirs, Kurmis, and Pasis, on the other.

The political sensitization of the Kanya-Kubja Brahmans has been transient and largely a product of Congress's freedom movement. Yet it has never been involved on a caste-collective basis. Individuals and families have been drawn into the political vortex, many of whom have slipped back into a search for modern occupational eminence. Both the context and history of this caste group indicate limited political mobilization—so limited that the sabhas have virtually ignored it as a possible direction of development. They praise and value political achievements of Kanya-Kubja individuals but do not make it a caste-collective pursuit. If Kanya-Kubja Brahmans and their sabhas are distinctive in this regard, they are so because they have kept themselves depoliticized.

But, then, political mobilization is only one of the many emphases that modern caste sabhas can possibly acquire.

The Kanara Saraswat Brahmans, for example, indicate their

main emphasis as religious and sectarian. Their various branches in Calcutta, Bangalore, Chopan, Coondapur, Guregaon, Hubli, Karwa, Madras, Mangalore, and so on, are administratively coordinated; and all of them can be found organizing guru worship, *bhajan*s (religious group songs), sectarian fasts, festivals and *poojā*s (worships), and pilgrimages (*The Kanara Saraswat* 1965).

The Gujarat Kshatriya Sabha supplemented economic emphasis with that of the positional problem of the lower local Kshatriyas so as to strengthen the organization to help achieve both the aims effectively at the "federation" level (Kothari and Maru 1965, pp. 35 ff.). Although precise descriptions are required, numerous Vaishya (e.g., Agarwala and Rastogi), Mārwāri, Kayastha, and Kshatriya sabhas of Uttar Pradesh are known to have an emphasis on religion and business, education, and administration, respectively. The Kanya-Kubjas overlap with Kayastha sabha aims, especially insofar as they emphasize education, modern advancement, and individualized progress.

Thus while the Kanya-Kubja Brahmans use their sabhas for kinship and marital purposes, the Kanara Saraswats employ them for organizing sectarian religion (in 1964, twenty-two out of twenty-three functions were organized for religious purposes according to their sabha journal). Although like the Nadars and Gujarat Kshatriyas they have better-organized, more-coordinated, and well-differentiated sabhas, they do not put their organizations to the same use. Like Kanya-Kubjas, the politics of ritual status improvement is useless to them. As Brahmans, Kanya-Kubjas emphasize kinship and their Kanara counterparts, religion—only caste-appropriate aims.

Strategic Interjacence of Tradition and Modernity

I have already summed up the main elements of this characteristic before. We saw that caste elites come to the fore in caste sabhas. They find paths between tradition and modernity and guide the common caste member. Unfortunately, no intensive studies exist on them as yet, although one does find mention of the importance of notable individuals in a caste sabha. For example, Kothari and Maru (1965, p. 36) name a "Western-educated noble of the high standing" and "another educated Rajput, a Tālukdār," who "were to be the two major influences in the course that the Kshatrya [*sic*] movement took in the next fifteen years. . . ." in Gujarat. For the Nadars, Hardgrave (1967, p. 21) notes that "it was not until 15 years later that Rao Bahadur Ti Rattinasami Nadar of Porayar, Tanjore, of a distinguished and wealthy family of *akbarī* contractors, sought to revive the association." Pocock (1955, p. 71) traces the initiation of an "upward" movement among the Patidars to "a few Kanbi families that had the title of Patidar," and refers to a Gujarati publication detailing them. For the Vanniya Kula Kshatrya [*sic*] Sangham, the Rudolphs (1960, p. 17) note that two suitable elites (a lawyer with experience in state-wide party activities, and a high school graduate, a "political elite") forged "caste solidarity for voting." These examples can once again be multiplied from the Census of India reports. For example, for the Illuva caste sabhas, the *Census Report* (1931 21: 261) noted that "the one force behind these changes and reforms was the unique personality of the late Sri Narayana Guru Swami whose teachings and influence galvanized the dormant community into vigorous activity, and whose enlightened leadership, more than anything else, was responsible for these achievements." (See also *The Kanara Saraswat* 1965, for caste elite participation.)

Sabhas and Caste Sentiments

Aims and achievements broadly correspond in modern organizations. The caste sabhas also follow this characteristic in a general way, except that since they are caste-centered, they parochialize and deparochialize any economic, political, educational and secular achievements in terms of an entire caste or some of its subgroups. Kothari and Maru (1965) provide an example of how a caste sabha may deparochialize to include certain other local, lower-ranked Kshatriyas on a regional basis, creating a caste "federation." This "fusion" process is also referred to by Srinivas (1968, p. 199). Achievements of the caste sabhas, therefore, can only be in terms of constituent sharing by local or regional "caste" or "subcaste" groups. However, the indirect consequence of such achievements may be examined under a much wider reference (see especially Rudolph and Rudolph 1960, 1967; Hardgrave 1965, 1966). However, several such differentiating criteria as direct and indirect, primary and subsidiary, "universal" (i.e., for all the potential and actual groups

213

or members of the sabha), "collective" (i.e., for only one or more constituent groups), familial and individual, and psychological must be employed to explicate the actual significance of caste sabha achievements.

Once again because expressive achievements (e.g., the "we," or "togetherness" feeling) are diffuse and intangible as against the instrumental, we should find ways which will allow us to evaluate the former either in terms of or through some types of social relationships. This study, for example, in the last chapter tried to track down the expressed feeling of "Kanya-Kubjaism" in actual instrumental activities that transpired between elites, and between elites and non-elites. It illustrates "strategies" which promote and yet prevent the expression of caste sentiments. It is only one useful way of "breaking down" a highly amorphous, but intensely expressive aspect of the modern caste system.

Further, we saw in the earlier discussion that caste sentiment may not always be a uniting or instrumental force. Sangave (1962) gives several examples of how people complain that their caste members do not help them when in need. Although the expression of the "we" feeling may be considerably boosted by the caste sabhas—and it may in itself be counted as a type of achievement—it is crucial to know how much, and in what disparate activities, it is actually being used by the sabha members. Then, how successfully and how consistently? We must also understand that caste sentiment is basically an *expressive* rather than an instrumental category (see DeVos 1966). In the absence of precise details, such workers as Ghurye (1961), Srinivas (1966), Bailey (1963b), the Rudolphs (1960, 1967), and Kothari and Maru (1965) have referred only to caste "sentiment" as a widely expressed but extremely vague element of the modern Indian caste.

"Caste" (jāti) is a still more generalized and vague referrent. In a highly politicized situation for a "centralized" caste group like the Vanniyars or the Nadars, it may promote pervasive centripetality in some social actions. But what is the duration of such centripetalism? It is a vital limiting question which must be answered for finding its actual sociological dimensions. For example, if the sabhas can be only temporarily geared as "vote-catching," "ticket balancing" devices, as the Rudolphs (1960, pp. 13 ff.) indicate, the "conversion rate" of caste sentiment into actual political behavior depends crucially on the context. The Nadar sabha is *not* a political party, although temporarily it may function very close to it.

Moreover, caste sentiment is a function of, basically speaking, intercaste situations. When directed at the intracaste level, it has only a limited-meaning effect—mostly by way of emphasizing "uniqueness" of a particular caste group. Whether for sharing power in a sabha, or for enhancing one's influence, the kith and kin loyalties become organizationally most effective at this level.

A sabha's achievements are only very crude indicators of caste cohesion. Diversification of sabha activities may not automatically mean wider sharing among caste members. As compared to the Kanya-Kubjas, the Kanara Saraswats, for example, have diversified sabha achievements, including a cooperative housing society, baby-welfare societies, convalescent-*cum*-holiday homes, infant welfare clinics, libraries, sports and games facilities, schools, pecuniary help funds, and movable supplies for festivals and ceremonies. They have an annual budget of about Rs. 200,000. Yet according to a published report (*The Kanara Saraswat*, June 1965, p. 222), the general membership of this sabha has grown from only 1,701 in 1959 to 2,291 in 1964—an increase of 590 new members. However, even this is a significant "upward" trend when we compare it with the Kanya-Kubja sabhas, who have either remained constant or have gone down in the same period. (Their variation is within a range of 10 per cent, with the all-Indian Lucknow sabha at the losing and the Indore local body at the gaining end.)

The "differences" in emphasis and analysis evident in the above comparative discussion seem to arise out of the major approaches and orientation of the investigators, and from the social history of different caste groups. Most of all, the inquiries in this area are still unsystematized, as they are far and few between. Accordingly, the anthropological description of the Kanya-Kubja sabhas of the north and of those described by the political scientists (Rudolph and Rudolph 1967) for the south may be found to differ in conceptual emphasis and approach. Even the same caste group, when handled by two different investigators (although both political scientists), may be found to receive a different emphasis, approach, and analytical frame of reference (cf. Hardgrave's [1969] presentation of the Nadars with that of

215

the Rudolphs, and Rudolph). Yet all these studies concur on major commonalities and provide a preliminary indication of the potentialities of this area of research. Indian caste has already received continuous intensive attention for a long time (for a useful summation and a viewpoint, see DeVos 1966, pp. 325–84; Berreman 1967), and now its modern adaptation must be understood in a wider comparative context. Its ethnographic reality should be handled in relation with idealized native and anthropological conceptions.

CONCEPTUAL VIEWS OF THE CASTE GROUP (INTRACASTE LEVEL)

The Kanya-Kubja sabhas have been described in this study in terms of ethnographic reality. This emphasis requires that I should make explicit two related perspectives which have been used here in viewing the caste group. First, it has been examined primarily from within, emphasizing interpersonal, intracaste relations. Second, it has focused on accounting the actual field-recorded social behavior of the Kanya-Kubja Brahmans. It does not analyze ideal types; however, it examines reality in terms of these types alluded to explicitly or implicity. The following remarks are intended here to clarify this perspective (enunciated in chapter 1).

Network of Kith and Kin

A Kanya-Kubja sabha's arena is composed of numerous overlapping kin groups uniformly obeying both the caste principles of birth and endogamy. Yet no single kin group, much less a caste member, can claim to know or be acquainted with *all* the members of one's caste group. In a dispersed caste group like the Kanya-Kubja this is even more difficult to achieve. From a caste member's point of view, a caste group has several other kin groups, some related and others unrelated; but it is the latter type ("kith") which is approached and controlled by several contextual conditions, and the route regarded as most favorable is attempted. The sabha activities being caste activities, therefore, restrict themselves to, and heavily rely upon, this kind of caste-elite and caste-member support. In modern urban living, both types of contacts are suitably used, depending upon availability and appropriateness.

216

The above considerations indicate, therefore, that a modern caste group may also be viewed as an overlapping but "loose" assemblage of kin groups, families and persons, each seeking occupational, economic, and positional aims in terms of the diverse demands of modern living and its extra-kinship organizations. The greater the number of caste elites involved with modern organizations, the more circumspect they have to be to insulate their kith and kin roles. If they emphasize the latter, their organizational impersonality may be affected; and if they overplay the "officialdom," they lose the kin and kith sympathies crucial for the performance of certain institutional obligations. Finally, although achieved position is important in kinship and caste obligations, and may allow certain flexibility in manipulating institutional norms, the latter can never be overthrown, as for example in marriage, kinship, and commensality. If this is attempted, there will be appropriate resistance from kin groups and even from society at large. (This seems to be a situation parallel to African lineage and state loyalties as described by Fallers [1965, pp. 230–31] for the Soga.)

Interrelations of the Ideal and the Actual

Another question relates to "what is" and "what ought to be" included under the modern Kanya-Kubja caste system. This issue, at a general all-Indian level, has been under anthropological discussion now for about a decade (e.g., see Leach 1960; Srinivas 1961, 1962, 1966; Bailey 1963a and 1963b; and Fox 1967). The discussion began when Leach (1960, pp. 1–10) summarized his opinion on the modern "doings" of caste: The papers that he was editorializing reported "caste labor unions" as symptoms of caste disintegration (Gough) on the one hand, and a "caste welfare society" as a symptom of caste resilience to changing circumstances, on the other. Leach, writing in terms of "typical" or "ideal types" and "principles" (from the very beginning of his Introduction, see pp. 1 ff.), applied the simple principles of Durkheimian "mechanical" vis-à-vis "organic" relations, "with each particular caste and subcaste filling a distinctive functional role." He made a logical conclusion: "It [caste] is a system of labor division from which the element of competition among workers has largely been excluded" (p. 5). He pushed this preliminary sociological distinction further in *ideal*

217

levels and relationships and surmised: "My own view is that wherever caste groups are seen to be acting as corporations in competition against like groups of *different caste,* then they are acting in defiance of caste *principles*" (p. 7, second italics supplied). In modern "class" competition, Leach saw the violation of *cordon sanitaire* of Indian caste groups made up of intergroup cooperation reinforced by ritual rules.

This statement became a topic of discussion, particularly by Srinivas, who produced the "resiliency argument" by emphasizing the "reality" of caste behavior (but without denying, I think, the idealized sociological opposition that Leach indicated, see the last italicized part of the following statement):

> I am at a loss to understand why the starting of a labor union, welfare society, bank, cooperative society, hostel, hospital, or journal on the basis of caste should be regarded as evidence of caste disintegration. . . . [He then cites some evidence on how modern caste actually has been organizing itself; and he concludes—] I find it difficult to understand why this is not to be taken as evidence of caste resilience even if it is *assumed* that such resilience *carries within itself the seeds of the destruction of the caste system.* [Latter italics supplied.]

Bailey (1963a, p. 121) in referring to this discussion observed that "it can be shown that this must be a dispute about the use of words, and not about the *reality* underlying them [italics provided]." He also thought that Srinivas was in fact saying the same thing that Leach was, and he concluded (p. 123): "While we may call the new caste associations (or the more amorphous caste categories) 'castes' in a loose way, they are certainly not operating in a caste system." Bailey's statements skirt around the central issue because, although maintaining the same sociological distinction that Leach raised, he only goes halfway to meet it. He terms caste associations " 'castes' in a loose way," probably attributing this looseness to the weakening of the "natural" *cordon sanitaire* of a modern caste through the adoption of modern economic competition and its appropriate organizations, including bureaucracy. At the same time, however, he tries to cope with ideal conflict and actual interjacence. Accordingly, he does not want to equate a caste bank or corporation with a state organization, yet he wants to differentiate it from all that is the traditional structure of caste. His phrases "amorphous caste categories" and "reality" (while actually meaning underlying idealized principles) further obfuscate the distinction between the ideal and the actual, although this is what he wants to clear up to convey his idea of the "structure" of modern caste.

The above discussion is significant not so much for discovering a serious non sequitur between the Leach-Srinivas-Bailey "positions" as for understanding how these persistent obscurities can be avoided. I suggest that the issue here is of treating the ideal and the actual at their proper levels—an issue which is of wider social anthropological importance. For example, the "alliance theory" debate (for a recent summary, see Buchler and Selby 1968, pp. 105–49) tells us that much of the discussion has been misplaced primarily because of our eagerness to "fit" ethnographic variations in an idealized type. As Buchler and Selby (1968, pp. 125–27) put it, "When the ethnographic reports are at variance with the elements of the model (idealized type), then, the errors must lie in ethnography." Actually, the debate conveys even more, for

> the type (idealization) . . . is by definition *nondisconfirmable* by reference to the empirical content; its value is entirely heuristic. Therefore, we need not seek an empirical case that fits the idealization. Whether an empirical replica can fit the model or not (and it surely can not), the idealization retains its value.

This lesson is most clearly derived from the works of Lévi-Strauss (see especially Lévi-Strauss 1949, 1953, 1956, 1960, 1963, 1965, and 1966). Leach, who initiated the discussion of idealized caste types, has been specially cognizant of such pitfalls in his own work on Ceylon and Burma (e.g., see his work on alliance systems—1945, 1954, 1963).

It follows from the above that provided one does not make the mistake of reifying the idealization (i.e., Leach's "ideal type" of caste) and begin searching for it in actuality, one is at liberty to discuss the modern caste system in terms of the ideal types. Accordingly, if Leach excludes "class" competition between caste groups because it is against the ideal principle of "organic" interdependence on which castes distinguish themselves all the time, it is a valuable heuristic and sociological distinction to keep in mind, especially when dealing with interjacent organizations like sabhas. But this does not imply that *in actuality* the caste members thereby become incapable of competing (within specified limits) among themselves and with other caste members on economic and secular bases of modern life.

The ideal type is usually very simplified while the ethnographic reality is diverse, dynamic and complicated. It is flexible and full of alternatives; it accommodates and becomes accommodated. The present study substantiates this point, when it views a caste group from the end of ethnographic reality. It shows how a "caste welfare body" remains a unit defined and identified in terms of caste members and caste welfare. Yet it shows how pervasive is the emphasis on modern economic and class achievements, and how "class" considerations come to interface and to compete with kith and kin relations. In actual life, Kanya-Kubjas deal with them without the fierce conceptual conflicts that a social anthropologist thinks exist between the idealized a priori categories like ascription and achievement, caste and class, tradition and modernity, and kinship and bureaucracy. It is not that such conflicts are not noted by the modern caste members but that they almost always have several ways of dealing with them "within a scheme of cultural priorities." This is why one does not confuse his caste sabha either with his modern office, or with a marriage party. Actually, for a caste member a sabha is no more than a modern dimension of caste groups which sponsor and run them with explicit caste-specific welfare aims. Ideally, when a caste group acts as a "corporation" competing against "like groups of different caste," it is acquiring a mode of interaction that is extraneous to caste system (and Leach is of course right in emphasizing it). Actually, however, caste corporations are not "real" corporations (i.e., they do not have the required organizational complexity) because they are organized *within* the limitations of a caste group or groups. They can be deparochialized but not completely universalized, or they will no longer be caste sabhas. But as this entire study shows the enthnographic reality is neither so simple nor are the caste elements so dramatically and completely replaceable.

Actually, the above is a complex all-Indian tendency, in which the modern Indian achiever, whether a politician or an administrator or a professional, is not a new man (and he does not want to be); he is a link of cultural continuity between his ascendants and descendants. He has been socialized by the former and is ready to socialize the latter. He makes many daily adjustments to modernization and ritualization, which as individual behavioral *fluctuations* remain small-scale, functional and individualized changes, but which exert a subtle influence both ways. Thus, although the new does not replace the old and is integrated in a more or less functional manner without a real change of substance, one neither makes a tabula rasa of the old, nor does one commit oneself unreservedly to the modern and Western.

Appendixes

A Minutes of a Typical Sabha Executive Committee Meeting

ORDER OF BUSINESS

1. The proceedings of the last meeting were read and passed.

2. This meeting expresses profound and heartfelt grief over the sad demise of Pundit X, retired Deputy Post Master General, Uttar Pradesh, and the Vice-President of Sri Kanya-Kubja Pratinidhi Sabha, and it prays to God that He may give *moksha* to the departed soul and strength to the bereaved family.

3. "Resolved that out of the amount in the current account of Sri Kanya-Kubja Pratinidhi Sabha, Lucknow, with the X Bank Ltd., Lucknow, a sum of . . . be invested in fixed deposit with the aforesaid bank for a period of nine years, bearing interest at Rs. 6–8 per cent, per annum and that the said account be operated jointly under the signature of . . . Hony. Secretary and . . . Hony. Treasurer of the sabha and that their specimen signatures be sent to the bank for the purpose."

4. "Resolved that specimen signatures of the Hony. Secretary . . . and . . . Hony. Treasurer of Sri Kanya-Kubja Pratinidhi Sabha be sent to the X Bank Ltd., Lucknow, and they are authorized to operate on the current account of Sri Kanya-Kubja Pratinidhi Sabha with the aforesaid work."

5. Resolved that the all-Indian general body meeting be called in May or June, 1965. For its organization the Hony. Secretary is hereby authorized to begin necessary actions and that he should report to the executive committee at its next meeting.

The proceedings of the Akhil Bhārtiya Sri Kanya-Kubja Pratinidhi Sabha's executive committee meeting (Kanya-Kubja Office, Lucknow, 4 October 1964) appeared in Hindi, except for the third and fourth resolutions, which are in English.

223

B Distribution and Main Languages of the Major Caste Journals

The following information (obtained with thanks from Maureen Patterson, who is collecting it for her own independent study), although preliminary and rough, is presented here to convey the general idea of the different languages used by modern caste journals in various parts of India. It is noticeable that migrant caste groups use either their own regional language or Hindi or English. Several journals listed below are multilingual in the sense that they may simultaneously use two or more languages—for example, Hindi/English, Gujarati/English, Urdu/Hindi, English/Hindi, Urdu/Hindi/Punjabi, and so on. However, in all such cases there seemed to be one main language in which most of the matter was expressed most of the time. The second table classifies the main languages of journals from seven states on this basis.

State	Number of Caste Journals
Andhra Pradesh	2
Assam	. . .
Bihar	2
Delhi	17
Gujarat	49
Jammu & Kashmir	. . .
Madhya Pradesh	3
Madras	4
Maharashtra	53
Mysore	1
Orissa	. . .
Punjab	8
Rajasthan	12
Uttar Pradesh	35
West Bengal	9

SOURCE: *Press in India*, "Part II: Tenth Annual Report." The Registrar of Newspapers (New Delhi: Government of India Publications, 1966).

MAIN LANGUAGES OF THE CASTE JOURNALS

	Hindi	English	Urdu	Punjabi	Gujarati	Marathi	Bengali	Not Mentioned
Delhi	7	1	7	2	..	..	..	..
Gujarat	..	..	..	..	49	..	..	..
Maharashtra	2	3	..	..	29	8	..	11
Punjab	3	..	5	..	..	..	..	..
Rajasthan	11	1	..	..	..	..	..	..
Uttar Pradesh	32	1	1	1	..	..	..	..
West Bengal	7	..	..	..	..	..	2	..

C Frequency Distribution of Agnatic Ancestral Groups

This appendix presents comparative distributional data provided by some published genealogies in Hindi and Sanskrit, which have been popular for help in settling modern Kanya-Kubja marriages (Bajpai 1946, Narain Prasad Misra 1959, Munni L. Misra 1966, and Shastri 1966). Of these, I have relied most on Misra (1959) because his data are substantiated and comprehensive. Yet there is no way of ascertaining if the genealogies are really exhaustive; it is likely that there may be many unreported AAGs of the geographically distant—the Kanya-Kubjas of the "fringe."

Biswā Scale	Khatkul Cluster (Six Gotras)							
	Kashyap	Shāndilya	Kātyāyan	Bharadwāj	Upmanyu	Sānkrit	TOTAL no.	%
Highest 20	12	23	24	42	47	13	161	17.3
19	4	10	21	13	13	3	64	6.9
18	5	9	9	16	23	5	67	7.2
17	7	6	5	7	14	..	39	4.2
16	1	8	9	8	9	1	36	3.9
15	2	9	4	7	8	3	33	3.5
14	4	6	9	15	3	1	38	4.0
13	1	5	4	12	4	..	26	2.8
12	1	5	2	23	3	2	36	3.9
11	3	1	1	11	5	..	21	2.2
10	40	4	19	40	16	3	122	13.1
9	8	..	..	5	4	1	18	1.9
8	23	2	2	11	12	2	52	5.6
7	15	4	1	8	7	1	36	3.9
6	8	1	1	2	1	..	13	1.4
5	36	5	2	24	22	6	95	10.2
4	18	5	1	13	6	1	44	4.8
3	3	13	1	5	1	..	23	2.5
2	..	1	..	2	4	..	7	0.7
Lowest 1								
TOTAL	191	117	115	264	202	42	931	100.0

Kāshyap	Garg	Gautam	Bhāradwāj	Dhananjaya	Vatsa	Vashistha	Kaushika	Kavista	Pārāshar	TOTAL no.	%	GRAND TOTAL no.	%
			MADHYAMA CLUSTER (Ten Gotras)										
												161	13.6
												64	5.4
												67	5.6
												39	3.3
												36	3.0
												33	2.8
												38	3.2
												26	2.2
												36	3.0
												21	1.8
1	..	..	..	..	..	..	..	..	..	1	0.4	123	10.4
10	..	..	..	..	..	..	..	..	..	10	3.9	28	2.4
..	1	..	3	..	..	..	..	..	..	4	1.6	56	4.7
5	..	..	..	..	2	..	..	..	..	7	2.7	43	3.6
..	..	..	1	..	..	..	..	..	..	1	0.4	14	1.2
5	1	1	8	..	2	..	..	..	..	17	6.6	112	9.4
11	1	5	7	..	16	..	..	..	2	42	16.3	86	7.2
9	4	1	11	5	4	9	6	4	3	56	21.8	79	6.6
11	14	12	19	7	10	7	6	8	7	101	39.3	108	9.1
..	2	2	..	..	3	1	5	2	3	18	7.0	18	1.5
52	23	21	49	12	37	17	17	14	15	257	100.0	1,188	100.0

D Summaries of Class Indicators of Some Modern Elites

ELITE A
Education
B. Sc., LL.B.
(brilliant student)
Career
College teacher
Deputy collector (recom-
mended by a university)
Promoted to I.C.S. (now
Indian Administrative
Service)
Deputy secretary, Finance
Department, Uttar Pradesh
government
Secretary, Board of Revenue
and Finance, Uttar Pradesh
government
Deputy inspector general of
civil hospitals (Uttar
Pradesh)
Deputy transport commis-
sioner (Uttar Pradesh)
Finance secretary of Madhya
Bharat
Occupation
Indian Civil Service
Civic Honors
Order of the British Empire,
Rai Bahadur
Honorary treasurer, Indian
Red Cross Society, Uttar
Pradesh Branch
Vice-president, Automobile
Association, Uttar Pradesh
Vice-president, Uttar Pradesh
Tuberculosis Association
Member, executive committee
of a university

President, Women's Service
Board
Community Welfare
Built a hospital as a memorial
to his father and wife for
Rs. 100,000 (now operated
by the state government)
Guest house—*Dharamshālā*
(memorial to mother;
Rs. 10,000)
Road construction and a river
bridge (elite induced but
government sponsored)
Other
Sport—lawntennis player

ELITE B
Education
1911–15—barrister-at-law,
London
Career
1915—barrister-at-law,
Avadh Chief Court
1915–48—active
congressman
1921—jailed for participating
in the Noncooperation
Movement of Indian
National Congress
Occupation
Barrister-at-law, Lucknow
High Court
Jāti Welfare
Active member: Kanya-Kubja
College and Kanya-Kubja
Vocational College,
Lucknow; Kanya-Kubja
College, Bhagwantnagar

SOURCE: *Kanya-Kubja* 1963–67.

Vice-president, All-Indian Sri
Kanya-Kubja Pratinidhi
Sabha, Lucknow

ELITE C
Education
(all traditional diplomas)
1916—Madhyamā, Queen's
College, Banaras
(?) Sāhityāchārya
(?) Vyākaraṇ Shāstri
(?) Āyurveda, Vāchaspati
(?) D.Sc.A. (honorary)
Ayurvedic Unit, Jhansi
Career
1917–19—Sanskrit professor,
D.A.V. College, Dehradun
1919–25—professor, super-
intendent, assistant gov-
ernor of the school,
Gurukul Kāngri, Haradwar
1925–27—principal, Hindi
Vidyā Peeth, Allahabad
(?)—founder, Ayurvedic
hosiptal, Lucknow
Editor, *Kanya-Kubja*
(8 months)
Editor, *Ajantā* (a periodical)
Director, Sanskrit Bhāṣā
Prachār Samiti
Member, Hindi Academy
Secretary, Ayurveda Academy
Principal, Ayurveda School
Lecturer in Hindi, Osmania
University
Honorary member, Indian
Medical Board, Andhra
Pradesh
Registrar, Hindi Prachāriṇi
Sabhā, Hyderabad
Author of books in Sanskrit
and Hindi on Ayurvedic
medicine, Gita, etc.

Occupation
Ayurvedic physician,
Hyderabad
Jāti Welfare
Since 1933, member of
Kanya-Kubja Sabha and
supporter of the journal
Kanya-Kubja-Ke-Shiroratna

ELITE D
Education
Mārwāri Commercial High
School
Career
Businessman
Political and social worker
Member, Bombay Pradesh
Congress Committee since
1930
Past president, Zila Congress
Committee
1947—honorary magistrate,
Bombay Presidency
Titled "justice of peace"
1952—member, Bombay
Municipal Corporation
1954–63—chairman, Depart-
ment of Market and
Gardens
1933—chairman, New Grain
Dealer's Association
President, Indian Grain
Dealers Federation
Chairman, Kerosine Oil
Committee
Executive committee member,
Federal Retail Cloth
Dealers Association
Executive committee member,
All-Indian Food Grain
Dealers Association, Delhi
Occupation
Businessman, Bombay

Jāti Welfare
Founder, Hindi High School, Bombay
Founder, girl's school
President (8 years), Kanya-Kubja Mandal, Bombay

ELITE E
Education and Academic Honors
1921—B.Sc. from Muir Central College, Allahabad; received Sir Charles Elliot Scholarship from a university and from the government
1923—M.Sc. in zoology in the first division and provincial government scholarship for the Ph.D.
1926—D.Sc., Lucknow University
1931—D.Phil. from Oxford and the University of London
1931–32—research in Berlin and Vienna
1936—research at the Imperial University, Japan
Government representative, Fifth Entomological Conference, London
1938—sectional president, International Congress of Entomology, Berlin

1960—sectional president, International Congress of Entomology, Vienna
1938–60—twenty students received D.Sc. and Ph.D.
1960–67—life president, Zoological Society of India
1930–67—fellow, Zoological Society, London; fellow, Royal Entomological Society of London; founder, Banaras School of Zoology; research committee member, Zoological Survey of India
Career
1926–60—teaching at Banaras University, professor and head of the zoology department
1945–47 and 1951–52—dean, faculty of science
1947—pro-Vice-chancellor
1952–55 and 1958(?)—university registrar
Principal, agriculture college
1959–60—principal, science college of the university
1961—until death, research professor, Central Drug Research Institute, Lucknow
Occupation
Professor and educator

Glossary

NOTE—This listing includes only those Hindi terms that have been used frequently throughout the text. Although many of these terms have more than one meaning, the one relevant to the textual discussion is given here.

Achkan A medieval, tight-fitting long coat worn by traditionalists or conservatives during the earlier decades of this century.

Ādābarz "Rendering respect"; a mode of Muslim greeting, also adotped by Hindus in appropriate situations.

Alla See Ānk.

Angarkhā A traditional, orthodox upper garment still used by some orthodox priests.

Ānk (also alla) Literally meaning number (a corruption of *ank* according to some informants); here it refers to various lineal ancestral names of the Kanya-Kubja Brahmans, especially as an element of their intracaste hierarchy.

Artha Wealth, worldly riches; also regarded by Hindus as one of the four goals of man.

Āshirvāda "Blessings"; traditionally spoken or bestowed by superiors in response to a greeting.

Āspad Ritual surname or title among the Kanya-Kubja Brahmans; an element of intracaste hierarchy.

Baithakā A rural north Indian term for drawing or living room.

Banuan A word used by Kanya-Kubjas to denote a spurious rise on their Biswā ranking scale.

Bétī Daughter

Béndā A woman's ornament worn in the middle of the forehead as a symbol of wifehood, particularly in northern India.

Bhāi (synonymous with bhaiyā) Brother.

Bhaiyā See Bhāi.

Bhajan A devotional song of a particular deity or deities; sung singly or by a group.

231

Bhāt   Literally rice; here it means a specific marriage ceremony called by the same name, involving the eating of boiled rice as a ranked food transaction.

Bilaitihā   Of or belonging to England, especially as used earlier by the Kanya-Kubja to refer to those who undertook foreign travel for education and occupation.

Biswā   Literally a traditional land-measuring unit (20 biswā equal one bighā, the latter being one-third of an acre); here meaning a numerical ranking scale of twenty divisions, applied to all Kanya-Kubja Brahmans along ānks (ancestral names).

Brahmachāri(n)   A celibate or a religious student; also the first stage of the ideal life prescribed for the Hindu student residing with his preceptor.

Charansparsh   "Touching the feet"; a normative mode of respectfully greeting a superior or an aged person.

Chauk   A wall or floor design usually drawn during a ceremony or a worship.

Churidār (paijāmā)   The tight-fitting lower garment worn by traditionalist men (now also a part of modern woman's dress); often worn with the achkan or sherwāni, the complementary upper garments.

Chotī   The sacred tuft of hair on the top of the head—a ritual symbol for the twice-born, particularly Brahmans.

Dān   A religious gift most usually offered to Brahmans.

Dash-gotra wālé   Of or belonging to ten gotras. See *Dhākara.*

Dhākara   The lower gotra-grouping among the Kanya-Kubja Brahmans, composed of ten gotras.

Dhotī   Lower garment (unsewn) used by males; usually a white cloth of five yards length.

Ekādashī vrat   Fasting on the eleventh day of a lunar fortnight; especially significant for a devotee of the god Vishnu.

Girdā   A long, round pillow, usually placed behind a person's back when one sits on the floor.

Gotra   A sage-founded exogamous and patrilineal "clan," usually characterized by widely dispersed membership.

Havana   Oblations to fire for religious purposes, or for "feeding" the fire god itself.

Jajmān   A client (for a priest); also, the *jajmānī* system of hereditary patron-client relationships, emphasizing economic and ritual interdependence of castes, prevalent in northern India.

Jāmā   A traditionally auspicious upper garment (much like a gown) worn by a groom during his marriage ceremony.

Jāti   Normally a term for the caste as an endogamous group; technically, it is now considered a better term for referring to many actual dimensions of a caste group.

Jātiya kosh   A fund collected on behalf of a caste group for its social welfare activities.

Juntā (janatā)   "People"; especially used today to refer to a body of people, political or otherwise.

Kachchā (kaccā)   "Raw, unripe"; used here to refer to the food type which requires greater ritual cautions in handling within and across caste groups.

Kanyādān   "Offering of a virgin," especially as a central ceremony in Hindu marriage.

Kathā   A recital of sacred story, usually drawn either from a scripture or an oral tradition.

Keertan (kīrtan or kīrtana)   An individual or group singing of devotional songs (*bhajans*), usually with musical accompaniment.

Khādī   Hand-spun and hand-woven cloth; especially a symbol of Gandhian philosophy.

Khạrāun   Wooden sandals used mostly within the house by the orthodox.

Khatkul   The higher six-gotra cluster of the Kanya-Kubja Brahmans.

Kulīn   "Of pure kin group"; particularly referring to adherence of ritual, marital, and commensal rules among the Kanya-Kubja Brahmans.

Kulīntā   In a state of being kulīn.

Kurtā   A traditional long shirt with or without a collar.

Lén-dén   Economic transactions (both in cash and kind), especially as during the course of marriage.

Madhyam   "Middle"; here it refers to, and is synonymous with, the lower ten-gotra cluster of the Kanya-Kubja Brahmans. See also Dhākara.

Mandapa   Canopy; particularly as erected in the center of a courtyard for marriage ceremonies.

Mardānā   Men's apartment or "section" in a traditional house.

Masnad   Synonymous with *Girdā*.

Mohallā   A residential ward of a north Indian city.

Namaskār   A common Hindu mode of greeting, usually by speaking this word, while folding the hands and bowing the head.

Namāz   The Muslim prayer conducted singly or in group, and privately or in a mosque.

Nath (nuth)   Nose ring; woman's ornament worn especially during the marriage.

Pān Betel leaf; also the whole leaf along with associated ingredients (lime paste, areca nuts, etc); usually offered as a symbol of respect and welcome to any visitor or guest.

Panchāyat "Coming together of five persons"; a council of five or more members; especially a caste panchāyat assembled to judge petty disputes and to reinforce caste rules.

Pān-supāri Betel leaf with areca nut; synonymous with *Pān* in meaning.

Paumān-yajña A special scriptural sacrifice; here referred to in the context of caste welfare.

Prabhātī A devotional song particularly suited to the morning hours for "waking up" one's deity.

Poojā (pūjā) Worship, particularly a systematic adoration of one's deity.

Pranām The Hindu mode of greeting the respected and the aged; in intent similar to charansparsh.

Prasād (prasāda) Food sanctified by having been presented to a god for his "eating"; usually eaten and/or distributed as an especially beneficial food.

Pravāsa Living away from one's original place; emigration to a distant place.

Pundit (pandita) A wise or learned man; particularly a learned Brahman; also applied to a Brahman priest.

Punya Religious merit.

Purushā (Purkhā) A close agnatic ancestor; standing nearer than ānk for the Kanya-Kubja Brahmans.

Rakshā "Protection"; especially the ritual tying of protection threads around one's wrist during a festival (Rakshā Bandhan) falling in July-August every year.

Rotī Unleavened Indian bread; figuratively, one's livelihood.

Sāfā Turban; also a symbol of one's social prestige.

Sahbhoj A group dinner or a commensal feast.

Samāj "Assembly, company"; society.

Samkaksh var A bridegroom belonging to the same social "class" as the bride.

Sanad A degree or certificate.

Shérwāni A knee-length upper garment, much like the achkan, except that it is styled and shaped differently—a little less snug.

Shākhā "Branch"; here, ritual peculiarities based on scripturally stated "branches" of ritual practice; especially as applicable to Kanya-Kubja Brahmans within the north Indian Brahman grouping (Panch Gauda).

Shulk A fee.

Sīdhā   Raw food-grains; especially a full plate of raw, uncooked foods for offering to a Brahman.

Susthān   A geographic location of original ancestral concentration, reckoned in respect to agnatic ancestral groups (ānks) of the Kanya-Kubja Brahmans.

Tālukdārs   A large landowner; especially in Uttar Pradesh.

Tambākhu   Tobacco; usually referring to the type chewed with the betel leaf by the Kanya-Kubja Brahmans.

Tilak   Sacred sandalpaste marks on the forehead, particularly among the religious and the orthodox.

Upjāti   "Subcaste"; a part of jāti.

Upvarga   A subcategory of varga.

Uttama   Another name for the higher gotra cluster of the Kanya-Kubja Brahmans. See Khatkul.

Vaidya   A traditional medical practitioner following the Ayurvedic system of medicine.

Vamshāvali   A genealogical account, usually of the entire caste group and compiled and published by a learned caste member.

Varga   A category of ritual classification assigning a distinct ritual place for each Brahman group; however, not widely known today.

Varna   "Color, class"; one of the four social layers of society in Vedic times, and of the ideal-typical scheme of social classification today.

References

Almond, Gabriel A., and Coleman, James S., eds.
1960　*The Politics of the Developing Areas.* Princeton, N. J.: Princeton University Press.
Apter, David E.
1965　*The Politics of Modernization.* Chicago: University of Chicago Press.
Aron, Raymond
1950　"Social Structure and the Ruling Class." *British Journal of Sociology.* vol. 1.
Bailey, F. G.
1963a　"Closed Social Stratification in India." *Archives Europeannes de Sociologie.* vol. 4.
1963b　*Politics and Social Change: Orissa in 1959.* Berkeley and Los Angeles. University of California Press.
Bajpai, A. P.
1946　*Upmanyu Vamshāvalī* (Hindi and Sanskrit). Banaras: Pathar Gali Kashi.
Barth, Fredrik
1967　"On the Study of Social Change." *American Anthropologist.* vol. 69.
Beattie, John
1964　*Other Cultures.* New York: The Free Press of Glencoe.
Bendix, Reinhard, and Lipset, Seymour Martin, eds.
1966　*Class, Status and Power: Social Stratification in Comparative Perspective.* 2d ed. New York: The Free Press of Glencoe.
Berreman, Gerald D.
1967　"Caste as Social Process." *Southwestern Journal of Anthropology.* vol. 23.
Bhāgwata Purāṇa
1896　*The Srimad-Bhāgbatam.* Translated by J. M. Sanyal. 5 vols. Calcutta: Oriental Publishing Co.

Bohannan, Paul
1963   *Social Anthropology.* New York: Holt, Rinehart and Winston.
Bottomore, T. B.
1964   *Elites and Society.* New York: Basic Books.
1967   "Cohesion and Division in Indian Elites." In *India and Ceylon: Unity and Diversity.* Edited by Philip Mason. New York: Oxford University Press.
Brass, Paul R.
1965   *Factional Politics in an Indian State: The Congress Party in Uttar Pradesh.* Berkeley and Los Angeles: University of California Press.
Buchler, Ira R., and Selby, Henry A.
1968   *Kinship and Social Organization: An Introduction to Theory and Method.* New York: The Macmillan Company.
Census of India
1891   vol. 11. *The Central Provinces and Feudatories.* "Part I: The Report." Calcutta: Office of the Superintendent of Government Printing.
1901   vol. 6. *The Lower Provinces of Bengal and Their Feudatories.* "Part I: The Report." Calcutta: Bengal Secretariat Press.
1911   vol. 7. *Bombay.* "Part I: Report." Bombay: Printed at the Government Central Press.
1931   vol. 3. *Assam.* "Part I: Report." Calcutta: The Government of India Central Publication Branch.
1931   vol. 7. *Bihar and Orissa.* "Part I: Report." Patna: Superintendent, Government Printing.
1931   vol. 5. *Bengal and Sikkim.* "Part I: Report." Calcutta: Central Publication Branch.
1931   vol. 8. *Bombay Presidency.* "Part I: General Report." Bombay: The Government Central Press.
1931   vol. 14. *Madras.* "Part I: Report." Calcutta: The Government of India Central Publication Branch.
1931   vol. 21. *Cochin.* "Part I: Report." Ernakulam: The Superintendent, Cochin Government Press.
Cohn, Bernard S.
1955   "The Changing Status of a Depressed Caste." In *Village India: Studies in the Little Community.* Chicago: University of Chicago Press.
1961   "From Indian Status to British Contract." *The Journal of Economic History.* vol. 21.

238

REFERENCES

1962   "Political Systems in Eighteenth Century India: The Ba-
        naras Region." *Journal of the American Oriental Society*.
        vol. 82.
1968   "Notes on the History of the Study of Indian Society and
        Culture." In *Structure and Change in Indian Society*.
        Edited by Milton Singer and Bernard S. Cohn. Chicago:
        Aldine Publishing Company.
Crane, Robert I., ed.
1967   *Regions and Regionalism in South Asian Studies: An Ex-
        ploratory Study*. Program in Comparative Studies in South-
        ern Asia, Monograph no. 5. Durham, N. C.: Duke Uni-
        versity.
Crooke, William
1896   *The Tribes and Castes of the North-Western Provinces and
        Oudh*. vol. 3. Calcutta: Office of the Superintendent of
        Government Printing, India.
Dalton, Dennis
1967   "The Gandhian View of Caste, and Caste after Gandhi."
        In *India and Ceylon: Unity and Diversity*. Edited by Philip
        Mason. New York: Oxford University Press.
Davis, Kingsley, and Moore, Wilbert E.
1966   "Some Principles of Stratification." In *Class, Status,
        and Power*. Edited by Reinhard Bendix and Seymour
        Martin Lipset. 2d ed. New York: The Free Press of
        Glencoe.
DeVos, George
1966   "Motivational Components of Caste." In *Japan's Invisible
        Race: Caste in Culture and Personality*. Edited by G. DeVos
        and H. Wagatsuma. Berkeley and Los Angeles: University
        of California Press.
District Gazetteers of the United Provinces of Agra and Oudh
1903   *Bahraich*. Allahabad: Superintendent, Government Press.
1903   *Sultanpur*. Allahabad: Superintendent, Government Press.
1903   *Unnao*. Allahabad: Superintendent, Government Press.
1904   *Lucknow*. Allahabad: Superintendent, Government Press.
1909   *Cawnpore*. Allahabad: Superintendent, Government
        Press.
1911   *Farrukhabad*. Allahabad: Superintendent, Government
        Press.
1920   *Pratapgarh*. Allahabad: Superintendent, Government Press.
1921   *Bara Banki*. Allahabad: Superintendent, Government Press.
1922   *Hardoi*. Allahabad: Superintendent, Government Press.

1923   *Sitapur.* Allahabad: Superintendent, Government Press.
1924   *Rai Bareilly.* Allahabad: Superintendent, Government Press.
1927   *Kheri.* Allahabad: Superintendent, Government Press.

Dumont, Louis
1967   "The Individual as an Impediment to Sociological Comparison and Indian History." In *Social and Economic Change, Essays in Honour of D. P. Mukherji.* Edited by Baljit Singh and V. B. Singh. Bombay: Allied Publishers.

Durkheim, Emile
1933   *The Division of Labor in Society.* Translated with an Introduction by George Simpson. New York: The Macmillan Company.

Dutt, N. K.
1931   "Notes on the Kayasthas, Nāmasudrās, Baidyas, etc." Appendix 3 in Census of India, 1931. vol. 5. *Bengal and Sikkim.* "Part I: Report." Calcutta: Central Publication Branch.

Easton, David
1959   "Political Anthropology." In *Biennial Review of Anthropology.* Edited by Bernard J. Siegal. Stanford: Stanford University Press.

Etzioni, Amitai
1962   *Complex Organizations: A Sociological Reader.* New York: Holt, Rinehart and Winston.
1965   *Modern Organizations.* New Delhi: Prentice-Hall of India (Private) Ltd.
1967   "Toward a Theory of Societal Guidance." *The American Journal of Sociology.* vol. 73.

Fallers, Lloyd A.
1965   *Bantu Bureaucracy.* Chicago: University of Chicago Press.
1966   "Social Stratification and Economic Processes in Africa." In *Class, Status, and Power.* Edited by Reinhard Bendix and Seymour Martin Lipset. 2d ed. New York: The Free Press of Glencoe.

Fox, Richard G.
1967   "Resiliency and Change in the Indian Caste System: The Umar of U. P." *The Journal of Asian Studies.* vol. 26.

Ghurye, G. S.
1961   *Caste, Class and Occupation.* Bombay: Popular Book Depot.

240

REFERENCES

Gusfield, Joseph R.
1967 "Tradition and Modernity: Misplaced Polarities in the Study of Social Change." *The American Journal of Sociology.* vol. 72.
Hall, Richard H.
1968 "Professionalization and Bureaucratization." *American Sociological Review.* vol. 33.
Hall, Richard M.; Hass, J. Eugene; and Johnson, Normal J.
1967 "Organizational Size, Complexity, and Formalization." *American Sociological Review.* vol. 32.
Hardgrave, Robert L., Jr.
1964 "Caste in Kerala: A Preface to the Elections." *The Economic Weekly.* vol. 16.
1965 "Caste and the Kerala Elections." *The Economic Weekly.* vol. 17.
1966 "Varieties of Political Behavior among Nadars of Tamilnad." *Asian Survey.* vol. 6.
1967 "Organiaztion and Change among the Nadars of Tamilnad." Mimeographed. Chicago: University of Chicago.
1969 *The Nadars of Tamilnad: The Political Culture of a Community in Change.* Berkeley and Los Angeles: University of California Press.
Hodge, Robert W.; Siegal, Paul M.; and Rossi, Peter H.
1966 "Occupational Prestige in the United States: 1925–1963." In *Class, Status, and Power.* Edited by Reinhard Bendix and Seymour Martin Lipset. New York: The Free Press of Glencoe.
Horowitz, Irving Louis
1965 *The New Sociology.* New York: Oxford University Press.
Hsu, Francis L. A.
1963 *Clan, Caste, and Club.* Princeton, N. J.: D. Van Nostrand.
Howard, Richard C., gen. ed.
1965 "Bibliography of Asian Studies 1964." *The Journal of Asian Studies.* vol. 24.
1966 "Bibliography of Asian Studies 1965." *The Journal of Asian Studies.* vol. 25.
1967 "Bibliography of Asian Studies 1966." *The Journal of Asian Studies.* vol. 26.
The Kanara Saraswat (Organ of the Kanara Saraswat Association)
1965 June. Bombay.
Kanya-Kubja (Organ of Akhil Bhartiya Sri Kanya-Kubja Pratinidhi Sabha)

1910–20   vols. 4–13.
1957   special golden jubilee issue.
1963–68   vols. 56–61.
Kanya-Kubja Chārucharitavali (Special Biographical Publications of the *Kanya-Kubja*)
1935–45   Lucknow: Misra Press.
Kapadia, K. M.
1962   "Caste in Transition." *Sociological Bulletin.* vol. 11.
Khare, R. S.
1960   "The Kanya-Kubja Brahmans and Their Caste Organization." *Southwestern Journal of Anthropology.* vol. 16.
1962   "Domestic Sanitation in a North Indian Village: An Anthropological Study." Ph.D. dissertation, University of Lucknow, Lucknow, India.
1966   "A Case of Anomalous Values in Indian Civilization: Meat-Eating among the Kanya-Kubja Brahmans of Katyāyan Gotra." *The Journal of Asian Studies.* vol. 25.
1968   "On Parentage and Progeny Rank Determination in North India." (Manuscript.)
Kothari, Rajni, and Maru, Rushikesh
1965   "Caste and Secularism in India." *Journal of Asain Studies.* vol. 25.
Leach, Edmund R.
1945   "Jinghpaw Kinship Terminology." *Journal of the Royal Anthropological Institute.* vol. 75.
1954   *Political Systems of Highland Burma.* Cambridge, Mass.: Harvard University Press.
1963   "Determinants of Cross-Cousin Marriage." *Man.* vol. 63.
Leach, Edmund R., ed.
1960   *Aspects of Caste in South India, Ceylon and Northwest Pakistan.* Cambridge Papers in Social Anthropology, no. 2. Cambridge: Cambridge University Press.
Lévi-Strauss, Claude
1949   *Les structures élémentaires de la parenté.* Paris: Presses Universitaires de France.
1953   "Social Structure." In *Anthropology Today.* Edited by A. L. Kroeber. Chicago: University of Chicago Press.
1956   "Les organizations dualistes existent-elles?" *Bijdragen tot de Taal- , Land- , en Volkenkunde.* vol. 112.
1960   "On Manipulated Sociological Models." *Bijdragen tot de Taal- , Land- , en Volkenkunde.* vol. 116.
1963   *Structural Anthropology.* New York: Basic Books.

REFERENCES

1965   "The Future of Kinship Studies." *Proceedings of the Royal Anthropological Institute (1965).*
1966   *The Savage Mind.* Chicago: University of Chicago Press.
Lynch, Owen M.
1967   "Rural Cities in India: Continuities and Discontinuities." In *India and Ceylon: Unity and Diversity.* Edited by Philip Mason. New York: Oxford University Press.
Madan, T. N.
1962   "Is the Brahmanic Gotra A Grouping of Kin?" *Southwestern Journal of Anthropology.* vol. 18.
Marriott, McKim, ed.
1955   *Village India: Stuides in the Little Community.* Chicago: University of Chicago Press.
Marriott, McKim
1968   "Multiple Reference in Indian Caste Systems." In *Social Mobility in the Caste System in India.* Edited by James Silverberg. The Hague: Mouton.
Mason, Philip
1967   *India and Ceylon: Unity and Diversity.* New York: Oxford University Press.
Mayer, Adrian C.
1966   "The Significance of Quasi-Groups in the Study of Complex Societies." In *The Social Anthropology of Complex Societies.* Edited by Michael Banton. Association of Social Anthropologists of the Commonwealth, Monograph no. 4. London: Tavistock Publications.
Mehta, Surinder K.
1968   "Patterns of Residence in Poona (India) by Income, Education, and Occupation (1937–65)." *The American Journal of Sociology.* vol. 73.
Merton, R. K.
1949   *Social Theory and Social Structure.* Glencoe, Ill.: The Free Press.
Merton, R. K.; Gray, A. P.; Hockey, B.; Selvin, H. C.
1952   *Reader in Bureaucracy.* Glencoe, Ill.: The Free Press.
Misra, B. B.
1961   *The Indian Middle Classes.* New York: Oxford University Press.
Misra, Munni L.
1966   *Kanya-Kubja Vamshāvali* (Hindi). Kanpur: Sri Krishna Press.
Misra, Narain Prasad

1959   *Kanya-Kubja Vamshāvali* (Hindi and Sanskrit). Bombay:
        Venkateshwar Press.
Misra, R. S.
1940   *Chārucharitāvali* (Hindi and Sanskrit). Lucknow: Misra
        Press.
Naegele, Kasper D.
1961   "The Institutionalization of Action." In Parsons *et al.*,
        Theories of Society. vol. 1. New York: The Free Press of
        Glencoe.
Nandi, Proshanta K.
1965   "A Study of Caste Organization in Kanpur." *Man in India.*
        vol. 45.
Parsons, Talcott
1951   *The Social System.* Glencoe, Ill.: The Free Press.
Parsons, Talcott, *et al*
1961   "Introduction to Part Two." In *Theories of Society.* vol. 1.
        New York: The Free Press of Glencoe.
Pocock, David F.
1955   "Movements of Castes." *Man.* vol. 55.
1957   "Inclusion and Exclusion: A Process in the Caste System
        of Gujerat." *Southwestern Journal of Anthropology.* vol.
        13.
Press in India
1966   "Part II: Tenth Annual Report." The Registrar of News-
        papers for India. New Delhi: Government of India Publi-
        cations.
Rao, M. S. A.
1964   "Caste and the Indian Army." *Economic Weekly.* vol. 16.
Random House Dictionary of the English Language
1967   Unabridged Edition. New York: Random House.
Risley, Herbert
1915   *The People of India.* Edited by William Crooke. 2d ed.
        Calcutta: Thacker, Spink and Company.
Rudolph, Lloyd I.
1961   "Urban Life and Populist Radicalism: Dravidian Politics
        in Madras." *Journal of Asian Studies.* vol. 20.
1965a   "The Modernity of Tradition." *American Political Science
        Review.* vol. 59.
1965b   "Barristers and Brahmans." *Comparative Studies in Society
        and History.* vol. 8.
Rudolph, Lloyd I., and Rudolph, Susanne Hoeber
1960   "The Political Role of India's Caste Associations." *Pacific
        Affairs.* vol. 33.

REFERENCES

1967   *The Modernity of Tradition: Political Development in India.* Chicago: University of Chicago Press.
Sangave, Vilas A.
1962   "Changing Pattern of Caste Organization in Kolhapur City." *Sociological Bulletin.* vol. 11.
Schwartzberg, Joseph E.
1965   "The Distribution of Selected Castes in the North Indian Plain." *Geographical Review.* vol. 15.
1968   "Caste Regions of the North Indian Plain." In *Structure and Change in Indian Society.* Edited by Milton Singer and Bernard S. Cohn. Chicago: Aldine Publishing Company.
Shastri, Lalmani
1966   *Kanya-Kubja Vamshāvali.* Kanpur: Yogendra Press.
Shils, Edward
1961   *The Intellectual between Tradition and Modernity: The Indian Case.* The Hague: Mouton.
Silverberg, James, ed.
1968   *Social Mobility in the Caste System of India: An Interdisciplinary Symposium.* Comparative Studies in Society and History, Supplement III. The Hague: Mouton.
Singer, Milton, ed.
1959   *Traditional India: Structure and Change.* Philadelphia: The American Folklore Society.
Singer, Milton
1968   "The Indian Joint Family in Modern Industry." In *Structure and Change in Indian Society.* Edited by Milton Singer and Bernard S. Cohn. Chicago: Aldine Publishing Company.
Singer, Milton, and Cohn, Bernard S., eds.
1968   *Structure and Change in Indian Society.* Chicago: Aldine Publishing Company.
Smith, Donald Eugene
1963   *India as a Secular State.* Princeton, N. J.: Princeton University Press.
Spear, Percival
1963   *The Nabobs: A Study of the Social Life of the English in 18th Century India.* London: Oxford University Press Paperbacks.
Srinivas, M. N.
1955   *India's Villages.* Calcutta: West Bengal Government Publications.
1961   Review of Leach, "Aspects of Caste in South India, Ceylon and Northwest Pakistan." *Man.* vol. 61.

1962   *Caste in Modern India.* Bombay: Asia Publishing House.
1966   *Social Change in Modern India.* Berkeley and Los Angeles: University of California Press.
1968   "Mobility in the Caste System." In *Structure and Change in Indian Society.* Edited by Milton Singer and Bernard S. Cohn. Chicago: Aldine Publishing Company.

Weber, Max
1962   "The Three Types of Legitimate Rule." Translated by Hans Gerth. In *Complex Organizations: A Sociological Reader.* Edited by Amitai Etzioni. New York: Holt, Rinehart and Winston.
1966   "Class, Status and Party." In *Class, Status, and Power.* Edited by Reinhard Bendix and Seymour Martin Lipset. 2d ed. New York: The Free Press of Glencoe.

Weiner, Myron
1962   *The Politics of Scarcity.* Chicago: University of Chicago Press.

Index

Achievement, economic, 107–10

Ādābarz, 69

Administrator, 127, 139–44, 170–74, 179, 182, 191

Age, and traditional position, 110

Agnatic ancestral groups (AAGs). *See* Ānks

Almond, Gabriel A., 8

Ānks, 20, 96, 98, 99

Apter, David E., 8

Aron, Raymond, 129, 131

Artha. *See* Achievement, economic

Āshirvāda, 60

Āspads, 19–20, 96, 98

Astrology, 106

Bailey, F. G., 6, 8, 13, 15, 96, 196, 206 n, 214, 217, 218

Bajpai, A. P., 19, 21, 99

Barth, Fredrik, 167

Beattie, John, 11, 13

Bengal, West, 54

Berreman, Gerald D., 216

Bhāgwata Purāna, 102

Bihar, 54

Biswā scale, 22–24, 96, 97–100, 101

Bohannon, Paul, 11, 14 n

Bottomore, T. B., 25, 118, 129

Brahmans: Kanara Saraswat, 211–12; Kanya-Kubja (*See* Kanya-Kubja Brahmans); Panch Gauda, 3

Brass, Paul R., 119

Buchler, Ira R., 219

Bureaucracy, defined, 26

Caste, 13, 16–17, 191–92, 214, 217–20; federations, 207–8; group, 6, 13–14; mobility, 208; panchāyats, 206–7; political aspirations, 210; sentiment, 214, 215

Census of India, 6–7, 196, 208, 213

Ceremonies: expenditures for, 109–10

Charansparsh, 60

Class, 115. *See also* Status

Clerks, government, 126

Cohn, Bernard S., 7, 200, 201, 206

Coleman, James S., 8

Commensality, 5, 103; and marriage, 104

Courtyard, inner: indicator of familial ritual behavior, 145,

247

Courtyard, inner—*Cont.*
146; prestige indicator, 142, 143, 144
Crafts, sacred, 106–7
Crane, Robert I., 7
Crooke, William, 3, 17, 45

Dalton, Dennis, 8
Davis, Kingsley, 147
DeVos, George, 14 n, 203 n, 216
Dhākaṛa cluster. *See* Madhyama cluster
District Gazetteers, 17, 196
Dowry, 104, 108; Biswā scale basis for, 22–23; "rates," 101
Drawing room: as prestige indicator, 135, 139–40, 142, 143, 144
Dress practices as prestige indicators, 89–91, 107
Dumont, Louis, 157
Durkheim, Emile, 10 n
Dutt, N. K., 209

Easton, David, 201
Elites, 119, 129, 197, 212–13; changes during lifetime of, 150, 152–55; defined, 25, 151; geographic distribution of those participating in Kanya-Kubja sabhas (map 3), 130; participation in caste sabhas, 204–5; praxeology of, 111–14, 134–37; prestige indicators, 129, 131–46; social interfaces among, 146–50; younger, 154

Engineering, as prestigious occupation, 117, 127
Etzioni, Amitai, 12, 15 n, 52, 161, 162, 163, 201 n, 204

Fallers, Lloyd A., 137, 217
Fasting, 105
Food, ritual purity in, 103–4
Fox, Richard G., 3, 8, 96, 192, 203, 206, 206 n, 207, 217

Ghurye, G. S., 12, 197, 206 n, 214
Gotra clusters, 19–20, 96, 97
Gray, A. P., 153, 165
Gujarat Kshatriya Sabha, 212
Gusfield, Joseph R., 16 n

Hall, Richard H., 16 n, 163
Hardgrave, Robert L., Jr., 8, 198, 206 n, 207, 208, 210, 213, 215
Hass, J. Eubene, 153
Havana (sacrifice), 68
Headgear, significance of, 58
Hierarchy, traditional and modern, 95
Hindi, use of in a Kanya-Kubja college, 69
Hockey, B., 163, 165
Hodge, Robert W., 120
Horowitz, Irving Louis, 12
House: formal and informal interactions in, 137-46; prestige indicator, 131-32
Hsiu, Francis L. A., 15 n

"Institution," defined, 11

Johnson, Normal J., 163
Judiciary, 120, 125, 217

Kanara Saraswat, 76 n, 198, 212, 213, 215
Kanara Saraswat sabhas, 212, 215
Kanya-Kubja, 17–18; achievement motive among, 24, 26; ascriptive status among, 24, 96–101; conception of bureaucracy, 26; in Congress movement, 45–46; educational institutions, 39–44, 66–71; elites, 25, 111–14, 119, 129–55; hierarchal-marital problems among, 50; hierarchy, 19–22; marriage among, 21–22, 24; military service, 45, 119; non-elites, 26; periodicals, 37–39; secular advancement among, 49; spatial mobility, 21–22, 46
Kanya-Kubja (the caste journal), 17, 32, 33, 34, 38–39, 43, 45, 47, 48, 53, 55, 72, 105, 106, 107, 108, 116, 121, 134, 136, 150, 151, 175, 197; caste-related matters in, 81–82, 84–85; contributions by location, 86–87; correspondence column, 85–86; donations to, 76; editor of, 58, 78–79; format and content, 80–81; geographical distribution of titled members, 74, 75 (map 2); lower middle class, 119; "marital affairs" in, 49–50, 85; matrimonial advertisements in, 72, 76, 77, 83, 100; membership in, 72,

73–76, 77–78, 84; photographs in, 87–91; "sabha affairs" in, 49–50, 85; youth participation in, 86
Kanya-Kubja Anglo-Sanskrit Mahājani Pāthshāla, 39, 41, 54, 66–70
Kanya-Kubja Bandhu, 32
Kanya-Kubja College, Bhagwantnagar, 43, 54
Kanya-Kubja Education Trust, 31
Kanya-Kubja Intermediate College, Kanpur, 43, 54
Kanya-Kubja Province, 3
Kanya-Kubja sabhas, 9, 26–27, 34 (table 1), 35–36, 44–46, 91, 195–99; achievement, 213–14, 215; Ahmedabad, 36; Ajmer, 32; aims, 47–50, 208–9; all-Indian, 32–33, 47–48, 55, 70; Amravati, 36, 37, 44, 48, 53, 71; Banaras, 56–57; bank account, 55; Bhopal, 36, 37, 48; Calcutta, 32; conceived in terms of caste, 169; Dohad, 36, 53; educational institutions and, 40, 70–71; elite participation in, 204–5; founding of, 56–57; fund-raising, 57–58; formalization indicators of, 163; geographical distribution (map 1), 35; Hyderabad, 53; incipient bureaucracy, 203–4; Indore, 36, 37, 44, 48, 53, 65, 71; interjacent organization, 161–62, 200; Jaipur, 36, 53;

Kanya-Kubja sabhas—*Cont.* Jodhpur, 66; Kanpur, 31, 32; Karnatak, 57; Khatkul Hitaishini, 51; Lashkar (Gwalior), 36, 37, 44, 53, 65, 71; Lucknow, 31, 33, 53, 54, 55–56, 59–65, 71; membership, 50–51; meetings, 59–66, 166; officers of, 165–70; organization, 15–16, 51–56, 127–28, 163–65, 190, 192, 201; political sensitization, 211; Rajasthan, 36; Sagar, 53
Kanya-Kubja Samāj, 38
Kanya-Kubja Vocational Degree College, 41–43
Kapadia, K. M., 206 n
Karma, 133
Khare, R. S., 4, 19, 19 n, 20, 23, 24 n, 45, 99, 103, 110, 119, 144, 197
Khatkul (Kulin) cluster, 96, 97, 98, 99
Kinship, 13, 14, 216, 217; influence, 175–79, 182–90, 191; quarrels, 149–50
Kitchen, and prestige indicator, 142, 143–44, 145
Kith, 205, 216, 217
Kothari, Rajni, 8, 198, 206 n, 207, 212, 213, 214
Kulīntā, 24

Law, as prestigious occupation, 116–17, 125, 127
Leach, Edmund R., 7, 8, 14 n, 17, 96, 206 n, 217, 219
Lévi-Strauss, Claude, 104, 219

Lucknow, 147, 148–49
Lynch, Owen M., 132

Madan, T. N., 19 n
Madhya, Pradesh, 54
Madhyama cluster, 96, 97–98, 99
Maharashtra, 54
Māheshwari, 38
Marriage, 5, 104–5, 179–83; between emigrated and susthān Kanya-Kubjas, 21–22; and commensality, 104; tests ascriptive hierarchy, 100–101
Marriott, McKim, 7, 10 n, 15 n, 206 n
Maru, Rushikesh, 8, 198, 206 n, 207, 212, 213, 214
Mason, Philip, 7
Mayer, Adrian C., 13
Medicine, 117, 127; Ayurvedic, 106, 126
Mehta, Surinder K., 132
Merton, R. K., 16, 153, 165
Migration, 20–22
Misra, B. B., 116, 117, 119
Misra, Munni L., 99
Misra, Narain Prasad, 3, 21, 98, 99
Misra, R. S., 21

Nadar sabha, 208–9
Naegele, Kaspar D., 10 n
Namaskar, 68
Nandi, Proshanta K., 8, 31, 206, 206 n
Neighborhood, caste makeup, 147–49
Non-elites, defined, 26

Observances, ritual, 145–46
Office, modern, 170–72
Organization: defined, 11–13; interjacent, 16, 17

Parsons, Talcott, 10, 16 n, 198
Peons, 172
Physician: drawing room of, 144; kitchen of, 145
Pocock, David F., 15 n, 209, 213
Possessions, prestige indicators of, 132–33
Praṇām, 68–69
Priest: drawing room of, 144; inner courtyard of, 144; kitchen of, 145; living patterns of a traditional, 111–14
Priestcraft, 106
Priesthood, 126, 127
Pundit. See Elites
Puṇya, 58, 67
Purushā, 20

Rao, M. S. A., 119
Risley, Herbert, 103
Rossi, Peter H., 120
Rudolph, Lloyd I., 8, 9 n, 96, 198, 206 n
Rudolph, Lloyd I., and Rudolph, Susanne Hoeber, 8, 9 n, 53, 70, 96, 161, 198, 199, 201, 213, 216 n, 208, 209, 210, 211, 213, 214, 215

Sabhas, 3, 6, 12, 18, 46. See also Kanya-Kubja sabhas; individual sabhas

Samkaksh var, 25
Sandal-paste mark, 105
Sangave, Vilas A., 206, 206 n, 214
Sanskritic learning, 106
Schwartzberg, Joseph E., 210
Selby, Henry A., 219
Selvin, H. C., 163, 165
Shastri, Lalmani, 99
Shils, Edward, 8, 177
Siegal, Paul M., 120
Silverberg, James, 7
Singer, Milton, 7, 200, 206
Smith, Donald Eugene, 8
Spear, Percival, 137
Srinivas, M. N., 7, 8, 21, 96, 150, 153, 197, 206 n, 208, 213, 214, 217, 218
Status: occupational, 115, 120; ranking, 120–27; stratification, 95–96, 155–57, 201–2; traditional, 102–3, 105, 115

Tālukdārs, 121, 125
Teaching, as prestigious occupation, 127
Thread, sacred, 105–6
Tuft, sacred (chotī), 105

Uttama. See Khatkul (Kulin) cluster
Uttar Pradesh, 21, 54, 116, 117

Weber, Max, 95, 115, 172
Weiner, Myron, 8
Westernization, 116–18
Worship, traditional and modern aspects, 105

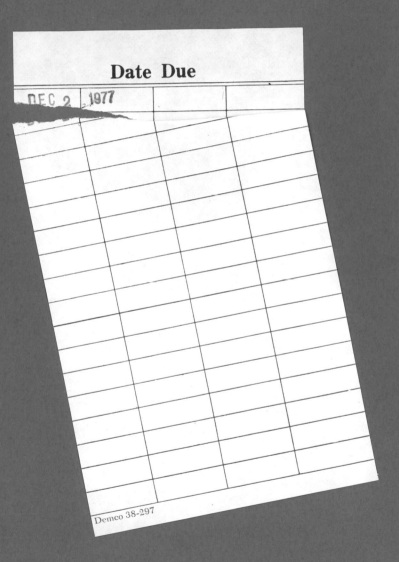

Date Due

DEC 2 1977			

Demco 38-297